D0540383

GOD AND THE ATLANTIC

GOD AND THE ATLANTIC

AMERICA, EUROPE, AND THE RELIGIOUS DIVIDE

THOMAS ALBERT HOWARD

UNIVERSITY PRESS

2011

OXFORD
UNIVERSITY PRESS

Great Clarendon Street, Oxford OX2 6DP

Oxford University Press is a department of the University of Oxford.
It furthers the University's objective of excellence in research, scholarship,
and education by publishing worldwide in

Oxford New York

Auckland Cape Town Dar es Salaam Hong Kong Karachi
Kuala Lumpur Madrid Melbourne Mexico City Nairobi
New Delhi Shanghai Taipei Toronto

With offices in

Argentina Austria Brazil Chile Czech Republic France Greece
Guatemala Hungary Italy Japan Poland Portugal Singapore
South Korea Switzerland Thailand Turkey Ukraine Vietnam

Oxford is a registered trade mark of Oxford University Press
in the UK and in certain other countries

Published in the United States
by Oxford University Press Inc., New York

© Thomas Albert Howard 2011

First published 2011

British Library Cataloguing in Publication Data

Data available

Library of Congress Cataloging in Publication Data

Library of Congress Control Number: 2010935046

Typeset by SPI Publisher Services, Pondicherry, India
Printed in Great Britain
on acid-free paper by
MPG Books Group, Bodmin and King's Lynn

ISBN 978–0–19–956551–1

10 9 8 7 6 5 4 3 2 1

For Elizabeth, Hannah, and Benjamin

Acknowledgements

The great Swiss–German historian Jacob Burckhardt opened his *Civilization of the Renaissance in Italy* (1860) with these memorable words:

This work bears the title of an essay in the strictest sense of the word. No one is more conscious than the writer with what limited means and strength he has addressed himself to a task so arduous.... In the wide ocean upon which we venture, the possible ways and directions are many; and the same studies which have served for this work might easily, in other hands, not only receive a wholly different treatment and application, but lead also to essentially different conclusions. Such indeed is the importance of the subject that it still calls for fresh investigation, and may be studied with advantage from the most varied points of view. Meanwhile we are content if a patient hearing is granted us, and if this book be taken and judged as a whole.

I shall happily allow Burckhardt's sentiments to stand for my own. Indeed, in completing an "essay," an attempt, on a complex and multifaceted topic, I feel that his words ring inescapably true. And while I do not expect that the current volume will enjoy near the life of Burckhardt's seminal book, I stand with presumably every other author in hoping that it might receive a "patient hearing" and be "taken and judged as a whole."

While individual judgment and exertion certainly had their place in conceiving and executing this project, I am acutely and gratefully aware of the support and encouragement that I have received from many others. I am eager, therefore, to recognize the following debts.

The seeds for the present book were sown in the academic year 2003–04 while I was in residence working on another project at the Erasmus Institute at the University of Notre Dame. I filched a little time from that project to sketch the agenda for this book, so let me express my thanks, again, to this fine institution (now subsumed within Notre Dame's Institute for Advanced Studies) and its erstwhile directors, James Turner and Father Robert Sullivan.

I am indebted to the Lilly Endowment for generously supporting my work as a scholar–teacher over the years. Since 2003 I have directed a Lilly-funded project at Gordon College on the idea and practice of theological vocation. While this project has entailed many teaching and administrative obligations, it has also provided me with the time and resources for scholarly pursuits. At the Lilly Endowment, I am especially grateful to Craig Dykstra and Chris Coble within the Endowment's Religion Division, and also to Kim Maphis Early, who directed the Program for the Theological Exploration of Vocation (PTEV).

The German Academic Exchange (DAAD) has supported my scholarship on several occasions. I am thankful for a study-travel grant in the spring semester of 2009 that allowed me to travel to the University of Bayreuth in Bavaria. There I appreciated the open-armed *Gastfreundlichkeit* of Georg Kamphausen, whose scholarship on the idea of America in modern German social thought is of the highest order. While in Bayreuth, I gained valuable feedback from Gabriele Cappai and Thomas Brockmann. In 2009, I also benefited from a grant from the Earhart Foundation, which allowed me to take great strides toward bringing this project to completion.

I remain abidingly thankful for my home institution, Gordon College, particularly for allowing me to take two semester-long research leaves of absence, in 2008 and 2009. Portions of both of these leaves were spent in residence at the Studio for Art, Faith, and History in Orvieto, Italy. Situated in a former convent that dates from the 1200s, overlooking the Umbrian countryside, this program is ideally situated for the task of reading and writing, thinking and talking. The staff there deserves special thanks, which with its founding director John Skillen also include Alessandro Lardani, Laura Menichetti, and Matthew and Sharona Doll. *Mille grazie a tutti.*

From Orvieto, I traveled on several occasions to Rome to conduct research at the library of the Pontifical Gregorian University. Winding my way through its labyrinthine periodical stacks in pursuit of the serendipitous ranks among the more memorable parts of my work. And this was only one of numerous libraries that contributed to my research. I am thankful for the helpful and courteous staff at a number of others, including Harvard's Widener Library, the Andover–Harvard Theological Library, Harvard's Houghton Library, the Library of the University of Bayreuth, the Library of the University of Notre Dame, Cornell University's Olin Library, the Library of Congress, and Dublin's Trinity College Library. Not least, I am thankful for the staff at

Gordon College's own redoubtable Jenks Library, and especially for the ongoing, tireless assistance of Martha Crain, who has handled more Interlibrary Loan requests for me than either of us would care to count.

I am grateful for a number of professional societies and scholarly institutions where I have been able to present portions of my work. These include the Kongress der internationalen Schleiermacher-Gesellschaft in Berlin, the Garaventa Center at the University of Portland, the American Society of Church History, Calvin College's Seminars in Christian Scholarship, and the Boisi Center for Religion and American Public Life at Boston College.

Besides these institutions, numerous individuals have provided criticism, commentary, and/or encouragement along the way. Let me thank then Stephen G. Alter, Peter Berger, Ian Marcus Corbin, Richard Crane, Joanna Epling, Stan Gaede, James Davison Hunter, Ahmet T. Kuru, Timothy Larsen, Andrei S. Markovits, (the late) Ralph McInerny, Wilfred McClay, Mark A. Noll, Klaus Penzel, Richard Pierard, Jonathan Sarna, and Alan Wolfe. In addition, I remain abidingly indebted to Allan Megill and H. C. Erik Midelfort, who taught me the craft of historical scholarship.

I am thankful to be granted permission to reprint here some previously published materials. These include "Philip Schaff: Religion, Politics, and the Transatlantic World," *Journal of Church and State* 49 (Spring 2007), 191–210 and "American Religion and European Anti-Americanism," in Jonathan Chaplin, ed., *God and Global Order: The Power of Religion in American Foreign Policy* (Baylor University Press, 2010).

For their research help and highly competent assistance in so many other ways, I thank Sarah and Andrew Carlson-Lier, Joshua Hasler, and M. Ryan Groff. The completion of this project owes much to their patient and diligent work.

This is the second book that I have published with Oxford University Press. I remain grateful and impressed by the professionalism, courtesy, and assistance of this venerable press. Tom Perridge and Elizabeth Robottom, among other editors with whom I have worked over the years, deserve abiding respect and admiration.

With respect to languages, my eagerness to learn sometimes exceeds my ability to master. While any lingering missteps are my own, I am grateful for translation advice on a number of points from my colleagues at Gordon College, including Gregor Thuswaldner (German),

Emmanuelle Vanborre (French), and Graeme Bird (Latin). My longsuffering, cherished, Slovak-heritage, "Italianate" wife, Agnes R. Howard, also helped with several passages in *la lingua più bellissima*.

Alas, family is often mentioned last because first in affections. Not only did my wife Agnes help with translation, but she read the whole manuscript several times over, providing trenchant commentary and helpful suggestions. Without our three children—Elizabeth, Hannah, and Benjamin—this project would likely have been completed much sooner. But their frequent interruptions point to higher states of being and a deeper sanity. For this I am thankful and this book is dedicated to them.

Thomas Albert Howard
Georgetown, Massachusetts, May 2010

Table of Contents

And sometimes she wondered whether America was the great death-continent, the great No! to the European.... The continent whose spirit of place fought purely to pick the eyes out of the face of God. Was that America?

—D. H. Lawrence, *The Plumed Serpent*

In a land where much is allowed, religious life too will more often witness the wildest growths.

—Adolf Zahn, *Outline of the History of the Protestant Churches in America* (1889)

America, you have it better.

—Goethe

I

Introduction

The states of America are a country where there are thirty-two religions, but there is only one course at dinner—and it's bad.

—Charles Maurice de Talleyrand, 1790

America's cultural peculiarities (as seen from Europe) are well documented: the nation's marked religiosity ...

—Tony Judt, 2008

The Presence of the Past

In Act I, Scene III of William Faulkner's *Requiem for a Nun*, the character Gavin Stevens utters among the more famous lines in twentieth-century literature: "The past is never dead. It's not even past." At one level, this book might be considered an extended meditation on this theme: the insistent presence of the past, how historical experience and the narratives derived from it inform, disturb, illuminate, burden, and/or simplify the present. And how different interpretations of past developments and events lead to specific reflexes of thought, habits of perception, moral judgments and disagreements—and, in turn, to further interpretations. And so it goes.

In particular, I focus on *images* and *explanations* of religion in American history and within the American political order as conceived and articulated by prominent European intellectuals, travelers, and writers—principally those of the nineteenth and early twentieth century. More specifically, I examine how religion figured into the stories and explanations given by Europeans to understand the political emergence of the United States, its place in world history, and its relationship to the so-called "Old World." At first glance, this might appear a peculiar stretch of modern history, but if one has the patience to follow it long enough one arrives at vistas that open onto one of the more significant developments of recent times: what we might call *the transatlantic religious gap*, the abiding religiosity of the United States and the contrasting secularity of Western Europe; and, concomitantly, the geopolitical confusions and disaffections that this cultural divergence has produced and portends to lead to in the future.[1]

Two anecdotes might shed some preliminary light on the topic. The first involves a young German woman studying at the University of Virginia on a Fulbright scholarship in the 1990s. Graduate students in history together, we had become friends and I once asked her offhandedly what she found most remarkable about the United States. She thought for a minute and then told a story about being an exchange student on the West Coast as a teenager. She was taken aback, she remembered, when the (evangelical Christian) woman hosting her told her about the daily "prayer journal" she kept. This would be an unusual thing for a German to undertake, my friend remarked, but what positively dumbfounded her was that her host's entries were logged on a home computer more advanced than those she had encountered in her native Germany at the time. The marriage of evangelical piety and cutting-edge technology seemed a strange brew, unmistakably American on the one hand, but somehow at odds—worrisomely at odds—with what modernity for her was *supposed* to look like.

The second anecdote comes, over a decade later, from an outburst at an academic conference. I was providing commentary on a panel on trends in the historiography of modern Europe. During the question-and-answer period, the conversation somehow turned to religion, politics, and transatlantic relations. At one point, a Scandinavian woman in the back of the room stood up and proclaimed, with a somewhat exasperated tone, that for many Western Europeans, Sigmund Freud was simply right: religion is a childish illusion, and clinging to it a form of neurosis. It followed that for Europeans of a secular bent, the pronounced religiosity in American society could only be regarded as a historically neurotic phenomenon, a stubborn holdover from less enlightened times, but one informing the politics of the most powerful country on earth.

Events of recent decades such as the ending of the Cold War, the attacks of September 11, the conflicts in Iraq and Afghanistan, and the worldwide financial crisis have highlighted various and sundry transatlantic divisions, including the religious ones suggested by these anecdotes. Writing in the *New York Times* in 2004, the respected German journalist Peter Schneider noted that "the war in Iraq has made the Atlantic seem wider, but in reality it has had the effect of a magnifying glass, bringing older and more fundamental differences between Europe and the United States into focus." Religion topped Schneider's list. The United States is a deeply religious nation, he noted, "while in Europe the process of secularization continues unabated."[2] A major reason for America and Europe "growing apart," Jeffrey Kopstein and Sven Steinmo echo, lies in the religious sphere: "Whereas churches in Europe are more likely to be filled with tourists than worshipers, American churches are thriving."[3] A few qualifications are in order, to be sure, but the empirical data largely support these broad claims.[4]

Various contemporary European intellectuals have expressed similar, if less dispassionate, sentiments, agitated in the extreme that the moral pitch of post-9/11 US foreign policy—first set in motion by a cabal of religion-friendly "neoconservative" intellectuals and "evangelical" electoral shock troops—constituted no episodic phenomenon, but expressed something embedded, and irredeemable, in American history and culture. "To Europeans," wrote the editors of *The Economist*, "religion is the strangest and most disturbing feature of American exceptionalism."[5] European visitors are regularly "confounded," noted Reinhard Heinisch in the *Wiener Zeitung*, "when they are confronted by the religiosity of the average American."[6] American democracy, opined Jean-François Colosimo, is not cut from the same cloth as that of the secular, enlightened European variety; it should be understood as a distinctive "*théodémocratie*."[7] The Swiss politician and publicist Gret Haller has untiringly expressed similar opinions, making the case for the limits of transatlantic policy interests. America's "unsecular" path to modernity, she believes, incapacitates durable "solidarity" with Western European countries and the European Union; in addition, the most energetically religious sectors of American society represent for her a threat to European values on par with that of Islamic extremism.[8]

While the above sentiments certainly do not testify to a monolithic attitude toward religion in the United States, such views resonate with a considerable and influential sector of elite opinion in Western Europe. Leaving legitimate policy considerations aside, the condescension and derision often informing such analyses bear witness to an established secular historical consciousness in European societies, the exponents of which have been at once uncomfortable with and dismissive of the contours of religious expression found in the United States—what Klaus-M. Kodalle calls Europeans' profound uneasiness (*Mißbehagen*) with the dynamics of American religious life.[9]

For sociologists preoccupied with questions of religion and modernity, the transatlantic religious divide has emerged as something of a truism (if a perplexing one) in recent scholarship. While once sociologists held that modernity led almost inexorably toward secularization or "the disenchantment of the world" in Max Weber's well-known formulation, most now concede that this is not necessarily the case: the United States presents at once a thoroughly modernized nation, indeed the paradigmatic example of modernity in many respects, and is simultaneously "awash in a sea of faith," especially when compared to most Western European societies, where the secularization thesis still seems plausible, if not entirely beyond criticism.[10] One may speak of the "exception religieuse américaine," the French sociologist Raymond Boudon has noted, reflecting an older consensus; this "profoundly enigmatic" phenomenon appears to him to defy some of the basic precepts of modern social science.[11]

But if sociologists, journalists, and some policy analysts have become attuned to the growing religious divide, it has not been terribly high on the agenda of historians of the modern Atlantic world and among those interested in the genealogy of European attitudes toward the United States.[12] Scholars of these topics often emphasize political, diplomatic, and socioeconomic issues, when in fact, as I shall contend, a substrate of prior cultural and religious factors should also be taken into consideration. What is more, the accretion of perceptions of difference in the cultural–religious sphere often functions as a prism of interpretation that informs, at once subtly and profoundly, judgments and attitudes about numerous contemporary issues. Students of transatlantic realities dismissive or inattentive to religion risk inadequately grasping the abiding presence of the past.

Beyond Tocqueville

Since its founding in the late eighteenth century, the United States has never suffered from a shortage of curious European commentators, whether or not they braved the Atlantic to behold the *novus ordo seclorum* for themselves. The many who did visit certainly came with a full and varied agenda, but the opportunity to observe first-hand the fate of Old World religion(s) in a New World was a persistent topic of interest, rarely failing to elicit fascination.[13] "Prominent European visitors who wrote on America," Seymour Martin Lipset has observed, "have been unanimous in remarking on the exceptional religiosity of the society."[14] The stark contrast between the Old World's longstanding environment of state-managed churches and the "voluntary" religious free-for-all of the upstart nation often proved jarring and gave rise to much worry and derision among Europe's conservative classes. Conversely, for progressive-minded and politically radicalized Europeans—the emerging "Left" sympathetic to the anticlerical ethos of the French Revolution—the American system, although liberal, stood out for remaining on too-friendly terms with traditional religion, even encouraging of obscurantist and sectarian expressions. Curiosity-inspired excursions to observe the Shakers, the Amish, or the Mormons in their New World habitats emerged as *au courant* activities for many educated Europeans visiting America in the nineteenth century. "There is a deep religious consciousness living in the people," the German scholar Hugo Münsterberg summed up; it's "a religiously inclined population."[15] The United States is a "nation with the soul of church," G. K. Chesterton famously observed.[16] With respect to religion, a contributor to the *Edinburgh Review* wrote in 1824, "Americans can be ranked at the head of all the nations in the world."[17] More recent, high-altitude descanters on "America," such as Jean Baudrillard, Bernard-Henri Lévy, or Simon Schama, have arrived at comparable conclusions.[18]

Of course, the French aristocrat Alexis de Tocqueville, who visited the United States in the 1830s, ranks as among the more insightful, probing, and most frequently cited European commentators on the American religious scene—indeed, the first and final word on the subject for many today, on both sides of the Atlantic. It was Tocqueville who made the significant observation that religion in the United States is at once formally separated from the political realm, but paradoxically exerts considerable influence over society and politics alike—precisely because of the formal separation. Indeed, religion, which he called "the first of their political institutions," did not detract from democracy and republican freedoms, but profoundly contributed to them. In words often quoted, Tocqueville remarked that upon my arrival in the United States it was the religious aspect of the country that first struck my eye. As I prolonged my stay, I perceived the great political consequences that flowed from this new state of things. In France I had seen the spirit of religion and the spirit of freedom almost always move in contrary directions. But in America I found them united intimately with one another: they reigned together on the same soil.[19]

Tocqueville's line of analysis has been adopted by numerous subsequent scholars, particularly those eager to affirm the exemplary character of state–church arrangements in the United States. Unlike in Europe where "secular" implies a hostility to religion, as one scholar drawing from Tocqueville has argued, the United States sought to disestablish religion so that it might flourish: "The American concept [of the secular] is grounded in the firm belief in the incomparable value of the religious life.... The separation of state and church is thus in the American creed primarily a need of religion itself."[20]

When such Tocquevillean analyses are linked up with the countless tales of beleaguered minorities and persecuted sects leaving the Old World for freedom in the United States one comes away with a rather positive image of the American religious experiment. John T. Noonan's *The Lustre of our Country: The American Experience of Religious Freedom*, a celebratory account of the American Bill of Rights' First Amendment and its legacy, serves as an apt case in point. In a playful conclusion, a so-called "ten commandments for understanding American religious liberty," Noonan enjoins the reader to "read Tocqueville for his celebration of the holy union of freedom and religion... and meditate on his conviction that religion is the foremost of our political institutions."[21]

But one cannot live by Tocqueville alone. Leaning on him too heavily, *at least as an historical source*, obscures aspects of the United States that the young French aristocrat, however insightful, might have ignored, exaggerated, or misunderstood. More importantly for our purposes, it obscures the historical significance of other European assessments of religion in the United States, particularly the outpouring of more negative, condescending, even vituperative accounts. In fact, if one wants to understand the historical underpinnings of counter- or anti-American sentiment vis-à-vis religion in Europe today, Tocqueville might prove an especially unreliable guide. His generally constructive (if far from flattering) assessment of the promise of American democracy and religion stands out as unusual when compared to many other European elites who traversed or peered across the Atlantic.[22] Where Tocqueville saw privatized religiosity contributing significantly to a voluntary spirit, philanthropy, and the march of freedom, others saw rampant sectarianism, a hatchery of heresy, religion mixing with commerce and individualism, the *reductio ad absurdum* of Protestantism according to some Catholics, or—according to many European socialists and secularists—the modernity-defying survival of "the opiate of the people" and its worrisome, rejuvenating proliferation in a vast and exotic western "frontier." In contrast to European nations, the polity of the United States—long considered a refuge for the Old World's religious outcasts and troublemakers—had given birth to a system seemingly intent on maximizing religious anarchy and cultural disarray. "The states of America are a country where there are thirty-two religions, but there is only one course at dinner—and it's bad," grumbled Charles Maurice de Talleyrand during his brief exile from France in the 1790s. "It must be admitted," wrote Achille Murat in 1832, "that looking at the physiognomy of the United States, its religion is the only feature which disgusts a foreigner."[23] North America is a "monotonous continent" in the clutch of "religious hypocrisy" (*Scheinfrömmigkeit*), griped the historian Karl Lamprecht.[24]

But if too frequently invoking Tocqueville can obscure the extent of negative assessments of New World religiosity, it also overshadows the voices of other more generous, high-minded European commentators. Besides examining the roots of European misgivings about and hostility toward American religious life, therefore, I also aim to retrieve European voices who offered more constructive engagement. In particular, I shall highlight the thought of the Swiss–German, Protestant church historian Philip Schaff (1819–1893) and that of the French, Catholic philosopher Jacques Maritain (1882–1973). Both scholars commented insightfully on America and, while known by some specialists, have been eclipsed by Tocqueville's long shadow.

This book, then, has two main components: a) analyses of negative assessments of American religious life, which, whether insightful or prejudiced, might help us grasp some of the deeper cultural currents of anti-Americanism afoot in contemporary Europe, and b) a retrieval of more positive, but often neglected European interpreters of the American scene, whose comments and interpretations—alongside those of the indispensable Tocqueville—provide insight into the distinctive character of the religious dynamics in the United States as well as into the history and current shape of some of today's transatlantic divisions.

But a few caveats are in order. The term "anti-Americanism," which I shall (circumspectly) employ, is an admittedly difficult, protean, and politically-freighted one. While I am persuaded that the focus and material of this study cast light on the depth and contours of at least *some* currents of anti-American sentiment in Europe today, I do not intend to suggest any simple causal relationship between past and present, nor do I mean to discount the powerful and persistent currents of philo-Americanism in European history. Anti-Americanism and philo-Americanism are in fact often structurally linked with one another, in that anti-American statements frequently constitute responses to *European* philo-American perspectives, not necessarily to America per se. What is more, attitudes toward America in Europe have a long and complex history, which belies any attempt to frame them as monolithic, ideologically determined, or predictable phenomena.[25] At the same time, the high levels of anti-Americanism in Europe in recent years—worrisome to some Europeans as much as to Americans—cannot be explained strictly in terms of contemporary developments, divergences on social questions, or recent foreign policy disagreements, as some would argue, although these factors are certainly not unimportant.[26] Much deeper historical forces are at work. One gains more insight, then, by regarding contemporary anti-American sentiment as a convergence of causes, in which two sets of factors—one more diachronic, the other more synchronic—together produce an effect that is significantly greater than the sum of the parts. Obviously, I am largely interested in the diachronic, the deeper historical antecedent structures, and will happily leave the synchronic to comparative sociologists, political scientists, policy experts, and others with relevant competence. Still, my arguments throughout rest on the view that contemporary levels of animosity and a more general cultural divergence—a widening Atlantic or an "Atlantic gap" as some have called it—cannot be adequately explained apart from efforts to examine deeper historical sources, particularly those in the religious sphere.

The term "Europe" requires a measure of qualification. This is a work largely of cultural and intellectual history, and more particularly one about the history of perceptions and interpretations. Accordingly, I focus preponderantly on commentary about and images of the

United States emanating from western Continental Europe, whose leaders, journalists, and scholars, if certainly not representative of the actual geographical Europe, have exerted a disproportionate influence on European intellectual life as a whole, not to mention on broader trends of thought in many other parts of the globe.[27] In the language of the great social theorist Edward Shils, I focus on the "centers" of the Continent, defined in terms of cultural influence, not on its many "peripheries."

Great Britain too will receive due attention, even if it admittedly represents a special case, for of course it shares a religious and (broadly Lockean) political patrimony with the United States far more extensively than any other European nation.[28] This shared patrimony, at times, has engendered considerable overlap and sympathetic feelings toward the United States and its religious life. But quite often, the same disparaging attitudes and hostilities voiced by Continental thinkers can be found among British ones as well. Anglican church leaders worrying about American revivalism and sectarianism, English aristocrats contemning American mass society and commercialism, and Oxbridge intellectuals disdaining the cultural vulgarity and lack of refinement in the upstart nation mirror broader patterns on the Continent. But, significantly, such lines of criticism directed against Americans in Great Britain were frequently directed against "Anglo-Saxon" civilization by Continental thinkers, many of whom were inclined to see the American experiment as a particularly degenerate and gangly offshoot of historical tendencies first incubated and nourished across the English Channel.[29] A 1910 entry on "Engländerei" (Englishism) in one of Germany's leading theological reference works, for example, lamented the "disastrous influence" in church life "not only of English but also American incursions."[30] In sum, then, let us consider Great Britain partially "European," but partially, and complexly, its own thing—an identity conundrum that persists and has taken on new life in recent decades.[31]

The modern abstraction "religion" possesses a singular power to vex scholarly precision. In the pages ahead, I would humbly ask the reader to endure its fluid usage as at once problematic and indispensable. In places, I employ it in a more functional sense, to denote the complex array of attitudes, practices, and beliefs that flow from any society's efforts to relate to the divine. More often, in the American context, it will denote the various forms of evangelical Protestantism, *the* juggernaut force in the nineteenth century, while also connoting the broader political–legal context of church disestablishment and religious voluntarism, which affected other forms of religious expression (Catholic, Jewish, Unitarian, Mormon, Deist) extensively.[32] The revivalist vitality and splintering of Protestantism ("sectarianism") together with official disestablishment ("religious freedom") constituted, by far, the most frequently noted items of interest—and points of departure from the Old World—in the eyes of European commentators, irrespective of their country of origin or confessional identity. These disparities, James Bryce wrote in his monumental *American Commonwealth* (1888), constitute "the most striking differences between all the European countries on the one hand and the United States on the other."[33]

Right, Left, and Master Narratives

In broad historical perspective, European misgivings about America in general and American religious life in particular possess both a traditionalist (Right) and a progressive (Left) dimension. These misgivings have been nourished at the far ends of a distinctly European political spectrum that first took shape in the aftermath of the French Revolution and Napoleonic era. In his classic *The Liberal Tradition in America*, Louis Hartz argued that, absent the "feudal and clerical oppressions of the Old World," American liberalism sprang forth in exceedingly favorable circumstances, "in the magnificent material setting found in the New World."[34] This set of conditions led to a profound, if often insufficiently acknowledged, consensus about the purpose and appropriateness of liberal forms of government. Liberalism, Lionel Trilling could remark in 1950, is really America's "sole intellectual tradition."[35]

Since the late eighteenth century, this reality has separated the trajectory of American political experience from that of Europe, where liberalism was bitterly contested from its infancy, from the Right and the Left. In practically every country in post-revolutionary Europe, one could find a counterrevolutionary program hoping to restore Church and Crown, but opposing them stood intellectual forces and (later) political parties equally determined to realize yet more radical forms of democracy, secularism, and socialism to accomplish what the

French Revolution—so the argument went—had only begun. European traditions of leftist–socialist thought, Hartz wrote,

[are] largely an ideological phenomenon, arising out of the principles of class and the revolutionary liberal revolt against them which the old European order inspired. It is not accidental that America, which uniquely lacked a feudal tradition has uniquely lacked a socialist tradition. The hidden origin of socialist thought everywhere in the West is to be found in the feudal ethos. The *ancien régime* inspires Rousseau; both inspire Marx.[36]

In the pages that follow, I take as a starting point that Hartz was essentially correct—in the big picture if not always in the details—and seek to transfer Hartz's insights from American politics alone to religio-political dynamics in transatlantic perspective. Put more fully, while Hartz's main aim was to demonstrate how the *absence* of a feudal order and established church affected American institutions and political habits, I intend to show how the *presence* of a feudal order and established churches (and their dialectically precipitated poles of opposition: more thoroughgoing socialist and anticlerical tendencies) have structured European attitudes toward the United States, particularly toward the American experiment in religious freedom, and in the seemingly unabating religious vitality that this system has since produced.

The nineteenth century is especially significant because after the apparent failure of the French Revolution in 1815, the United States constituted the only country of size in the world guided by what many in Europe regarded as the dangerous and discredited ideas of democracy, equality, and religious freedom.[37] To grapple with the contours and meaning of modernity during this time, a real or imagined "America" was a frequent topic of reflection among Europe's knowledge classes, even if the unsettled legacy of the French Revolution often presented itself as a more immediate subject of concern. The political enthusiasms and revolutionary tremblings of 1830 and 1848 only intensified interest in the American experiment, both as a beacon (for some) of what Europe might become, but also as a cautionary tale of what Europe must avoid, or of what excesses or deficiencies European states, while modernizing, must guard against.

Writing during a time of expanding rates of literacy and education, intellectuals played crucial roles during this period as interpreters of experience and shapers of perception. Since perceptions are often the mother of social reality, intellectuals figure preeminently in this study, even if I freely admit, following the philosopher Charles Taylor, that ideas do not exhaust the causal nexus, even as they remain a significant point of entry into the large and complex phenomena of the past. The accumulation over time of similar interpretations and perceptions powerfully contributes to what Taylor calls a "social imaginary," the broader and deeper, often inchoate and prearticulate, "environing backgrounds of thought" that people draw upon when they consider social reality, how things ought to fit together, where their selves and their collectives fit in the matrix of time and space.[38]

Intellectuals' conceptions of history during and after "the age of democratic revolution," to use R. R. Palmer's famous phrase, constitute my particular area of concern. During this era, two especially influential "master narratives"—one establishmentarian–reactionary, one secularist–progressive—are discernable among European writers; they arose to make sense of the often dizzying, discontinuous experience of early modernity and the powerful symbolic role of America therein. Whether of the Right or Left, these "master narratives" should be understood here in the spirit of Weberian ideal-types, widespread tendencies or patterns of thought, the contours of which are more recognizable with the benefit of hindsight than they would have been to contemporaries.[39]

The way these particular narratives took shape in post-1789 Europe carried far-reaching implications for how European intellectuals and wider educated and elite circles (what Edward Shils has nicely called "the penumbral world of intellectuals") understood the meaning of the new American polity and the nature of its religious dynamics. The stark subsequent contrast in religious trajectories, and the layers of transatlantic observation and commentary derived therefrom, have enduringly shaped European perceptions and interpretations of the United States.[40]

The traditionalist or conservative narrative, as one would expect, accents declension and dereliction, a regrettable movement away from "the world we have lost," encompassing a rich and varied critique of the Enlightenment and modern revolutionary ideologies. This version of conservatism received its most forceful expression among those with a vested interest in the *Ancien Régime*: aristocrats, Romantic artists and writers, churchmen, scholars, and others who had a proprietary or nostalgic stake in the complex network of corporative and local identities prior to the *esprit révolutionnaire*. Since the United States lacked a hereditary aristocracy and an established church at the national level, this particular strand of conservatism has never really existed on American soil (with the partial exception of Southern Agrarianism). The conservatism of the United States has always been on more friendly, if often guarded, terms with the Enlightenment and classical liberalism than its European counterparts. "From a European perspective," as two British journalists, in the spirit of Louis Hartz, have pithily remarked, "American traditionalism has a bit too much democratic millenarianism and not quite enough noblesse oblige."[41]

Religious concerns saturated the reactionary sensibilities of the early nineteenth century in Europe. In the "throne and altar" formula of the era, altar was every bit as important as throne, and in some respects more so. Opposition to the French Revolution, especially to its secularizing and anticlerical tendencies, helped bring various reactionary forces together into a recognizable European-wide conservative movement. Besides key statesmen such as Count Metternich of Austria, significance should be accorded to figures such as Edmund Burke, Adam Müller, Franz von Baader, Novalis, Friedrich von Gentz, Rafael de Vélez, Joseph de Maistre, Louis de Bonald, René de Chateaubriand, among others. A periodical published by Chateaubriand in 1815, *Le Conservateur*, gave the conservative movement its name. Books such as Burke's famous *Reflections on the Revolution in France* (1791) and Müller's *On the Necessity for a Theological Basis for Political Science* (1819) called for the "organic" development of political institutions and the indispensability of traditional religious sentiment and ecclesiastical institutions for civilized life. Others, notably de Maistre, emphasized stable and firm religious authority as an antidote to the "satanic" bloodshed and confusion that the French Revolution had brought forth.[42]

Underlying and informing traditionalist assessments of the *Zeitgeist* was the long-standing reality of confessional state–church establishments, which traced their origins, at least on the Continent, to the Peace of Westphalia of 1648, and ultimately back to Emperor Constantine. The influential formula *cuius regio, eius religio* had proven, many held, a prudential and necessary measure for assuring religious tranquility throughout Europe and guaranteeing religious stability within individual countries.[43] What is significant about the post-revolutionary period was the degree to which confessional partisans, long divided historically by doctrinal conflicts, were forced to confront a larger common threat in the irreligion and liberal principles of the Revolution. And even if any confessional rapprochement during this period proved shadowy and fleeting, its existence is of notable historical significance.[44]

Among the more salient examples of this phenomenon was the so-called Holy Alliance of 1815, one of a series of alliances tied to the Congress of Vienna and the Restoration, which sought to stanch any recrudescence of the spirit of 1789. Signed by (Orthodox) Tsar Alexander I of Russia, (Catholic) Francis I of Austria, and (Protestant) Friedrich Wilhelm III of Prussia, the Alliance sought to provide a united religious front against the revolutionary tide. Governments of Europe, it stipulated, should "take for their sole guide the precepts of that Holy Religion...[,] which, far from being applicable only to private concerns, must have an immediate influence on the councils of Princes."[45] The recognized enemies of the Holy Alliance were movements and governments that championed voluntary religion, anticlerical and anti-monarchical sentiment, and democracy. Diplomats and statesmen sympathetic to the Restoration expressed acute concern about the revolutionary movements sweeping Latin America in the 1810s and 1820s, and harbored brooding disquiet about the very existence of the United States, a haven for many liberals and Bonapartists who had fled Europe during the Restoration.[46]

The recognition of the new Latin American republics by the United States in 1822 and the proclamation of the Monroe Doctrine of 1823 came as unsettling developments to the European powers bent on stifling revolutionary principles and reasserting Old World colonial prerogatives. For a period, members of the Holy Alliance considered joining the restored monarchies of Spain and France in warring against the new republics, ignoring the Monroe Doctrine. Although this did not happen, it should not go unnoted that the assertion of American interests in the western hemisphere highlighted a stark *ideological* parting of ways between the Old World and the New. The "political system" of the European powers, President Monroe had said, "is essentially different in this respect from that of America" and European meddling against the "just principles" of the new South American republics would therefore be considered "as dangerous to our peace and safety." The actions of the United States, Count Metternich later opined, served as a way for the new nation "[to] clearly announce its intention, not only to set power versus power, but, to put it even more clearly, altar versus altar. This unfortunate declaration [of Monroe] cast criticism and contempt on European institutions worthy of greatest respect."[47] The phrase "altar versus altar" made clear that the polity of the United States in religious matters contravened the specific principles of the Holy Alliance and the broader principles of church establishmentarianism central to Restoration-era thought. The United States' commitment to religious "indifferentism" (*Indifferentismus*), as the Austrian jurist and diplomat Johann Georg Hülsemann added, represented a "strange" aspect of the new land and "a sharp point of opposition to everything that our [European] civilization rests upon."[48]

In contemning American principles, Metternich and Hülsemann did not stand alone. As shall be developed more fully later, the conservative case against America received bountiful support in the Romantic and nostalgic literature of the era. Indeed, the era of European Romanticism, as Dan Diner has noted, "can with all justification be considered the main workshop for lasting anti-American images and metaphors."[49] These images and metaphors created a bountiful repository of familiar sentiments that later generations of intellectuals, whether of the Right or Left, could draw upon with the assurance of receptive listeners. The Romantics' disapproval of America went hand in hand with their more general hostility to liberal ideologies; with their denunciations of materialism and mass society; with their rejection of "abstract" constitutional thought; and with their regret of the leveling tendencies of modernity, which threatened to upend divinely-sanctioned hierarchies and traditions.

Romantic-era critiques of America drew particular strength from two ideas about the course of recent historical developments. The first was the view that the American Revolution, while a child of European ideas, in turn helped precipitate and, at some level, was of a piece with the French Revolution and its excesses. Friedrich Schlegel wrote in his *Lectures on the Philosophy of History* (1828) that "North America had been to France and the rest of Europe the real school and nursery of all these revolutionary principles."[50] Chateaubriand had earlier made the same argument.[51] As the political experiments of France receded in memory after 1815, the growth of the American republic and its turn toward popular democracy under President Andrew Jackson served for conservative European thought as a cautionary tale against the unruly consequences of liberal principles and religious freedom. Those European travelers who witnessed first-hand the frontier revivals, camp meetings, church divisions, and myriad other religious enthusiasms of this period—commonly referred to by American historians as the "Second Great Awakening"—often concluded that nothing good could come from a society where religion had a compromised sense of authority and no civil organizing principle. The British Tory Frederick Marryat was no lone voice when in 1839 he denounced the American religious milieu as a "great evil," a source of "continual discord and the unhinging of society, instead of that peace and good will intended by our divine Legislator."[52]

Critiques of America also gained saliency among Romantic and conservative authors because many, despite holding negative views of the United States, felt that the economic and political forces associated with the new nation might well prove inexorable and come to dominate all of modern society. A brooding resignation toward a contemptible historical inevitability, one that equated modernity with America, first reared its head in Romantic-era thought. This idea would have a long life. Victor Hugo warned young people, for example, against idealizing a nation "without anchor, without past, without history, without art."[53] America was a nation of "shopkeeper souls stinking toward heaven" (*himmelanstinkende Krämerseelen*), opined the Austrian Romantic poet Nikolaus Lenau in 1833, "who bring death to all spiritual life."[54] When the French poet Baudelaire coined the verb "américaniser" in 1855, he did so in a tirade against "the idea of progress," a "very fashionable error," a "grotesque idea, which has flowered upon the rotten soil of modern fatuity."[55]

In the final analysis, the European rightist or conservative interpretation of the United States regularly associated the new American polity with the rational and liberal ideas of the Enlightenment and European revolutionary thought, with the foreboding early stirrings of commercial capitalism, with mass society and cultural mediocrity, and, not least, with an atomizing, anarchic spirit of religious zeal. Since European Jews often advocated religious freedom along American lines, the conservative case against the United States contained, too, no small measure of anti-Semitism or the potential thereof.[56] Together, these incipient anti-American sentiments did not represent a coherent ideology; they were rather an amorphous, contradictory mélange of ideas, uttered often as peripheral remarks (as most European thinkers disquieted by modernity focused on the French Revolution) and with significant national and confessional variations within Europe.[57]

Religious concerns, it should then be clear, appeared consistently in conservative critiques. The American path of purely "voluntary" religion simply had no historical precedent in European experience, except in what conservatives viewed as the farcical excesses of Enlightenment and revolutionary thought. To be sure, some divined that the United States stood on more friendly terms with religion than the French revolutionary tradition. But questions and doubts persisted. What would be the destiny of belief and piety in this *novus ordo seclorum*? What would happen to churches—not to mention to the theological idea of "the one, holy catholic and apostolic church"—which were dependent on voluntary support? What authority would ministers really have if congregations held the purse strings? Would not the inherent schismatic tendencies of Protestantism reach, under American conditions, their logical, ignominious end in splintering into an endless number of jealous and competitive sects? Implicit in all of these questions was the extent to which European Christianity had developed under conditions of state patronage and the sensibilities of the *Ancien Régime*, and to which these conditions had come to be regarded as customary, even normative. America represented then a radical departure, a plunge into the unknown. In 1844, shortly after his arrival in the United States, Philip Schaff (who later modified his views considerably, as we shall see) gave quintessential expression to this traditionalist perspective:

Tendencies, which had found no political room to unfold themselves in other lands wrought here without restraint. Thus we have come gradually to have a host of sects which is no longer easy to number, and that still continues to swell from year to year.... Such is the aspect of [this] land. A variegated sampler of all conceivable chimeras and dreams.... Every theological vagabond and peddler may drive here his bungling trade, without passport or license, and sell his false ware at pleasure. What is to come of such confusion is not now to be seen.[58]

★★★

The European secularist–leftist or progressive criticism of American religious life did not come into its own until later in the nineteenth century, and it did so not as a negative reaction to modernity, but as a positive, engaged devotion to it. While the traditionalist critique sought to associate the American with the French Revolution and with the disruptive principles of modern liberalism generally, the progressive critique sought to distinguish the two revolutionary traditions and uphold the French model as the more inspiring and exemplary, not least in its militancy in warring against ecclesiastical institutions and traditional expressions of faith. Of the modern bourgeois revolutions, as Friedrich Engels expressed it, "The Great French Revolution was...the first that had entirely cast off the religious cloak."[59] Or, as Gret Haller has recently opined, the Continental revolutionary tradition wanted "the freedom *of* the state in order to implement freedom *from* religion, whereas the United States needed freedom *from* the state in order to implement the freedom *of* religion."[60]

Indeed, a pronounced anticlericalism and secularism—what in France today is generally associated with the tradition of *laïcité*—might be considered as the ideological fundament informing the progressive standpoint, even if its exact meaning and expression varied considerably among different thinkers and when refracted through different national and political contexts.[61] Its deeper roots descend into the soil of eighteenth-century thought, in Voltaire's plea of "Écrasez l'infâme" and in Diderot's proposition "to strangle the last king with the entrails of the last priest." Only gradually—and notably in Tocqueville's writings—was this distinctly counter-*Ancien-Régime* manifestation of secularism recognized to contrast with the more religion-accommodating liberalism of the United States.[62]

But one finds rudiments of it already expressed in the *philosophe* Marquis de Condorcet's *Sketch for an Historical Picture of the Progress of the Human Mind* (1795), the Magna Carta of post-Enlightenment conceptions of historical progress. While Condorcet admired the American Revolution, it ultimately came up short when compared to the Revolution in France, the animating impulses of which were "purer, more precise, and more profound than those that guided the Americans." The French Revolution alone had waged a more successful struggle against "superstition" and ought therefore to be preferred, as it was "more far-reaching than that in America."[63]

Condorcet's conception of history presaged the emergence of various nineteenth-century universalizing visions of progress that, *mutatis mutandis*, equated human development with the attenuation, transformation, and/or eventual elimination of traditionalist expressions of religious belief, especially in their *institutional* manifestations. Collectively, these visions bear witness to what Dipesh Chakrabarty (among others) has identified as modern Europe's hallmark "stadial" or "stagist" conception of history, in which the "persistence" or "survival" of religion has often been taken as *prima facie* evidence of improper or uneven modernization.[64] Sometimes the more pointedly anti-Christian, anti-theological implications of the nineteenth-century visions were muted, or expressed elliptically and in residually religious language, especially during the post-1815 reactionary milieu (see Saint–Simon, for example). But they emerged in a more forthrightly anticlerical and secular idiom by the mid- and late nineteenth century, helping fuel a protracted European-wide *Kulturkampf* against forces of reaction and tradition. As such, they informed a range of ideologies and movements from this period, including liberal republicanism (at least in its more anticlerical guises), Comtean positivism, Left Hegelianism, Marxist Communism, and the platforms of various socialist and revolutionary parties that began to spring up across Europe in the late nineteenth century—the likes of which, in size and scope, had no comparable counterparts across the Atlantic.[65] Differences abounded in these intellectual currents and movements, but each in its way reflected a post-Enlightenment "stadial" conception of "secular historical time" that sought to substitute itself for more traditional theological conceptions of time.[66] (It bears noting, however, that thinkers such as Raymond Aron and Leszek Kolakowski have espied in these movements, and especially Marxism, an ersatz-religiosity or secularist confessionalism, a species of pious enthusiasm, not its counterpoint.)

Europe's liberal and progressive voices in the nineteenth century, to be sure, expressed considerable philo-Americanism, or at least much hopeful curiosity about a nation conjured up with neither a feudal past nor entrenched ecclesiastical powers. Indeed, America—or, at least, the European *idea* of America—was frequently placed on a pedestal by liberals, republicans, parliamentarians, idealists, and social democrats alike. "Amerika, Du hast es besser," as Goethe had famously written. During Europe's reactionary moods and phases in the nineteenth century, liberal and radical thought often had few sources of inspiration besides that of the New World; the United States therefore invited idealized projections of a break with the European past, pristine natural conditions, and unlimited potential for the realization of the New Man of modern democracy.[67]

Nonetheless, hints of worry about America's religious life began to surface from the mid-nineteenth century onward, building eventually into a powerful, distinctly *leftist* European tradition of criticism and repugnance toward the "sectarian," "puritanical," "moralizing" cast of mind found in *actual* American society. A French writer in the Saint-Simonian journal *Revue encyclopédique*, for example, could find much praiseworthy in the United States of the 1830s, but he castigated the "decrepit devotions" of its Christianity and lamented its "puritan austerity" (*rigorisme puritain*) for stifling the development of the fine arts in the New World.[68] Auguste Comte, patriarch of "positivism" and the discipline of "sociology," could peer across the Atlantic with some optimism, but not without taking a shot at the "innumerable and incoherent cults" that seemed to flourish on American soil, a problematic atavism in light of his three-stage theory of history that envisioned humankind advancing from a theological to a metaphysical and, ultimately, to a positivist–scientific plane of existence.[69] So-called republican "1848-ers" in Central European lands tended to idealize the United States, but once the mid-century revolutions collapsed, prompting many to flee across the Atlantic in the 1850s, they were quite often "mightily undeceived in America," Philip Schaff observed of them, "and begin at once . . . to scoff at the intolerable tedium of the . . . pharisaical church-going, the tyrannical priestcraft, and whatever else they may call *the pious habits and institutions of the United States.*"[70]

As shall be elaborated in chapter three, Karl Marx and Friedrich Engels expressed worries too, regarding North America as a most advanced bourgeois polity, but one where "religion and sectarianism" in a commercial, frontier environment contributed to "a certain backwardness of thought" that worked against the maturation of socialist theory and practice.[71] Socialist visitors to the United States in the late nineteenth century often groused about the pious attachments of American workers and the "deformed Puritanism" that permeated American society.[72] Early twentieth-century communist works on America—bearing such titles as *America, A World Menace* (1922) and *Le cancer américain* (1931)—could take it for granted that the untrammeled capitalist conditions of the United States explained the pitiable need for religious consolation among the population.[73]

As is well established, the emergence of the sociological concept of "secularization," although more a twentieth-century development, cannot be separated from the European experience of the nineteenth century and the ideological predispositions and inclinations of early theorists of social science. The aforementioned Comte and Marx are among the best known cases, but the generalization holds equally true for many other figures. The origins of secularization theory, Jeffrey

Hadden has noted, was never a matter of "value-free armchair scholars" simply watching a phenomenon unfold, but a theoretical assertion all too often beholden to a desired future outcome. Like anticlerical politicians in the French Third Republic, David Martin has echoed, early theorists of secularization were "not simply observing a sociological fact, but were doing all in their power to guarantee it and make it a reality."[74]

Although "secularization" as a theory, as many studies have shown, fails miserably in capturing the empirical realities of nineteenth-century Europe, its totalizing, forward-looking assumptions possessed a conceptual éclat highly attractive to intellectuals (especially, but not exclusively, of the Left) and influential in how many conceived of the "necessary" course of modern times. (For quite different reasons, it has attracted conservative critics keen to bemoan modern irreligiosity.) By the late nineteenth century, as David McLellan has observed, a "materialist metaphysics" intent on expunging religion from human consciousness colored much of Continental socialist thought,[75] irrespective of whether one opted for a more parliamentary path of socialist development, which emphasized constitutional religious freedoms, or for a more confrontational revolutionary path, which sought, as Marx put it, "to liberate the conscience from the witchery of religion" altogether.[76] In both cases, a correlation of the growth of socialism and the decline of religion was generally presumed; and in classical Marxist formulations, it became an article of certainty that overcoming bourgeois structures through working-class revolution, ipso facto, entailed the dissolution of "the opiate of the people" and its replacement by historical materialism.[77]

The twentieth century in Western Europe, especially since mid-century, was much kinder to notions of secularization, broadly understood. If the more utopian political projections of Marx have been widely discredited by the brutalities of left-wing totalitarian governments and, ultimately, by the events of 1989 and the collapse of the Soviet Union, Marxist projections about the withering of religion cannot easily be brushed aside when confronted by the high levels of church disaffiliation and personal unbelief found in the welfare states of Western Europe.[78] To what degree the relative advance of socialist ideas and realities in Europe actually accounts for this is certainly a contestable point, but the reality itself (whatever its causes) has undeniably conferred plausibility on the general teleological narrative of secularization, fostering a reflexive association of "the modern" and "the secular," marching together in progressive lockstep. And even if it has become increasingly clear that "secular Europe" presents an exceptional case when compared to the rest of the world's high levels of enduring religiosity,[79] the story-line of modernization-leads-to-secularity has been invoked frequently and insistently enough and bears sufficient sanction within the particular historical experience of Western Europe as to confer an aura of a *normative* historical teleology, a description of what, under appropriate circumstances, *should* be the case. "[T]heories of secularization in Europe," to quote the sociologist José Casanova, "have functioned as self-fulfilling prophecies to the extent that the majority of the population in Europe has come to accept the premises of those theories as a depiction of the *normal state of affairs* and as a projection of future developments."[80]

From this standpoint, it should not surprise that the United States' more vibrantly religious path to modernity—as my earlier story about the German Fulbright student suggests—appears as an "anomaly," a "puzzling" development in need of explanation. This, in rough terms, comprises the crux of the European-secularist perspective on American religious life. Not surprisingly, explaining why religion "persisted" in America—like explaining why socialism failed to find "appropriate" succor here—emerged as an intriguing "research problem" for many Western European academics, as well as for some American scholars heavily influenced by the contours of historical consciousness and patterns of social-scientific plausibility derived from the European experience and accepting of a "social imaginary" and comparative orientation that dropped its plumb line from Paris, London, or Berlin.[81]

For those who have advocated or assumed the historical normativity of the European route of secularization, the United States indeed appeared to have taken a peculiar road to modernity, one whose revolution, unlike the French Revolution, congenitally lacked sufficient secularizing impulses. From this vantage point, what distinguished the American system was not so much that it produced religious–cultural disarray (that is more the traditionalist criticism, outlined above), but that it preserved variants of dogmatic premodern religiosity all too well—sectarian and obscurantist variants, to be sure, and ones stubbornly impervious to enlightenment or elimination. Criticism from the Left thus focused more on *cultural backwardness* (a progressive fear) than *cultural anarchy* (a conservative fear). But *les extrêmes se touchent*, as the French say: the two outlooks, Right and Left, have certainly proven capable of blending together, as the condescension of the traditionalists and the incredulity of the secularists toward America's religious vitality have frequently cross-pollinated. The resulting reproachful glances across the Atlantic should figure in any assessment of the deeper historical currents informing transatlantic realities and relations.

Allow me to summarize. European misgivings about American religious dynamics reflect both a traditionalist-right and a secularist-left genealogy and corresponding historical perspectives. While these perspectives are at odds with one another at many levels, their respective narrations of the relationship between modernity and religion, willy-nilly, cast the religio-political character of the United States as ill-conceived, producing an erroneously religious society (Right) or an overly religious one (Left). These narratives owe their formation to the far ends of a distinctly European political spectrum that first took clear shape in the decades following the French Revolution. The traditionalist critique of America derives from a nostalgia for established churches and a host of attendant pre-democratic, culturally organicist sentiments; the United States, in this view, represents a disquieting departure from a more salutary ecclesiastical establishmentarianism, and a robust exercise of religious freedom has been met warily as indulgence in subjectivism and individualism. On the other hand, European skepticism of American religious life evinces a progressive–secularist mien, insofar as the French tradition of *laïcité* and various comparable ideologies and intellectual currents informing leftist and socialist thought and, later, secularization theory are invoked, or unconsciously assumed, as the benchmarks for appropriate historical development. In both cases, Right and Left, critics of American religiosity have often regarded the United States simply as the absence of certain specifically European conditions that are regarded as normative, or at least highly desirable. Both views, one might further argue, bear witness to an irrepressible nineteenth-century European *mission civilisatrice*, with the emerging United States serving to Europe at once as poor learner, oafish foil, and didactic counterexample.

Finally, both European accounts of the American religious scene suggest the inadequacy and historically shallow nature of many present-day analyses of anti-Americanism and transatlantic divisions. Various and sundry major geopolitical developments since the end of the Cold

War have certainly roiled and reconfigured transatlantic relations, raising policy questions of the highest order. But this should not obscure
the fact that an "Atlantic gap" between the Old World and the New is
more probingly examined by keeping in mind embedded cultural factors and the accretion of perceptions and interpretations over much
longer stretches of time. Contemporary European misgivings about
America ought to be understood against a backdrop of historical precedents—at least some of which certainly have to do with European
perceptions of American religion.[82]

The Historian and the Philosopher: Philip Schaff and Jacques Maritain

Examining images and perceptions of American religion through the
comparative political lens inspired by Louis Hartz, as sketched above,
promises insight into a little explored realm of European disquiet toward the United States. But to focus largely on the negative and
critical—and on the far ends of the political spectrum—would, finally,
offer an incomplete picture. From the wholly laudatory to the con-
structively critical, some Europeans have of course exhibited profound
sympathy with the United States and its religious life, offering insights
at once trenchant and distinctive to a foreigner's pen. In the final parts
of the book, I turn my attention—tipping my hat respectfully to Tocqueville, but looking beyond his imposing figure—to two underap-
preciated, largely sympathetic European commentators: Philip Schaff
and Jacques Maritain.

At first glance, this might appear an odd pairing. Denizens of different
eras and milieus, one Swiss–German, the other French; one a Protestant,
the other Catholic; one a church historian, the other a philosopher—
these two men might seem to possess more differences than commonalities. And, indeed, their differences help make for an interesting pairing,
as their respective standpoints offer diverse angles of observation and
interpretation.

But as their differences are often complementary, so their commonalities are often striking. Schaff and Maritain shared a fascination
with the United States, its constitutional order, and especially, as both
believed, its historically unprecedented experiment in religious freedom. Since both were men of faith, the latter interest should perhaps

not be surprising. What is more, neither were simply "visitors" to American shores; making their home in the United States for extended periods (in Schaff's case for the majority of his adult life), they were truly *transatlantic personalities*, traversing the Atlantic frequently and hence well-situated to mediate the New World to the Old and vice versa. Schaff departed Europe in 1844, accepting a call from the German Reformed Church in America to teach at its seminary in Mercersburg, Pennsylvania. Later he took a position at Union Theological Seminary in New York, teaching there until the year of his death in 1893. During his career, he made no less than fourteen return trips to Europe, often to lecture on conditions and events in the United States. From these lecture tours came several remarkable books and essays, particularly his *America: A Sketch of the Political, Social, and Religious Character of the United States of North America*, first published in 1854.

Born a decade before Schaff's death, Maritain, too, lived in the United States. He and his wife Raïssa fled war-torn France in 1940 for what was to be a brief exile abroad. As things turned out, he accepted academic appointments in New York and Princeton, and wound up living in the United States until 1960, punctuated by a three-year period as the French Ambassador to the Vatican directly after the war. His time in America, in other words, corresponded with the fascist undoing of Europe and the anxious early years of the Cold War. Publishing *Reflections on America* in 1958, based on a seminar given at the University of Chicago, he commented on the political and religious significance of the United States in numerous other works as well, including in *Scholasticism and Politics* (1940), *Christianity and Democracy* (1943), *Man and the State*, (1951), and *On the Philosophy of History* (1957).

Neither Schaff nor Maritain withheld criticisms. Schaff frequently criticized the religious and cultural life under the social conditions of American democracy, and he felt that educational institutions in the United States had much to learn from those in Europe, especially from the universities of Germany, where he had received his doctorate.[83] Maritain too made critical observations, worrying that Americans' overly practical mind-set and consumerist ways worked against appreciation of the *vita contemplativa*. Moreover, both Schaff and Maritain, along with numerous other foreigners, commented critically on the institution of American slavery and its unhappy legacy.

Nonetheless, Schaff and Maritain were ultimately constructive commentators, convinced that the United States truly represented a *novus ordo seclorum*, in politico-religious matters foremost, and one from which Europe had much to learn. Nowhere was this more evident to them than in Americans' commitment to and robust exercise of religious freedom and in the habits of mind and emphasis on self-government derived therefrom. Furthermore, both came to believe that the novel historical conditions of the United States were not readily grasped from traditional European categories and frameworks of interpretation, especially those pertaining to church–state relations. For this reason, both felt the need to explain America's distinctive conditions—not only to Europeans, but to Americans as well—and countermand streams of anti-American sentiment that both men regarded as excessive and misguided among Europe's elite, opinion-shaping classes.

Schaff and Maritain, however, went about their tasks quite differently. A Reformed Protestant and, intellectually, a child of the early nineteenth century, Schaff sought to situate the United States in an unfolding, quasi-Hegelian scheme of history, one which accorded America great significance for awakening humanity to the voluntary principle in religion and to its many related virtues, such as individual initiative, personal responsibility, private philanthropy, and a sense of even the lowliest's dignity before God—virtues, he felt, that were inhibited from coming to full expression under the prevailing European system of "state-churchism" (*Staatskirchentum*). Not surprisingly perhaps, Schaff felt that America's religious voluntarism bore witness to a distinctly *Protestant* achievement, one that could not have occurred in a country where Catholicism predominated, and one greatly assisted by the particular historical circumstances of America's founding era and early history.

Maritain came to similar conclusions about church–state relations in the United States and the voluntary principle in religious matters. As an observant Catholic, however, he was compelled to make his arguments within a tradition that in the nineteenth century had witnessed Vatican decrees against religious freedom (associated with the error of "indifferentism") and against "Americanism," a shadowy collection of putatively erroneous religious traits believed to stem from the political climate of the United States. It was Maritain's genius to return to some of Catholicism's own most revered intellectual authorities, Thomas

Aquinas foremost, to argue that modern ideas of democracy, individual rights, and religious freedom, particularly as represented by the United States, could be developed from latent but dynamic possibilities within scholastic thought. His arguments on these topics contributed significantly to the Second Vatican Council's epochal decree on religious freedom, *Dignitatis humanae* (1965), a momentous theological defense of religious freedom on the basis of human dignity.[84]

In the final analysis, Schaff and Maritain's personal experiences in and intellectual reflections on the United States led them to reevaluate and reengage their respective theological traditions and their European heritage, in an attempt to validate American religious freedom and many of its associated virtues and principles. To accomplish this, both felt the need to challenge criticisms of the United States and its religious life—criticisms which, as chapters two and three will show, had become entrenched and self-perpetuating within many high-brow circles of Europe. The efforts of Schaff and Maritain are themselves not above criticism, but, together, they provide a rich and relevant legacy today, for peoples of good will on both sides of the Atlantic— and beyond.

2

The Traditionalist Critique: A "Ranting and Raving Tumult"

> With regard to religion in America, the Government affords it no support whatever, it being left entirely to the voluntary zeal of its professors.... The country, therefore, what between powerful preachers and cunning builders, is overrun with churches, and it is not easy to predict where this popular movement is to stop.
>
> —J. H. James, *Rambles in the United States and Canada* (1847)

Introduction

In 1835, the year that the first volume of Alexis de Tocqueville's *Democracy in America* appeared in France, a young American, Robert Baird (1798–1863), set sail for Europe. An agent of the American and Foreign Christian Union, Baird had received a mandate to encourage Sunday School organization, Bible distribution, and temperance reform abroad. What he discovered in Europe took him aback: boundless curiosity about religious life in North America, but also much derision toward it. This unsettling encounter led to subsequent trips abroad to lecture on American political and religious institutions. Eventually he published a book, *Religion in America* (1844), among the first major efforts by a citizen of the United States to explain the new nation's religious dynamics to a foreign audience.

Baird conceived of his task as delicate and difficult. European visitors to the United States, he felt, tended to focus on the excesses and unseemly elements of religious freedom, "and such abuses have been trumpeted throughout the world with the view of bringing discredit

on the religion of the country." "Many, who have never visited America," he complained, "owe all their ideas on that subject to writers
whose own information was partial and incorrect, and who . . . wished
to give piquancy to their pages by working up for the wonder and
amusement of their readers every false and exaggerated statement, and
foolish anecdote, which had been poured into their ears."[1]

While one might correct for an element of nativist defensiveness on
Baird's part, his impression of European attitudes was not unfounded.
What is more, negative assessments of the United States were not restricted to the religious domain, but touched upon politics, society,
culture, and more. Although the Revolutionary War and the drafting
of the American Constitution had elicited much enthusiasm from proponents of Enlightenment and liberalism in Europe, this enthusiasm
had decidedly waned in the early decades of the nineteenth century,
as travelers with means (which often meant those with aristocratic
backgrounds) and conservative publicists and intellectuals (now with
images of Jacobins and guillotines etched in their minds) mounted
stronger and stronger arguments against the United States and its democratic institutions as models for European development.[2]

But even the late eighteenth century was no golden age of philo-
Americanism. During this time, appreciation of the early American
republic competed with an influential body of putatively "scientific"
literature on the "degeneracy" of the New World, its impoverished
natural and social conditions, from which little good could be expected, and certainly not the high civilizational standards of Europe.
Exemplified in the writings of Cornelius de Pauw, Georges Louis
Leclerc, Comte de Buffon, and the celebrated encyclopedist Guil-
laume Thomas Raynal, this literature provoked a debate—the so-called
"Dispute of the New World" in Antonello Gerbi's formulation—that
raged in Europe and across the Atlantic in the late eighteenth and early
nineteenth century, drawing in figures from Immanuel Kant and Alexander von Humboldt to Thomas Jefferson and Alexander Hamilton.[3]

Positions in the debate were sharply drawn. On one side stood
European travelers, explorers, and emigrants, drawing on earlier mythic
accounts of the New World, who extolled the virtues of natural man, the
pristine wilderness, the chance for humanity to refashion itself in a new
world. On the other side—the one that frequently commanded more
scholarly respect in the salons and academies of Europe—stood those
intent to puncture such grandiose accounts of America by pointing out

its myriad deformities and insufficiencies. North America in particular presented a dreary, inhospitable natural environment—"a fetid and boggy terrain" in some places, "a vast and sterile desert" in others—that promised to weigh upon all efforts of political and cultural achievement.[4] In some formulations, the New World was dismissed as a gigantic mistake, destined to deteriorate all institutions and peoples unwise enough to transplant themselves from Europe. Unfit for human habitation, "so ill-favored by nature that all it contains is either degenerate or monstrous," the discovery and conquest of the New World "has been the greatest of all misfortunes to befall mankind," summed up Cornelius de Pauw in his *Recherches philosophiques sur les Américains* (Berlin, 1768–69).[5]

While many aspects of this dispute seem comical in retrospect (the presumed inferiority of dogs' ability to bark in the New World, the unseemly size of American frogs!), the "degeneracy thesis," as it is sometimes called, would leave a lasting impression on *Homo sapiens Europaeus* (Thomas Jefferson's term), especially in shaping the cultural and historical categories available to size up the fledgling polity of the United States.[6] The eighteenth-century savants "who rediscovered America from their studies in Paris and Berlin," notes Philippe Roger, were inclined to see a "geographical flaw," the site of prevailing and future "stagnation." "[J]ust as the New England colonies were solidifying their aspiration for a *vita nuova*, the most listened-to voices in Europe were consigning America to sterility and death."[7]

Whether directly or indirectly influential, the rhetorical contours of the degeneracy thesis are relevant to nineteenth-century traditionalist assessments of American religion, even if a more immediate point of influence is traceable to fears about the *esprit révolutionnaire* gripping the modern world. Criticisms from the conservative standpoint, as previously indicated, could of course vary considerably, depending on the critic's national identity and confessional allegiance. But these criticisms also shared significant common ground, in the conviction that transplanting beliefs, traditions and institutions from the Old World to the New entailed their degeneration and the unraveling of proper religion as such.

One hears rudiments of this line of argument already in the Frenchman Jean de Crèvecoeur's well-known *Letters from an American Farmer* (1782), where he writes of the "strange religious medley" in America, inclining people to "religious indifference." The expatriate believed that this condition betokened the demise of coherent belief and the rise of a type of spiritual individualism. The situation in America "leaves every one to think for themselves in spiritual matters...and worship the Divinity [according] to their own peculiar ideas." Just as national differences blurred in America, so too did creedal traditions and religious communities: "all sects are mixed as well as nations; thus religious indifference is...disseminated from one end of the continent to the other.... Where this will reach no one can tell.... [Z]eal in Europe is confined; here it evaporates in the great distance it has to travel; there it is a grain of powder enclosed; here it burns away in the open air, and consumes without effects."[8]

Variations on such lines of reasoning were legion in nineteenth-century European opinion and travel literature, even if one may fairly conclude that Crèvecoeur more accurately foresaw American Christianity's fragmentation than its dissipation. In what follows, I concentrate on three distinct but related strands of Old World traditionalist critique. The first focuses on British voices loyal to the Anglican church, supportive of its civil connections, and appreciative of its nurture of cultural refinement and social propriety. Such Tory voices from the erstwhile "mother country," oscillating between parental disapproval and sibling rivalry, tended to interpret religion in America as a consequence of the dangers of popular democracy and the weakening of rightly-constituted authority. As we shall see, these interpretations often tell us as much about domestic issues in Britain as about the United States per se.[9]

Continental–Romantic criticisms, secondly, will receive attention, particularly those emanating from German-speaking parts of Europe, the heart of the Romantic movement in the nineteenth century. In this literature, one comes across ample criticism of the United States on traditionalist, nostalgic grounds, in which an idealized pre-revolutionary, religious past and an organically-constituted society, respectful of the distinctions of *Volk* or race, provide the cultural benchmarks, from which the United States—with its religious divisions and populism, commercial spirit, abstract constitutionalism, and mish-mash of European peoples—fundamentally deviated. From this standpoint, the United States might be regarded as a religious nation, but a misguided one, lacking profundity and Spirit (*Geist*) in the desired cultural sense.

Finally, the Catholic Church, embattled against modernity ever since Napoleon reduced the Eternal City to capital of the French *département* of the Tiber, can lay claim to its own distinctive attitude toward the United States. From Rome, and her ultramontane allies throughout Europe, the United States tended to be viewed through the prism of the French Revolution, the revolutions of 1848–49, and the Italian *Risorgimento*, which led to the dissolution of the Papal States. What is more, the United States, connected in its formative periods to the heirs of John Calvin, constituted, at root, an expression of *Protestantism*; the dangerous principle of "private judgment" that first had erupted in Wittenberg in 1517 had come home to roost in a land of deficient, fissiparous manifestations of Christianity. "Protestantism is the *sans-culottisme* of religion," Joseph de Maistre had written, and while the United States had not witnessed the violent anticlericalism of France, the upstart nation ought to serve neither as a model for Europe's religious life nor its political future.[10]

Sophisticates Abroad: The Anglican Visitation to American Democracy

> I am willing to love all mankind, except an American.
>
> —Samuel Johnson

"America was the China of the nineteenth century—described, analyzed, promoted, and attacked in virtually every nation struggling to come to terms with new social and political forces."[11] If this generalization holds true for European nations as a whole, it especially holds true for Great Britain.[12] Although London never witnessed the revolutionary bloodshed of Paris, forces of liberalism, popular democracy, and religious dissent roiled British society and were hotly debated in parliament and tavern alike. As a former colonial possession, the United States occupied a position of singular symbolic importance in these debates, dividing radicals, nonconformists, and progressive Whigs, who generally tilted toward pro-American positions, from representatives of the Tory–Anglican Establishment, who tended to regard the United States as a threatening counterexample to cherished political traditions and rightly-constituted religion.[13]

Embittered by memories of 1776 and 1812, disquieted by the rapid spread of free-market principles and practices, nineteenth-century

English conservatives had much to worry about from the upstart nation strictly on political and economic grounds. But religious matters were of a different and deeper order, ramifying into the most sensitive areas of culture, morality, and, indeed, eternal felicity; and it was simply taken for granted that an established church constituted a necessary pillar for political order and civilizational norms. "[T]he Church of England," as G. H. Guttridge has written, "was the central institution of Toryism—the state in its religious aspect, and the divine principle in monarchical government."[14] James Mill once opined in the progressive *Westminster Review*, that every evil in American society, in the eyes of conservatives, was regularly traced to the want of an established church.[15]

One should not over-estimate the extent and influence of Tory criticisms, for numerous British voices praised America's voluntary religious system and held it up to expose the shortcomings of tithes, religious tests, and other forms of Anglican privilege.[16] Even so, fears of a coarse and unruly religious populism, of rampant sectarianism, and of the general atomizing of society stretched well into center of the political spectrum. What is more, many of the most eloquent examples of transatlantic travel literature in the early nineteenth century were penned by conservatives, whose eagerness to diminish radicalism and nonconformism at home often resulted in extreme skepticism of American institutions and society. The domestic Tory press too—which found its center of gravity in the London-based *Quarterly Review*—had a reputation for relentless, satirical anti-Americanism. These realities—combined with the witty derision of the United States flowing from the pens of conservative literary lights such as Frances Trollope, Charles Dickens, Matthew Arnold, Thomas Carlyle, John Ruskin, James Fitzjames Stephen, and others—contributed by the late nineteenth century to a rhetorical arsenal of stock phrases, quips, and habits of thought, which cast the United States as a cauldron of confusions, deprivations, and misbegotten principles.[17]

English travelers in the early nineteenth century encountered an American society in the grips of one of the most formative religious revivals and expansions in the nation's history, the "profound religious upsurge" of the Second Great Awakening. While many of the denominations at the forefront of this expansion—Methodists, Baptists, Presbyterians—owed their roots to British soil, the American movements took place absent the authority of an established national church, under a federal government with few internal functions, and during a period of rapid westward expansion and massive population growth.[18] British conservatives abroad were regularly astonished, at a loss to describe the religious ferment and vitality of their erstwhile colonial possession.[19] This astonishment, combined with the desire to check anti-establishment sentiment at home, produced not only a highly critical literature on American religious life, but, for many, evidence of the instability of the fledgling democratic experiment. "The unreasonableness of the demands of the dissenters [for dis-establishment] in our own country," wrote the Tory novelist and sea captain Frederick Marryat, "will be better brought home to them by...pointing out the effects of the voluntary system in the United States."[20]

Recurring themes appear in the criticisms of conservative travelers, as well as in those of others who felt the urge to size up, second-hand, characteristics of American democracy. Nearly all believed, and were eager to document, that social chaos flowed predictably from a purely voluntary religious system. Few expressed this better than Bishop Samuel Wilberforce of Oxford, whose history of the Episcopal church in the United States (published in 1849) sounded a strong warning against the influence of democracy and religious freedom. "No where have the restless waters of the multitude of sects," he wrote, "tossed themselves in wilder madness than in the new world.... Every fantas-tic opinion which has disturbed the peace of Christendom has been re-produced in stronger growth on the other side of the Atlantic."[21] Charles Lyell, who visited the United States in 1841–42, was taken aback at how "the bitterness of sectarian dogmatism and jealousy" frequently divided family members"[22] After his visit to the United States, the Scottish writer and critic of democracy Thomas Hamilton complained that in America religious differences breed "argument, dis-pute, and bitterness of feeling," which in turn "rend society into shreds and patches."[23]

Frederick Marryat could admit that an established church, at some level, constituted a "species of coercion," but the absence of one in America, he felt, only produced the fracturing of religion and soci-ety. People in the United States "divide and split into many mole-cules[;]...they resemble the globules of water when expanded by heat, and like them are in a state of restlessness and excitement." Marryat cataloged some of the religious paths taken by individuals and communities in a land where "everyone worships the Deity after his own fashion." Time and again he returned to the view that the social environment only fomented confusion. In America, "even the Quakers," he noted, relishing the irony, "have split into controversy, and the men of peace are at open war in Philadelphia, the city of brotherly love." One then could not easily discount the virtues of an established church: "It would appear as if the majority were much too frail and weak to go it alone upon their heavenly journey.... The effects of an established church are to cement the mass, cement society and communities, and increase the force of those natural ties by which families and relations are bound together."[24]

If the American voluntary system produced "excitement" and divisions, as Marryat held, others faulted it for paving the way for heterodoxy, religious apathy, and irreligion—a line of reasoning not unlike that earlier voiced by Crèvecoeur. John Robert Godley, for example, held that the New World's sectarian impulse, although encouraging dogmatic divisions in the short term, led finally to a watered-down indifference toward all theological verities. For him, "the American mind" was at root "latitudinarian," possessing "a natural repugnance to anything which affects an exclusive or dogmatical character." "Like the ancient Romans, who would receive any number of additional divinities into their Pantheon,...the American will admit any sect...which receives the Christian Scriptures, and any doctrinal scheme which it thinks may be deduced therefrom, so long as it allows all others to be equally right who do the same."[25] While such a situation might secure civil peace, Godley believed that it ultimately undermined genuine faith, promoting "outward" religion and a hypocrisy that was at once "shallow and unphilosophical,...self-contradictory and suicidal."[26] "For my part," he concluded, "I prefer the earnest striving after truth," enjoined and assumed by Old World establishmentarianism, to "the carelessness about it," embodied in the American voluntary system.[27]

Unflattering depictions of clergymen appear routinely in travel literature. American pastors were charged in particular with a lack of education and culture, and with pandering to their congregations. Such accounts were meant less as an attack on the clerical profession in America per se than as an indictment of the voluntary system or, less scathingly, as a recognition that the United States had not yet had the time to develop high-caliber seminaries and institutions of higher learning. Isaac Fidler, for example, who journeyed to the United States in 1832, derided "the superficial learning of the best educated among the American population," illustrating his point by summarizing his encounters with so-called Methodist "ranters."

After any ranter had used an improper expression, or made an inconclusive [biblical] quotation, I begged him to explain himself and point out the justness of his [theological] inferences. Such incoherent and absurd expressions were hereby instantly suspended; for none I met with could explain himself or discuss religious subjects without extravagant metaphors. In less than five minutes, in every case, and mostly in less than one, we were all as mute and melancholy as if we had just emerged from the cave of Trophonius.[28]

Samuel Wilberforce worried that the lack of education among the clergy on the American frontier raised the specter of a host of "ardent, inexperienced, imprudent young men," whose shallow minds threatened "to obliterate civilization."[29] Thomas Hamilton bemoaned the "ignorant fanaticism" of the American clergy, opining that the endless theological controversies in the United States lacked the dignity of erudition: "The rival clergymen attack each other from the pulpit; newspapers are enlisted on either side; and religious warfare is waged with the bitterness if not the learning which has distinguished the controversies of abler polemics."[30]

For many observers, though, the greater misfortune of the voluntary system resided in clerical pandering. This amounted to an inadmissible state of affairs, Isaac Fidler believed, for the minister in America "is entirely at the mercy, and under the control of his flock. He is, in fact, their creature, however desirous he may be of concealing it from himself."[31] For Fidler, this arrangement boded ill for the clergy's prospects of attaining high levels of education and a respected social standing. "From the manner in which ministers are rewarded," he wrote, "it is clear to me that America can never, under her present form of government, possess a body of divines so learned and respectable as those in England." Instead of leading his flock to higher standards of knowledge and piety, the minister in America will be forced "to adapt his mode of delivery to the taste and temperament of his hearers," who hold the purse strings, thereby compromising and vulgarizing the vocation of ministry.[32]

In his travel reflections, Marryat traced the minister's compromised position directly to the political environment. "In a republic, or democracy," he wrote, the people will rule in everything: in the Congregational church they rule as deacons; in the Presbyterian as elders. Affairs are litigated and decided in committees and councils, and thus is the pastoral office deprived of its primitive and legitimate influence, and the ministers are tyrannized over by the laity, in the most absurd and unjustifiable manner.[33]

But if the general democratic milieu received censure, a more immediate bane came in the form of "camp-meetings" and "revivals," especially among the Methodists, in the country's vast, scantly populated frontier, "the waste lands which spread for countless leagues beyond the settled portions of the union."[34] "The Methodists in America are more enthusiastic than those in England," wrote Isaac Holmes in a fairly typical summary of a frontier camp-meeting:

They appear determined to take heaven by storm; their ministers are not well paid, and they have not many men of education amongst them.... [T]hey occasionally have camp meetings. They fix upon some place, where they erect tents, one portion of which is allotted for females to repose in at night. The morning is ushered in by singing, praying, and telling "their experience." Afterwards, there are sermons delivered, and the whole day is taken up in religious exercises. This...occasionally produces in some persons a partial derangement. I have no doubt that the promoters of these camp meetings do it with the best intention; but... [it] does certainly appear the height of folly.[35]

Whether based on direct observation or secondary sources, such derisory commentary on American revivals, camp-meetings and itinerant preachers is borne out in the travel literature with remarkable consistency.[36] To provide another example, T. H. Grattan, who served for a period as the British consul in Boston, complained of the "monstrous" religious displays in the American interior. Such displays, he elaborated,

throw the country into ranting and raving tumult, under the form of revivals, awakenings, and other deplorable scandals, bring[ing] disgrace and shame upon the very name of Religion they desecrate. The frightful descriptions of these periodical outbursts require no addition. The burlesque exhibitions of human weakness and hypocrisy mingled together are almost incomprehensible; and in witnessing their terrific effects on multitudes of people, the marvel is that there can be any limit to the epidemic insanity, and that the whole world does not go mad.[37]

Of the itinerant preachers who led the revivals, Grattan had only contempt, blanketly accusing the majority of them of insincerity and duplicity:

Thousands of men enter into holy orders of one kind or another, adopt the title Reverend and some peculiar garb of outward sanctity, and dash into the exercise of their profession, either as followers or founders of sects, outrunning each other in the race which seems to have no fixed starting-place, no limits, and no goal. Where these extraordinary persons come from, under what authority they act, or by what principles they are guided is all a matter of mystery.... [I] believe that the enormous majority of those ranting vulgarians, who mount into pulpits and penetrate into parlours, scattering threats of damnation and pictures of hell, like incendiaries flinging firebrands into a powder mill, are heartless hypocrites, living on the weakness and wretchedness of their dupes.[38]

Along with descriptions of frontier revivals among the Methodists and other denominations, accounts of excursions to the rarer religious communities, such as the Millerites and Shakers, became a staple for many conservative visitors, motivated in part by simple curiosity, but also by a desire to document first-hand the extremities of New World belief. Shakers communities in New York and New England emerged as such "a leading tourist attraction" that some even allowed at their meeting houses a special section reserved for onlookers.[39] While visitors often esteemed the industry of these communities, Shakers themselves were regularly depicted as imbeciles and dupes. "[T]heir extravagant superstition," Grattan wrote, "sinks them far below the scale of beings guided by sound views of life and rational principles of belief."[40] Charles Dickens, who loathed their austerity, quipped that Shaker women were so ugly that their celibacy was probably not entirely a matter of choice.[41] Millerites[42] too were regularly dismissed as among the more "grotesque and unreserved" of the American sects, while the emergence and success of Mormonism—and "the enormous iniquities of this erratic sect"—were widely regarded as proof-positive of the misguided principles animating the American religious experiment. By mid-century, Mormons came to exercise a tremendous fascination among European writers, largely displacing Shakers and Millerites as the great American religious curiosity. While few trekked out west to visit them, this undoubtedly contributed to knowledge of them being shrouded in suspicion and speculation.[43] Sir Arthur Conan Doyle's 1887 *Study in Scarlet* (in which Sherlock Holmes first appeared) contains a typically unflattering portrait of Utah, "the country of the saints."[44]

While travel books on America were published aplenty in the early nineteenth century, none emerged as a literary sensation quite to the degree of Frances (Fanny) Trollope's *Domestic Manners of the Americans* (1832). Its colorful author—part Tory traditionalist, part financial opportunist—traveled to the United States in 1827 and spent two years in the American interior, principally in and around Cincinnati, an emerging commercial city "freshly risen from the bosom of the wilderness."[45] Her acidly critical and satirical account of the republican experiment quickly went through several printings and translations after it first appeared in London. Arguably no other book in English penned in the nineteenth century provoked as much discussion about the United States or confirmed conservative prejudices more than this single volume. "I do not like them [the Americans]. I do not like their principles, I do not like their manners, I do not like their opinions," she bluntly concluded.[46] The New World that she described was a giant step backwards with respect to civilization, the unruly triumph of self-interest, vulgarity, and a tobacco-spitting mob. To "trollopize," meaning to abuse the American nation, entered the English language as a recognized verb.

Commentary on American religion occupies a significant portion of her book. In many respects, her perspective resembles that of other conservatives, and she covers predictable topics: revivals, itinerant preachers, camp-meetings, Methodists, Shakers, and so on. But her eloquence and erudition in connecting the want of an established church to the general lack of manners and culture, and her firm association of the decidedly non-aristocratic forms of American religious life with the shortcomings of democracy as such, make her, in some respects, a case apart. And, again, her influence in England and beyond, was formidable, particularly her skill in modeling a supercilious disapprobation toward the United States.

While many European critics esteemed religious freedom in principle, but pointed out its deficiencies in (American) practice, Trollope went a step further, arguing that the American example demonstrates that untrammeled freedom of belief engenders a "religious tyranny" more exacting than "the paying of the tithe," and that some form of ecclesiastical establishment, however unlikely, might arrest America's descent into venality and cultural anarchy. Along with others, she pointed to the sectarian impulse as an indictment of the voluntary system as a whole. "[I]t was impossible to remain many weeks in the country without being struck with the strange anomalies produced by its religious system.... The whole people appear to be divided into an almost endless variety of religious factions." The Catholics alone, she averred, appeared exempt "from the fury of division and sub-division" and "the outrageous display of individual whim" characteristic of American Protestantism. These anomalies, one might reason, were peculiar to the new nation's sparsely settled western regions, but Trollope insisted that they were embedded in the American polity itself, producing "the same effect everywhere."[47]

The influence of religion in general and over-zealous ministers in particular on American women received some of Trollope's most excoriating commentary. Without developed literary and cultural institutions in Cincinnati, women appeared to her to have few outlets for social activities, except in the churches. "I never saw, or read, of any country where religion had so strong a hold upon the women," she wrote, comparing the position of women in society to that of Southern European countries, where women suffocated, she held, under the undue influence of Catholic priests. Female energies that might have been channeled into the making of high society were exhausted in America by untoward religious pursuits. "Were it not for the churches I think there might be a general bonfire of the best bonnets, for I never could discover any other use for them."[48]

Revivals and camp-meetings elicited predictable derogation. After describing in minute detail a revival that she had attended, with its "most violent cries and shrieks," Trollope confessed to finding the whole experience "frightful," wholesome neither for religion nor for the American people: "For myself, I confess that I think the coarsest comedy every written would be a less detestable exhibition for the eyes of youth and innocence than such a scene." She similarly deplored a Methodist camp-meeting, "that most terrific saturnalia." Captivated by the "distorted figures" rapt in worship or repentance, she expressed "horror and disgust," comparing at one point the activities of the tents, where participants gathered in the daytime to pray and read Scripture, to "a cell in Bedlam" because of the raw emotion on display and the extemporaneous nature of the praying.[49]

In short, the American religious scene presented itself to Trollope as nothing short of a nightmare—formless, emotional, zealous, harmful to piety and worship alike, and a general social evil. To rightly criticize it, one ought not stop at half-measures, but address the root cause: the absence of an established church, and one guided by learned, aristocratic sentiment. "It is impossible, in witnessing all these unseemly vagaries," she wrote, "not to recognize the advantages of an established church as a sort of head-quarters for quiet unpresuming Christians, who are contented to serve faithfully, without insisting upon each a little separate banner, embroidered with a device of their own imagining." An established church would not only prevent "every tinker and tailor" from mounting the pulpit, but would help ensure the maintenance of a "salutary decorum" in social manners.[50] The American polity, by contrast, positively encouraged the passing of religion from aristocratic guardianship to the vulgarity of the mob, and with it the despoilment of refined social sensibilities.

From the mid-nineteenth century onward, few learned Britons who crossed the Atlantic or expressed curiosity about the new nation did so without some acquaintance with Trollope. And while she by no means constituted the final word on American life and manners, her sentiments vis-à-vis religion and other matters have enjoyed a long life, particularly in encouraging summary dismissals of the United States as an "uncouth nation," in the phrase of Andrei S. Markovits. "It was ultimately not simply the specific criticisms that she levied against America that made her book such a representative and influential text for the voice of modern anti-Americanism," writes Markovits; "rather it was her unwavering tone of moral indignation and righteous horror, this sense of the simultaneous absurdity and very real danger of America, that set a tone, and assured the book's international popularity."[51]

The linkage between populist, "uncouth" religiosity and a more general cultural deficiency became commonplace in later nineteenth-century assessments of the United States. Trollope's son, the accomplished novelist Anthony Trollope, for example, felt the term "rowdiness" best described American religious life, and its manifestations were both a sign and cause of deeper pathologies in American politics and society.

For myself, I love the name of State and Church, and believe that much of our English well being has depended on it. I have made up my mind to think that union good, and not to be turned away from that conviction.... I feel very strongly that much of that which is evil in the structure of American politics is owing to the absence of any national religion, and that something also of social evil has sprung from the same cause. It is not that men do not say their prayers. For aught I know, they may do so as frequently, or more frequently and fervently, than we do; but there is a rowdiness ... in their manner of doing so which robs religion of that reverence which is, if not its essence, at least its chief protection.[52]

Charles Dickens visited the United States in the early 1840s and made it the object of ridicule and scorn in two subsequent works: *American Notes* (1842), a travel essay, and a longer novel, *The Life and Adventures of Martin Chuzzlewit* (1843). Like Trollope before him, Dickens was repulsed by the populist currents of "Jacksonian" America, complaining that the Revolution of 1776 had produced a "degenerate child," populated by "dull and gloomy" people, quarrelsome, libelous, and self-seeking. Although he recognized that many of America's sects traced their origins to Great Britain, the New World had given them a roaming expanse and a political environment that encouraged their fecundity and growth.[53] A dissenting, anti-institutional spirit had emerged as such an embedded part of the national character, he believed, that even the remedy of an established church appeared now beside the point: "I think the temper of the people, if it admitted of such an Institution, being founded amongst them would lead them to desert it, as a matter of course, merely because it *was* established."[54] In religious matters, therefore, and in most everything else, the United States "is far from being a model for the earth to copy."[55]

Dickens' criticisms stung. But "trollopizing" America arguably reached its nineteenth-century apogee in the writings of Matthew Arnold, who visited the United States twice, in 1883 and again in 1886.[56] While the renowned aesthete and apostle of high learning admired aspects of the United States' political and social achievements, he felt that in matters of culture and spirit a desolate wasteland lay across the Atlantic—"a great void . . . in the civilization over there." Replete with obtuse, self-deceived people, lacking in history and sophistication, the new nation presented to his eyes a boorish, "uninteresting" phenomenon. "What really dissatisfies in American civilization," he complained, "is the want of the interesting, a want due chiefly to the want of those two great elements of the interesting, which are elevation and beauty." In contrast to Europe and presumably to other ancient civilizations, the United States lacked any sense of historical grandeur, and few objects of beauty presented themselves to ennoble the spirit. "If we in England were without cathedrals, parish churches, and castles," he wrote, "but had only the towns and buildings which the rise of our middle class has created in the modern age, we should be in much the same case as the Americans."[57] Upon hearing of President Abraham Lincoln's assassination, the dispassionate aesthete could only muster that this event at least "brings into their history something of the tragic, romantic, imaginative, which it has had so little of."[58]

Arnold's misgivings about America were nested in a broader critique of middle-class values and sensibilities.[59] Indeed, he regarded America's principal flaw as granting free reign to the appetites and aspirations of the middle class—a class extant in England too of course, but one existing there more self-consciously and uneasily, faced with an aristocracy above and an underclass below. While Arnold did not outright gainsay middle-class traits such as thrift and industry, he felt that the modern ascendancy of the bourgeoisie had, everywhere, lowered and coarsened cultural and religious sentiments. Middle-class existence brought with it "*its defective type of religion*, its narrow range of intellect and knowledge, its stunted sense of beauty, [and] its low standard of manners."[60] In England, these "middle-class misgrowths" were at least forced to struggle against the pervading "ancientness" of European civilization with its countervailing values and sensibilities. But this was not the case in the United States, where they spread like an infection without resisting antibodies. "That which in England we call the middle class is in America virtually the nation," as he expressed it. "[T]he great bulk of the nation" across the Atlantic was made up of "Philistines"—"a livelier sort of Philistine than our [English] Philistine," he could haughtily muse, "but [one] left all the more to himself, and to have his full swing."[61]

In spiritual matters then, one can deduce, America permitted "full swing" to a Philistine, "defective type of religion," and in particular to sectarian forms of Protestantism. While Arnold made no direct plea for an established church in America, he wholly contemned "the voluntary principle," which had been realized on a "grand and impressive scale" under American conditions. The guiding principle of American religious life, in his view, corresponded to that "of modern English nonconformity," which advocated that each individual be allowed "their own specially invented and indomitably maintained form of religion." In America "this type of religion is not, as it is here, a subordinate type, it is the predominant and accepted one. Our dissenting ministers think themselves in paradise when they visit America."[62]

The untrammeled growth of the voluntary principle, he held, rendered piety trivial and banal, depleting from it all noble forms and time-honored traditions. What is more, in the hands of the *demos*, the voluntary principle allowed for the widespread retention of supernaturalist forms of faith—forms which, in Arnold's more critical, immanentist outlook, were destined for extinction, to be replaced by modes of religion emphasizing cultural decorum and human intellectual development. Appeals by supernaturalists and their defenders to "freedom of conscience," the right of everyone to think for themselves, only exacerbated Arnold's worries—both about America and about religious nonconformism at home. He regarded "conscience" as an unstable category, always "wavering" and "undecided" in the minds of the people at large. Thus the plea of popular Protestantism in Great Britain and America was deemed insufficient when, appealing to conscience to justify obscurantist forms of religion, it "thinks that it has said enough." Put differently, freedom of conscience might sound well and fine, but in experience—not least in American experience—it allowed for the persistence of sectarian, supernaturalist manifestations of Christianity— wrongheaded manifestations, in Arnold's view, ones that had blithely failed to concede traditional orthodoxy's "melancholy, long, withdrawing roar," as he had famously written in the poem "Dover Beach."

The defective religion par excellence, Methodism, whether in Great Britain or America, Arnold regarded with particular disdain. Methodism, after all, had fractured the Church of England, and the United States had given it a congenial environment in which to spread. "In that universally religious country [the United States]," Arnold groused, "the religious denomination which has by much the largest number of adherents is . . . Methodism originating with John Wesley." For Arnold, this spoke poorly of America's present and signaled nothing promising for its future:

To live with one's mind, as to a matter of this sort [religion], fixed constantly upon a mind of the third order, such as was Mr. Wesley's, seems to me extremely trying and injurious for the minds of men in general. And people whose minds, in what is the chief concern of their lives, are thus constantly fixed upon a mind of the third order, are the staple of the population of the United States, in the small towns and country districts above all.[63]

In his essay *Culture and Anarchy*, Arnold associated Methodism with what he called "Hebraism," the narrow religious mind-set of the Old Testament, in contrast to "Hellenism," the more high-minded intellectual spirit associated with Greek thought. America, not surprisingly, was beholden to the former, not the latter: "From Maine to Florida, and back again, all America Hebraises."[64]

What possible cure could Arnold propose for America? At home, he felt it necessary for the Church of England, somehow, to try to corral and assimilate religious dissenters, to "cure" and "transform" their untutored minds.[65] But the situation in America appeared far more dire. At one level, he could esteem the intentions of America's ministers to supply the nation's uncivilized parts with greater infusions of piety. But given the generally defective religious landscape, the cure might prove worse than the malady: obscurantism could not remedy boorishness. Instead, he proposed that new nation needed first-order educational institutions supplying massive dosages of European high culture. What is more, Americans ought to de-emphasize religion's miraculous and other-worldly aspects and instead seek meaning in "a renovation and perfected human society—the ideal of the future."[66] Such a course might finally help render America "interesting." But as things actually stood, the unhappy marriage of Philistinism and obscurantism held sway, making the United States, "that universally religious country," among "the last countries in which one would like to live."[67]

A Land without "Spirit": German Thought, Religion, and America

We must energetically proclaim the true and only German mission of spirit: get away from America!

—Ferdinand Tönnies

The Americans, Matthew Arnold wrote in 1871, have "never been in touch with 'Geist,' only with claptrap."[68] If the cultural and religious currents of the United States held no charm for Arnold, those of the Continent did, especially those tied to the intellectual and literary efflorescence that took place in late eighteenth- and early nineteenth-century German-speaking lands. These currents are well captured in such words as *Geist* (spirit), *Bildung* (education), *Kultur* (culture); associated with figures as diverse as Herder, Schiller, Novalis, Fichte, Hegel, the brothers Schlegel, Schleiermacher, Wilhelm von Humboldt, Schelling, and a host of others; and usually lumped under the capacious and endlessly wrangled-over categories of "Idealism" and "Romanticism."[69]

German thought during this period, in the words of Dan Diner, has exerted a "definitive influence" on the European image of America, particularly in ideas and theories about society that dovetailed with the

reactionary, nostalgic milieu associated with the post-Napoleonic Restoration of 1815. Continental Romantics' disapproval of America went
hand in hand with a principled opposition to the Western Enlightenment, with an aversion to the spread of free-market ideas and practices
("*Manchesterismus*"), and with a rejection of "abstract" constitutional
development in favor of the "organic" growth of communities, rooted
in history, tradition, and piety. Some Romantics tended to scorn the
entire "revolutionary age" as an unnatural development, the imposi-
tion of foreign, often "Anglo-Saxon," habits of thought, ones emphasizing contracts, commerce, and individual rights to the detriment of
communal bonds and a more harmoniously ordered society.[70]

The Puritan–bourgeois ascendancy in England in the seventeenth
century, and subsequently (and consequently) the animating principles behind 1776 and 1789, had unleashed, west of the Rhine, the
makings of a contemptible, artificial civilization (*Zivilization*), which
under no circumstance should be mistaken for authentic culture (*Kultur*). As these categories developed linguistically in the nineteenth
century, *Zivilization* often came to stand for the merely "outward"
signs of progress: material comfort, utilitarianism in education, technological mastery of the environment, the rise of the masses, and an
unbridled commercialism and individualism. *Kultur*, by contrast, stood
for the more profound, "inner" development of humankind: cultural
refinement, communal solidarity, a general well-roundedness, and an
ethical and spiritual depth of soul—qualities of being weakened by
ideologies of trade and democracy, but still fortuitously, if fragilely,
embodied in the distinctive character of the German-speaking peoples and their cultural and educational arrangements.[71]

Indeed, the distinction between *Zivilization* and *Kultur* emerged as
a central component of what Fritz K. Ringer influentially defined as
the "mandarin ideology," which came into its own in the writings of
German elites during the late nineteenth and early twentieth century, when Germany founded itself embattled (after 1914 quite literally) against the cultural depredations of a putatively shallower
Western society.[72] Within the parameters of this ideology, Great Britain and France, however errant in modern times, could at least lay
claim to a deeper, pre-revolutionary past, one still capable of rendering individuals receptive—as the case of Matthew Arnold perhaps
illustrates—to the moral and educational repositories of *Kultur*. The
United States, by contrast, often appeared as an irremediable golem

of soulless modernity, an artificial construction, lacking both history and culture—a bewildering tangle of commercial transactions, the jumbling of all races, cultures, and creeds.

While some leading Romantics and their many nineteenth-century intellectual offspring could admire and write eloquently about the pristine New World wilderness, a lack of organic grounding (*Boden-losigkeit*) and a massive deficit of spirituality (*Geistlosigkeit*) summed up the social conditions of the United States for the nostalgic imagination. With strong echoes of the "degeneracy thesis," these wanting conditions, it was often assumed, colored virtually every aspect of American society, including that of the religious life. Admittedly, in the early nineteenth century, the new republic often appeared as a negligible curiosity shop of modern foibles, across a wide ocean. But by century's end, the emerging industrial colossus posed a more immediate threat—one regularly depicted as an obtuse, money-driven parvenu foisting its sensibilities upon more estimable and cultured peers. The "breathless haste" of America, Friedrich Nietzsche had written in the *Gay Science*, capturing a widespread fear, "is already beginning to infect old Europe with its ferocity and is spreading a lack of spirituality [*Geistlosigkeit*] like a blanket."[73]

The charge of *Geistlosigkeit*—literally, "spiritlessness"—and efforts to read American culture and religion through this lens has a venerable pedigree in nineteenth-century thought, and one that has enjoyed a long life afterwards; it is also a charge that has quite freely traversed the political spectrum, as shall become clear later. One hears intimations of it shortly after the formation of the new American republic in the writings of Dietrich von Bülow (1757–1803), who visited the United States twice in the early 1790s before publishing, in 1797, *Der Freistaat von Nordamerika in seinem neuesten Zustand* (Recent Conditions of the North American Republic). Seeking to counter optimistic emigrant accounts of the New World, Bülow saw America as a site of "moral degeneracy," where the political system seemed designed to encourage little other than a "spirit of commerce." He criticized the Americans for slavishly imitating European high culture, not developing their own, and he deplored the absence of any systematic national education:"The youth of the country are brought up in stupidity and license that goes on increasing." He arraigned the religious bodies of the country for their fanaticism, even contending that were it not for the mentality of the "enthusiastic sects," which had fled Britain, no

American Revolution would have taken place. As a consequence of the Revolution, anti-authoritarian and anti-ecclesiastical sensibilities had been given free reign, undermining social rectitude and diminishing the authority of the clergy. "The state does not care for [the clergy] at all," he complained, and "in this way pastors are placed at the mercy of their congregations." With other factors, this contributed to "the disturbing spirit of this nation."[74]

The philosopher Friedrich Schlegel (1772–1829), an enthusiastic subscriber to the degeneracy thesis, offered criticism from a similar angle in his *Lectures on the Philosophy of History* (1828). A deficient land zoologically and botanically prior to European settlement, the newly formed nation, ridden with sectarianism, appeared as both parasitic borrower from European culture while, politically and socially, constituting "the actual source of all these destructive principles" (*die eigentliche Pflanzschule aller dieser zerstörenden Principien*) that had roiled Europe since the storming of the Bastille.[75] Schlegel's Romantic kindred-spirit, the political theorist Adam Müller (1779–1829), offered a comparable analysis, asserting that true politics required an organic and theological basis, not the kind exhibited in the United States based simply on human contrivance and an appeal to abstract rights. It had taken Europe centuries to nurture its cultural, religious, and political sensibilities; and it would be better for all if the revolutionary, commercial spirit of the times would simply vanish across the Atlantic where it would find a more congenial, if inferior, abode in the United States.[76] The conservative jurist Friedrich von Gentz (1764–1832) seconded such a view, opining further that with the Monroe Doctrine "the separation between America and Europe is...irrevocably completed."[77]

A similar attitude of antipathy prevails in the writings of Heinrich Steffens (1773–1845), a Norwegian by birth, but an enthusiast for German idealist philosophy and science by academic training and vocation. An eyewitness to Napoleon's ravaging of central Europe in 1806–07, Steffens became a loyal believer in the mission and aptitude of the Prussian state, as it was reconstituted politically (in the Prussian Reform period, 1807–15) and intellectually (in the founding of the epoch-making University of Berlin in 1810).[78] With Hegel and other German idealists, Steffens affirmed the importance of a powerful, centralized state for shaping cultural and religious meaning for its citizens. By contrast, the American polity—to which he devoted a section in his *Die gegenwärtige Zeit und wie sie geworden*, "The Present Age and its

Origins" (1817)—had only given birth to "bourgeois freedom," "a negative fight against established order," but not to "authentic freedom," which required a "positive" vision about the correct ordering of society. He compared the United States to a statue, possessing the external qualities of statehood, but "without a living, beating heart in its breast." Commenting specifically on religious matters, he elaborated that "North America is a sad monument of a time, in which great strength is yoked with the absence of high purpose.... Religion [there] is a private matter of the individual, and thus it appears in a dismal, turbid form." Such a condition could supply citizens neither with deep connections to one another nor with ethical and transcendental ideals, nor could it promote serious scholarship and art. For all these things, one required that "spirituality [be the] life principle of the state" and that "state religion" be more than a formless reality or a "nothing," as the case appeared to be in the United States.[79]

Steffens' contemporary, the pessimistic philosopher Arthur Schopenhauer (1788–1860), likewise regarded the United States as deficient at several levels. He gave typical expression to the reactionary view that custom and tradition presided over by a powerful sovereign could never be replaced by "abstract" natural rights as the basis of political well being. The United States had attempted precisely this, however, compounding its error by presenting itself as a model for other nations to follow. Schopenhauer could admit that America had achieved a limited, purely material success. But even this was riddled with erroneous assumptions, for "the success is not enticing, for alongside the material prosperity of the land comes a dominant attitude of deplorable utilitarianism and its inseparable partner, ignorance, which stupid Anglo-Saxon bigotry, foolish conceit, and vicious crudeness... have prepared the way." He therefore concluded that "the specimen of a purely legal constitutional order on the other side of the planet offers cold comfort to republican forms of government," and it undermined by regrettable example "imitations" of the United States in the newly formed governments of Latin America.[80]

The Austrian Romantic poet and writer Nikolaus Lenau (1802–50) gave expression to influential negative commonplaces about the United States, even if his transatlantic travels and reflections might have languished in obscurity were it not for their being immortalized in the popular novel *Der Amerikamüde* (1855) by his fellow Austrian Ferdinand Kürnberger (1821–79). Aptly translated as "One Weary of

America," the novel follows a scholar and writer, one Dr. Moorfeld (modeled roughly on Lenau) from Europe to the United States, where his initial optimism about the New World turns into disenchantment as he encounters actual American society; and thus he learns the Romantic-era truism that while conditions in post-1789 Europe might present difficulties, America offered no redeeming hope and, indeed, was part of the problem.

The harshly critical tone of the book takes its cue from Lenau's actual sentiments, expressed in letters to friends and relatives back home during his sojourn to the United States in 1832–33. Like the character Dr. Moorfeld, Lenau was at first eager to encounter nature and society in the New World, but his experience abroad (for reasons not entirely clear) soured his attitude completely.[81] The America of his imagination was transformed, suddenly and profoundly, into that of an irredeemable dystopia, the refuge of the "Last Man" to use Nietzsche's well-known terminology—"the land of the end, the outer edge of man" in Lenau's own formulation.[82] Even the natural landscape, which he had longed to see, did not escape his wrath. In his letters, he grumbled repeatedly about the "monotonous and unimpressive" mountains and valleys. He complained of never hearing "any nightingale, indeed no true songbirds" in America and speculated that this somehow must have "a deeper, more serious meaning." He even invoked the eighteenth-century degeneracy thesis: "Buffon was right that in America man and animals degenerate from one generation to the next."[83]

But it was the cultural and "spiritual" life of the United States (or rather the lack thereof) that received his most scathing disapprobation. "The Atlantic ocean," he opined, "is the isolating cordon of *Geist* and all that pertains to higher life."[84] He followed this claim with an etymological meditation on the meaning of the word culture (*Kultur*), noting its close association with the cultivation of plant life, with roots and soil, with steady, patient development. The society of the United States lacked this sense of culture completely, he felt; everything was hastily borrowed or imposed, nothing developed "organically from within." True intellectual and spiritual life in his reckoning were therefore virtually impossible; only the practical and profitable could find succor in such a wasteland. "Here the practical man is developed in his most frightful matter-of-fact-ness." To a relative, he complained that "the petty-mindedness of these Americans stinks to heaven. They are dead to the life of the mind, dead as doornails." In short, American society exhibited a contemptible groundlessness (*Bodenlosigkeit*), and he felt that with this term he had captured the essence of the new land. "With the expression *Bodenlosigkeit* I think I am able to indicate the general character of *all* American institutions, including political institutions."[85]

Outfitted with such a comprehensive analytic indictment, Lenau believed that he had cured himself of earlier, misguided longings for America—of the sort felt by so many German-speaking emigrants at the time. He had learned to love his European fatherland again, for he had encountered a society where the idea of a fatherland (in the German sense) did not apply. "That which we call fatherland is in America nothing more than security for one's assets. The American knows nothing, seeks nothing but money; he has no ideas; consequently the state is not an intellectual and moral institution (fatherland), but merely a material convention." Indeed, Lenau's time abroad renewed his appreciation of aspects of German and European culture which he had previously neglected; "[it] cured me of the chimera of freedom and independence that I had longed for with youthful enthusiasm. There [in America] I became convinced that true freedom exists only in our hearts, in our desires and thoughts, our feeling and our actions."[86] America, in sum, was a beacon of false hope, a spiritual nullity, a mirage across the ocean.

Kürnberger drove Lenau's points home with great success in the *Amerikamüde*, a novel replete with all the familiar Romantic-era criticisms, and ones often focused explicitly on American religious life. (Incidentally, Max Weber in his *Protestant Ethic* drew freely on Kürnberger as an *historical* source, despite the fact that the Austrian writer had never set foot in America!)[87] In *Amerikamüde*, the offhand judgments of Lenau were intensified into fixed antitheses between things American and things German or European—the latter two categories praised, the former deplored. German profundity was thus pitted against American superficiality; the rich German language and literature against the impoverished English dialect of the Americans; German individuality against American conformism; the European love of good wines against the American spirit of temperance; and so on.[88]

In this vein, Kürnberger contrasted the "German religion," rich in history and tradition, against the "arid sectarianism" of the Americans, whom he felt were bereft of any sense of the church as an established,

culture-bearing entity. He illustrated this point by having the protago-
nist, Dr. Moorfeld, visit the city of Philadelphia and there encounter
Quakers and other religious communities. Moorfeld is taken aback at
the state of the American clergy, depicting them as divisive, hypocritical, and greedy to a man. In his journal, Dr. Moorfeld records:

> In Europe, where there are *established* churches, the clergy…exists with a
> fixed and distinguished position and with a feeling of corporate identity. This
> provides comfort, rendering them often amiable members of society. Things
> are different here, where the church as such simply does not matter, where
> religious communities form and dissolve like tea parties, where it is easier to
> protect a pasture from grasshoppers than keep a religious society together.
> Here importance does not rest on churchly authority, but rather on the
> authority of individual personality. Consequently, among the clergy [in
> America] a nest of Pharisees has been established, the repulsiveness
> (*Ekelhaftigkeit*) of which is hard to understand from a European standpoint.[89]

Castigating Philadelphia as a "Zion of religious hypocrisy," the fictional character consoles himself with the fact that "our governments
[in Europe] do not want to tolerate the formation of…sects," for
otherwise Europe would resemble America by giving free reign to a
"narrow spirit of obscurantism."[90]

Such experiences and others prompt Moorfield, in conservations
with another character in the novel, one Dr. Althof, to reflect more
broadly on the nature of religion in America. He wonders if sectarianism and enthusiasm were signs of America searching for its own "national form of religion." As Islam in the seventh century had borrowed
ideas and motifs from Judaism and Christianity but developed something new, he postulates that a similar, world-changing religious transmutation was afoot in the New World. But no elevating spirituality
appeared to be emerging, but only a strange and dull religion, reflecting the "colossal American national pathos." Dr. Moorfeld's interlocu-
tor, Dr. Althof, even offers a name for the new religion: "humbug."[91]
"Religion," he elaborates, "in Italy is a ballet, in Spain a pledge, in Germany a philosophical love, [but] in America it is a machine with so
much horsepower." The new religious spirit presented a "stark antago-
nism" to that of Europe. "Christianity announced to a suffering world
the desire for a better world"; this had inspired moving worship, great
art and architecture, and stirring music. By contrast, in America, "we
have the kingdom of practicality" (*Reich der Tat*) and a religious spirit
"absolutely incapable of achieving inner depth and profundity."[92]

In addition to Lenau and Kürnberger, writers and critics associated with the literary movement Young Germany (*Junges Deutschland*) occasionally remarked on the United States. Some, such as Ludwig Börne (1786–1837), could admire New World freedoms almost uncritically, but the majority of this loose literary "school" shared common ground with traditionalist–conservative criticisms, despite predilections toward liberalism and little affection for the reactionary status quo in Europe. The poet Heinrich Heine (1797–1856), for example, regularly deplored conditions in Europe during his lifetime, but the United States provided no example to follow. In fact, it appeared as the greater evil, as he mused in the poem "Now, Where To?" (1830):

> Sometimes I have thought to sail
> To America the free,
> To that great stable of freedom,
> Where all the boors live equally.
> But I fear a land where men
> Chew tobacco.
> There's no king among the pins
> And they spit without spittoons.

Elsewhere Heine described America as a "God-accursed land," a "monstrous prison of freedom (*ungeheuren Freiheitsgefängnis*), where . . . the most repulsive of all tyrants, the masses, practice their vulgar dominion!" He affirmed the Romantic association of America with the soulless triumph of commerce: high-minded ideals of liberty and exploitative moneymaking did not mix, rendering America not only a land of boors, but of hypocrites too—defilers of true religiosity even though they were a nation of "enthusiastic church-goers." "They have learned this hypocrisy from the English," he wrote, tellingly, "who incidentally have bequeathed to them their worst characteristics. Worldly practicality is their true religion, and money is their God, their only almighty God."[93]

Other figures associated with Young Germany offered comparable broadsides. Echoing sentiments of Lenau, the poet Hoffman von Fallersleben (1798–1874), in his poem "The New World," spoke of "the fetish of freedom" in America, of the "swindler spirit" and the unchecked "self interest" found there. American flowers, he wrote "have no scent, / No bird [there] can even sing a line, / And poetry its life is spent." Karl Gutzkow (1811–78) described citizens of the United States as "salesmen for one big banking house," while Heinrich Laube (1806–84), a close friend of Heine, expressed yet more extreme views. In his novel *Young Europe*, he summarily dismissed America as a "business school that claims to be a world.... No history, no free science, no free art! Free trade is the total freedom;... anything that does not bring money is useless, and that which is useless is unnecessary!"[94] (All of these sentiments, one should note, dovetail almost seamlessly with later criticisms of the socialist Left—which should perhaps not surprise given Karl Marx's affinities to and connections with the literary Young Germany.[95])

Not only German-speaking poets and philosophers, but historians too chided America for its shortcomings. An American-style republic, wrote the esteemed Roman historian B. G. Niebuhr (1776–1831), "is the most trivial and disgusting [one] that one can imagine."[96] Following Leopold von Ranke (1795–1886), the most influential of nineteenth-century historians, many German historians saw in the United States an emerging antithesis to older European values and institutions. Ranke regarded the American Revolution as an unprecedented event in human history, a "complete overturning" of established principles, the source of "all subsequent revolutionary efforts," and the origins of a profound and ongoing conflict between republican ideals and those of the European Old Regime. What is more, because of its "rapid rise" in the nineteenth century, the United States was ominously poised to effect "an unceasing influence on Europe."[97]

If America appeared as a *novum* in human history in some respects, its very lack of a past (*Geschichtlosigkeit*), when compared to Europe, contributed to its spiritual desolation, and made conditions ripe for ungainly expressions of religious belief. For the great Swiss–German historian Jacob Burckhardt (1818–97), for instance, a rich and deep spirituality was inextricably tied to an historical sense. Lacking such an historical sense, Americans were little more than present-day barbarians, justifiably held in contempt.

[B]arbarians... utterly lack history.... [A]mericans renounce history; peoples, that is, of unhistorical formations (*ungeschichtliche Bildungsmenschen*) who still cannot quite shake off the Old World. It clings to them parasitically in the shape of such things as the heraldry of the New York plutocracy, in the most absurd forms of Calvinism, [and in other] forms of spiritual nonsense (*Geisterspuk*).[98]

Burckhardt also worried about a spreading commercial mentality, warning Europe against a future path where everything "became simply business as in America."[99]

If Burckhardt's language suggests Max Weber's well-known Calvin-ism-to-capitalism interpretation of the United States, one finds an even more pointed harbinger of this in the writings of the aristocrat and Prussian nationalist historian, Heinrich von Treitschke (1834–96). Writing in the 1860s, longing to see a powerful German nation-state established, and eager to refute those who looked admiringly at the republican model of the United States, Treitschke argued that the re-cent American Civil War portended future splits; the minimally cen-tralized state of the United States could never contain future regional and ideological divisions. Accordingly, a "highly mannered and culti-vated Europe need not make room for such a crude political experi-ment," one that "restricted the state to only the most urgent needs." The origins of such a dubious political experiment he traced to the spirit of Calvinism run amok in the New World:

The dogmatic Puritan emigrants left behind in the Old World all aristocratic elements—the nobility, the established church—of English political life, [and] in counterpoint lugged faithfully across the ocean...[the] principle of self-government and there massively expanded it. One can say that this led to the establishment of a thousand little republics in the New World.... and [thus] the free church helped nurture a nation of republicans. Calvinism there devel-oped mightily all of its democratic ideas.... The entire political life of North America is rooted in democratic Protestantism.[100]

The Calvinist-republican nation possessed a knack for commercial en-terprise, the Prussian aristocrat freely acknowledged, but its spiritual and cultural impoverishment stood out, therefore, all the more glar-ingly. "In spite of their great material progress," he wrote, "the Ameri-cans have...failed to contribute anything to the great ideal possessions of the human race, and this failure is the more striking in comparison with their colossal productivity in all technical spheres." Nor did he expect much to issue from a "colonial" people who had broken "direct connection with the cradle of its race." "Colonies do not attain, even remotely, to the level of the mother-land's civilization."[101]

★★★

The waxing of American power in the late nineteenth century and its direct involvement in Europe as a consequence of World War I ampli-fied and hardened negative perceptions of the United States. During the early nineteenth century, conservative anti-American sentiment regularly possessed an air of confident condescension, with little at stake other than the opportunity to deride a distant, misguided upstart. During the fin-de-siècle era, however, images of America reflect fear added to contempt.[102] The staggering industrial growth of the United States at this time began to overtake that of many European countries, and America's dalliance in overseas imperial ventures awakened general alarm. In 1901, the British journalist William Thomas Stead published *The Americanisation of the World or the Trend of the Twentieth Century*, stirring in many European quarters worries that America's money-making spirit and mass society posed a global threat.[103]

But if anxiety about "Americanization" became a widespread European phenomenon at this time, German elites had some special concerns about the "American danger."[104] Germany had become a nation-state only in 1871 under the shrewd leadership of Otto von Bismarck, who after national unification pursued a conciliatory foreign policy with other European powers. After Bismarck's forced resignation in 1890, the mercurial young Emperor Wilhelm II set Germany on a rapid course of militarization, overseas imperialism, and cut-throat modernization—to the great consternation of Germany's neighbors. At home, these trends stimulated German nationalism and feelings of historical destiny, but they simultaneously heightened worries in many intellectual circles about the alienating and worrisome aspects of modernity, about an industry- and technology-driven future and the specter of mass society. With clear echoes of the Romantic era, intellectuals regularly adopted a stance of cultural pessimism toward the present while projecting anxiety about modernity onto foreign sources, not least on the United States. They also turned to an idealized past as a means of compensation, as a bulwark of true German "Kultur" against the depredations of "Americanization" or "Americanism" and all the negative modernizing forces that these terms had come to symbolize.[105] For numerous leading thinkers of this period, Fritz Stern has observed, "the bleaker their picture of the present, the more attractive seemed the past, and they indulged in nostalgic recollections of the uncorrupted life of earlier rural communities."[106] It was in this general context that the German sociologist Ferdinand Tönnies had published his highly influential work *Community and Society* (1887) in which he contrasted "society" or *Gesellschaft* (the impersonal "mechanical" relations between individuals characteristic of modern, market-driven existence) to "community" or *Gemeinschaft* (the tighter "organic" relations between individuals characteristic of traditional cultures).[107] "It must be pointed out," Tönnies remarked, "that the most modern Gesellschaft-like state [is] the United States of America."[108]

Admittedly, America was far from the exclusive target of anti-modern hand-wringing. The *gesellschaftlich* "West" in general, Great Britain and France foremost, actually took the brunt of the criticism in the prewar years. (These two countries, of course, posed the most immediate obstacles to Wilhelmine Germany's own "belated" great-power ambitions.) The Great War, however, reconfigured the geopolitical dynamics. The entrance of the United States into the fray in 1917; Germany's humiliation in the Versailles Treaty; and the postwar emergence on the European stage of Woodrow Wilson—widely criticized as sanctimonious and naïve—led during the Weimar period (1919–33) to what one scholar has called an "epidemic" of anti-American sentiment, but one with ample precedents in the prewar period.[109]

During this entire era, America's putative cultural or "spiritual" mediocrity, rootlessness, and vulgarity came under frequent attack from German travelers and intellectuals.[110] Commentators could draw from a wellspring of time-entrenched negative commonplaces generated throughout the nineteenth century. What strikes one about the fin-de-siècle commentary is the degree to which some observers sought to associate the peculiarities of American "voluntary" and "sectarian" religion with the dynamics of the nation as such.[111] In a few cases, most prominently that of Max Weber, America's religious ethos—i.e., its "sectarian" spirit unconstrained by superintending ecclesiastical or political powers—suggested an explanatory key for modernity in general, insofar as modernity entailed the *voluntary* individual initiative (and ascetic restraint) needed for the rise of entrepreneurial capitalism and other forms of "rational" organization.[112]

The United States at once fascinated and disquieted Weber. In 1904 he crossed the Atlantic with his wife Marianne and various leading German academics to present a scholarly paper at a conference sponsored by the St. Louis World's Fair. His famous essay on the Protestant ethic and capitalism was in the works at this time, and he saw the journey as a means of gathering further evidence and confirming his views. Indeed, America was practically regarded as the primary testing ground for his thesis. Not surprisingly, Weber evinced keen interest in what he called America's "very intense church-mindedness (*sehr intensive Kirchlichkeit*)."[113] During the trip, he made it a point to speak with numerous pastors, visit several churches and denominational colleges;

he even attended a Quaker meeting in Pennsylvania and an open-air Baptist baptism in rural North Carolina, where some of his distant relatives lived. "The power of the church communities [in America] is still tremendous," he wrote after visiting a chapel service at the University of Chicago. "In an elemental form [in North Carolina]," Marianne wrote in her biography of her husband, "he saw the life-forming effect of religious sects as well as their increasing replacement by orders and clubs of all kinds."[114] Not unlike Tocqueville before him, Weber believed that the social energy unleashed by a purely voluntary approach to the religious life contributed massively to modern social activity generally, including business practices. The teeming sectarian environment of America—an historical consequence of Calvinist–Puritan ecclesiology and doctrine, Weber believed—helped explain the existence in America of what today we might call "civil society"; it also contributed to the trustworthiness of business transactions and the myriad personal motivations and initiatives underpinning American capitalism. These were far from negative things in Weber's view, as he esteemed the vitality inherent in Calvinism over that of Lutheranism, which shared more in common with Catholicism in retarding the development of voluntary social engagement and organization.[115]

Nonetheless, Weber remained a child of his time, sharing much of the cultural pessimism about America prevalent in the German academy at large. In an essay, "The Protestant Sects and the Spirit of Capitalism," he implied throughout that motivations for "sect membership" in the United States often had scant to do with sincere piety, but were mostly a matter of keeping up appearances and pursuing economic self-interest. The transference of religion from the public to the private sphere helped account for the voluntary and "ascetic" character of American religious communities, to be sure. But, in his interpretation, this asceticism really only helped "put a halo around the economic 'individualist' impulses of the modern capitalist ethos."[116] Citing Tönnies' work at one point, he claimed to have defeated the absence of the "organic" in American sects, confirming for him how they bore witness to the pre-conditions of capitalist development.[117]

At several points in his *Protestant Ethic and the Spirit of Capitalism*, Weber drew uncritically on Ferdinand Kürnberger's (fictional) *Amerikamüde* to illustrate the utilitarian and time-obsessed aspects of American life. What is more, in the brooding, famous final passages of the essay, the only country mentioned by name is the United States, the site of capitalism's "highest development," before Weber mused, who will live in this "iron cage" of the future, this site of "mechanized petrifaction, embellished with a sort of convulsive sense of self-importance." America, a reader might reasonably infer, finally represented the menacing future, the land of artificial *Zivilization* and impersonal *Gesellschaft*, not a place of *Kultur* and *Gemeinschaft*: "For the 'last men' at this stage of cultural development, it might well be truly said: 'specialist without spirit, sensualists without heart; this nullity (*Nichts*) imagines that it has reached a level of human civilization never before achieved.' "[118]

But if at times Weber demonstrated a measured, or at least an ambivalent, attitude toward the United States, many of his contemporaries did not. In a finely argued study, Georg Kamphausen has shown how leading German social theorists during this time—Weber and Tönnies included, but also Werner Sombart, Ernst Troeltsch, Robert Michels, Georg Simmel, Karl Lamprecht, Karl Mannheim, and others—harbored deep antipathy toward American intellectual life and culture and often despised the manifestations of religion that they descried there.[119] Unlike Germany, and other European nations, the United States not only lacked, historically, the culture-molding force of an established church, but was bereft of any sense of the state as an agency to superintend the intellectual and religious life of the nation—something in central Europe, since roughly the late eighteenth century, assigned to a "ministry of culture" (*Kultusministerium*) and expressed in the idea of a *Kulturstaat*.[120] Absent such a state apparatus, religion and culture were cast to the whims of local communities and individuals, undermining the possibility of a cohesive, well-directed national communal life. In Kamphausen's interpretation, however, "European arrogance vis-à-vis the New World is mostly purchased at the cost of a heroic pessimism appealing to the essentialist gravity of an allegedly higher morality that only the state appears capable of guaranteeing." This had major epistemological and methodological consequences for the shaping of German (and, by extension, much of Western) social thought, embedding in some of its deepest assumptions and frameworks of orientation a certain wariness toward and opposition to the contours of American society. Kamphausen concludes that "a genuine cultural comparison did not take place" in the work of German social theorists of this era, because there was little genuine interest in the actual differences of American society, but mainly in their deviation from German and European patterns. Thus this generation of thinkers did not "discover" America in their analyses, but largely "constructed" (*erfunden*) it from the presuppositions of their own social location.[121]

While one might resist embracing Kamphausen's analysis too sweepingly, his thesis could easily be broadened to apply to many other intellectual arenas, given the voluminous interpretations of the United States of this time that highlighted shortcomings when compared to German/European models. Academic theology offers another example. "Americans are not 'theologians,'" complained the German theologian Hans Haupt, who spent an extended sojourn in the United States; Americans had produced no Schleiermacher or Albrecht Ritschl or Adolf von Harnack. In Germany, Haupt held, "'theology' [is understood] to be something very exclusive; it denotes a man whose whole interest lies in theological research.... The American people would hardly recognize such a profession; up until now they have produced no theologian of world renown." The nation was certainly overrun with enthusiastic preachers, Haupt noted, but these were generally "men of the people" and hardly qualified as "theologians in the German sense of the word."[122] Those who traveled with Weber to America in 1904—Ferdinand Tönnies, Werner Sombart, Karl Lamprecht, Adolf von Harnack, and Ernst Troeltsch—repeatedly offered up similar negative comparisons, touching upon various academic fields and cultural spheres.[123]

But if America might need an infusion of German academic gravitas Europe had best be on guard against practically all elements of American culture. Indeed, on the eve of the Great War, others remained less focused on the shortcomings of the United States per se, but on the worrisome "Americanization" of Europe. In a popular travelogue with the ominous title, *The Land of the Future* (1903), Wilhelm von Polenz, for example, warned Germans against too much receptivity to American culture: "For the Old World and especially Germany that would mean sinking from a higher level of culture to a lower one. Americanization of culture means trivialization, mechanization, stupefaction."[124] "I no longer love Paris," the poet Rainer Maria Rilke wrote in 1913, "partly because it is disfiguring and *Americanizing* itself." Anticipating the views of thinkers such as Martin Heidegger and Jean Baudrillard, Rilke regarded the United States as the site of pseudoculture and cheapened simulacra. "Now there comes crowding over from America empty, indifferent things, pseudo-things. *Dummy-life*. . . . A house, in the American understanding, an American apple or vine, has *nothing* in common with the house, the fruit, the grape into which the hope and meditation of our [Old World] forefathers had entered." (Not even American plant life escaped the depredations of American culture!) The modern catastrophe of materialism, he summed up, the "indefatigable, indifferent machine," represented by America, threatened to supplant a world "permeated by *Geist*."[125]

As indicated earlier, the World War and the subsequent involvement of the United States in European affairs led to the mushrooming of anti-American sentiment in Germany. The son of a Presbyterian minister, the American president Woodrow Wilson emerged as a particularly reviled figure, typifying for many a naïve American piety and hypocrisy. His strident moralizing was often seen as the personification of his nation's "messianic" soul, and his actions were interpreted as helping foment a cultural collision between the Old World and the New. The esteemed German scholar of antiquity Eduard Meyer was no lone voice when in 1919 he opined that, for Germany, "Wilson remains a type of unctuous hypocrite who brings together everything [in America] that contradicts the German nature and is loathsome to the core. But he will be remembered in the history of the world as the man who, by assuming a doctrinaire arrogance [,] . . . not only destroyed the ideals that Germany sought to achieve, but became the executioner of European culture."[126] In an academic address of 1917, Ferdinand Tönnies had warned against a "mechanization of life" and a "flattening of the world" that could be expected from the entry of the "American spirit" into global affairs.[127]

Adolf Halfeld adopted a comparable tone in his *America and Americanism: Critical Observations of a German and European* (1927), a commercial success that popularized much of the academic cultural pessimism toward America that had taken shape in prior decades. A journalist, Halfeld had lived in the United States, and had grown to despise its culture and its status as a rising power. Acutely worried about the "Americanization of Europe" in the postwar era, he sought to refute those who upheld the United States as a model for European development. To the contrary, America represented in concentrated form practically all of the ills of modern society, and it was imperative that someone "cleansed" the Old World of rosy images of the New. In his book, many of the negative generalizations about America that had developed in Romantic-era thought and reinforced in fin-de-siècle social theory were strung together with powerful rhetorical effect. A "petty-minded nation," the United States represented an artificial construction, harboring a wealth-obsessed, philistine population. The "cultural and historical undefinability of America" presented a sad spectacle, a site of "spiritual rootlessness" (*geistige Wurzellosigkeit*). The country possessed no sense of history of its own, for it had "developed too rapidly to have developed organically." To protect the "European spirit" Halfeld called on Germans and "Europeans" everywhere to recognize "Americanism" as a dangerous force and the actual United States as "[a] civilization of the mass man (*Zivilisation des Massenmenschen*) realized with utmost consistency."[128]

In Halfeld's view, the "Wilsonian" impulse in American history and foreign policy was not an isolated phenomenon, but the logical outcome of something long embedded in the American spirit: in the country's sibling devotions of capitalistic enterprise and religious fervor. In a type of simplified Weberian analysis served up for broader consumption, Halfeld gave expression to a commonplace that has pervasively colored perceptions of America; he decried "the peculiar two-sidedness in American life—idealistic, pathos paired up with wily business practices; the religious foundations of ambition; the preacher who is an entrepreneur; the proselytizer of morals; the businessman with God and ideals on his lips; [Wilson's] Fourteen Points; world peace with Wall Street's stamp of approval—in the end it all goes back to the Puritan ethic, the ethic of the self-liberating bourgeoisie."[129]

Halfeld commented yet more directly on American religious life. Adopting the mordant tone of American social critics such as H. L. Mencken and Sinclair Lewis, whom he greatly admired, Halfeld lampooned the "fundamentalist" beliefs and practices of those in the American interior. He decried the earlier "fanaticism" of New England that had given rise to the Salem witchcraft trials (failing to note that German lands witnessed the execution of thousands for witchcraft, in contrast to America's nineteen). He claimed that the notion of the separation of church and state in America was hypocritical, as all American presidents were practically required to be Protestants of Calvinist persuasion. While in typical fashion he disparaged the "numerous sects" in American society, he also felt that the exigencies of capitalist enterprise and mass society ultimately were leading to "the standardization of faith and thought."[130]

Halfeld was particularly keen to point how a society based on competition and advertising had forced clergymen to imitate business practices. "The methods that many American preachers use to bring its teachings to people do not differ in the least from those used by businessmen to sell their wares." To illustrate his point, he called attention to the advertisements churches placed in newspapers, and marveled at an electrically lighted cross on one church lawn. American evangelists and revivalists especially captivated him. He singled out the popular evangelist Billy Sunday, astonished at how such a figure could emerge as a "national institution" and among the best known people in America. But Sunday was no isolated case, Halfeld averred; similar figures traveled from coast to coast with their "spiritual stooges" in entourage, mesmerizing and deluding the people and "turning the altar into a stage."[131]

The American religious scene, finally, presented a "circus" to Halfeld's mind. But this should really not surprise, he remarked, given the mechanical, rootless fabric of society in the New World. In all of the aforementioned examples, Americans were simply reaping the religious fruits of a defective civilization. As Halfeld summed up:

The inner emptiness of these people and the spiritual sterility of a mass civilization, which subjugates people and land alike, becomes clear to us in such examples.... [R]eligious experience becomes a mechanistic exercise in a spiritually dead setting (*geistig toter Umgebung*). The whole idea of the American frontier suggests a boundless loneliness and isolation, not only in a spatial sense but in a cultural one as well. The people there do not know the folk dances and village festivals of old Europe. They live next to one another, but as beings accidentally planted in the ground, but with no relationship to it other than work and profit-taking.... And in this manner their inner life wastes away.[132]

Given the deficient state of things, he asked, was it any wonder that Americans looked to itinerant evangelists and revivalists for religious stimulation? An evangelist could at least provide a temporary "high ecstasy" of spiritual meaning. "And this," he concluded, "belongs to the psychology of mass man—the filling up of a barren inner life with compensatory excitements."[133]

Assessments of the American "Geist," or lack thereof, comparable to Halfeld's proliferated during the interwar period.[134] Although Halfeld sought to engage a wider readership, his book is best understood as an effort to mediate entrenched high-brow opinions downward to German society at large—a society, to his consternation, all too easily enthralled by American cinema and jazz. Meanwhile, at the higher altitudes of literary and academic sophistication, anti-modern, anti-American sentiments continued apace, as examples such as Oswald Spengler, Eduard Meyer, Ernst Jünger, Hans Freyer, Carl Schmitt, Alfred Weber, and Martin Heidegger well illustrate.[135] Spengler, for instance, opined that "life [in America] is exclusively determined by economic concerns and therefore completely lacks profundity. It lacks an element of genuine historical tragedy, of great purpose, which has deepened and matured the soul of Western peoples through the centuries. Its religion, originally a strict Puritanism, has become a type of obligatory amusement, and the [world] war was a new sport."[136]

The well-known philosopher Martin Heidegger cuts a particularly significant figure for our topic. Arguably, the German Romantic-cum-mandarin depiction of America as a spiritually deformed, economically utilitarian, and culturally shallow civilization reached its apogee in the writings of this influential thinker and in his highly symbolic conception of America—or Americanism—as the site of "cultural catastrophe." "No thinker in this [twentieth] century has had greater influence on the development of the idea of America than Martin Heidegger," writes James Ceaser, overstating things perhaps, but not without some warrant. "With Heidegger, America was transformed from a country to a major literary and philosophic category that intellectuals have since been unable to ignore."[137]

Heidegger grew up in provincial Baden in southwestern Germany. His father served as the church sexton in Messkirch (in the Black Forest). Early on, the young Heidegger sought to become a Jesuit, and he began his academic studies in Catholic theology. His early years, in other words, were seeped in a rural, conservative, highly religious milieu—in something akin to *Gemeinschaft* to use Tönnies' language. However, the ponderous anti-modern, anti-technological outlook that he developed—while finding resonance on the traditionalist Right—has arguably exerted even more influence on the Left in the twentieth century, in the form of existentialist philosophy, in and alongside various strains of Marxism, and in the ecological movement and the "green" political parties that have emerged from it. Here is truly a case where *les extrêmes se touchent*, where Rightist and Leftist images of America converge. In figures such as Herbert Marcuse (*One-Dimensional Man*) and Jean Baudrillard (*L'Amérique*), the Heideggerian image of "the American" as a history-less, culture-less "mass man" or "collective man," holding desperately to a simple and irrational faith, emerges as an article of certainty.[138]

But we should not bypass Heidegger himself in considering his influence. Already in his first major work, *Being and Time* (1927), Heidegger occupied himself with the problem of mass man (*das Man*), examining the loss of individual identity and authentic "Being" through immersion in various forms of collective identification and modern conformism. In this work, he made no specific mention of America, whether as an actual geographical place or as a symbolic principle of modernity, but it is "implicit in much of [his] interpretation of everyday human existence."[139] However, in his *Introduction to Metaphysics* (1935), a work unhappily reflective of his political milieu, Heidegger commented explicitly on "Americanism," likening it to "Bolshevism." Germany, he wrote, two years after the Nazis had seized power,

lies today in a great pincer, squeezed by Russia on one side and America on the other. From a metaphysical standpoint, Russia and America are the same, with the same dreary technological frenzy and the same unrestricted organization of the average mind.[140]

In 1942, as the Holocaust was underway, he ranked Americanism as the purest and most problematic form of modernity. "Bolshevism is only a variant of Americanism" he wrote; "[Americanism] is the most dangerous shape of boundlessness [*Maßlosigkeit*], because it appears in the form of a democratic middle-class way of life *mixed with Christianity*, and all this in an atmosphere utterly devoid of any sense of history [*Geschichtslosigkeit*]."[141] "Americanism," as he put it in yet another formulation, "is the still unfolding and not yet full or completed metaphysical essence of the emerging monstrousness of modern times."[142]

Heidegger's hallmark wooly prose sometimes prevents clear apprehension of his meaning. But the overwhelmingly negative image of America(nism) that emerges from these passages (and many cognate ones) is quite clear. Heidegger never visited the United States. But this is perhaps beside the point. His America has little to do with the actual human beings of Kentucky or Maine; it is largely a symbolic place-holder of an errant, rising form of human subjectivity, a defective state of mind as theorized within Continental thought. "America" embodied for him the malaise of modernity itself: human consciousness dominated and deformed by efficiency, the market, the masses, the mechanical, the utilitarian, the quantitative, and so on. Purely profit-driven, technological ways of thinking, or what he called technicity (*Technik*) or logistics (*Logistik*), constituted a primary culprit: "In America...logistics as the only proper philosophy of the future is thus beginning today to seize power over the spirit."[143] Such thinking brought a void of cultural authenticity in its wake, lack of historical depth, existential "homelessness," a myopic presentism endangering Old World culture, indeed all true culture. "Americanism is resolved to destroy Europe," he claimed during World War II. "The entry of America into this world war is not an entry into history, but is already the last American act of American absence of historical sense and self-devastation."[144]

The America of Heidegger's imagination represents, finally, a land of "spiritual" atrophy and death. As Michael Allen Gillespie has noted, Heidegger's America is at once foremost contributor and foremost symbol of a dangerously compelling force in the modern world, but one that fundamentally "misconstrues human spirituality."[145] While Americanism might appear "in the form of a democratic middle-class way of life *mixed with Christianity*" (Heidegger appears here attempting to square the modernity of the United States with its well-known religious energies), its underlying substance ultimately contravened "Geist," the authentically spiritual. By being complicit in elevating efficiency and technological mastery to absolute values, Americanism had prepared the way for modern "un-culture," the antithesis of all genuine thought, poetry and profundity.

In all of this, one of course hears powerful echoes of earlier Romantic-era critiques of the United States. Far from challenging or qualifying these critiques, Heidegger assumed their veracity and absorbed them into a highly sophisticated, and often compelling, philosophical framework, which powerfully resonated with culturally illiberal elitism in the 1920s and 1930s, and was enthusiastically taken up by the intellectual countercultural New Left in the postwar period.[146]

After the war, Heidegger grew yet more culturally pessimistic, and intellectually and politically cagey, convinced that the deleteriously modern forces symbolized by America(nism) had perhaps finally and fully engulfed the Western world, leaving little room for insightful reflection or the reassertion of authentic "Being." On occasion, he proffered gnomic, quasi-religious references to some "event" or "happening,"—mediated from beyond, from "the gods"—that would arrive, Savior-like, to rescue advanced modernity from its self-incurred depredations.[147] If Germany—and Europe—were to "receive" this happening, however, he made clear that the "American model" must be forcefully rejected, sending it back to the other "hemisphere."[148]

"Indifferentism" and "Americanism": Embattled Catholicism and the American Experiment

Heidegger's drift away from the Catholicism of his youth was a protracted process, and one in which elements of a reactionary, religious anti-modernism arguably persisted in his thought, albeit in residual and submerged forms.[149] But, of course, Heidegger cannot be regarded as emblematic of Catholicism per se. From the standpoint of Rome—and her ultramontane allies throughout Europe—the image of the United States and perceptions of its religious freedoms had long posed a challenge of a different sort, one bound up with the dangers of revolution and political liberalism, to be sure, which had roiled the Church in Europe ever since 1789, but also with the abiding problem of Protestantism, especially in its Calvinist guises, which had engaged in a death struggle against "Popery" and "Jesuitism" for the soul of Western Europe since the late sixteenth century.

In the nineteenth century, then, the United States posed a double-edged challenge to the reactionary Catholic imagination: a nation congenitally imbued with Calvinist forms of Christianity and one juridically committed to the principle of religious freedom.[150] Admittedly, the French Revolution and its far-reaching aftermath often constituted the more urgent vexation from the standpoint of Rome. Some Catholic thinkers even felt that the American example offered a more promising contrast to the "ideas of 1789." "If we compare the American and the French Revolution," the Spanish traditionalist Jaime Balmes (1810–48) wrote, "we find that one of the principal differences between them is that the American Revolution was essentially democratic and the French...essentially impious."[151] In 1793, at the height of the Jacobin ascendancy in France, Baltimore's John Carroll, the first bishop and archbishop in the United States, received word from Rome that because of "the most severe wounds which have been inflicted upon the catholic faith in Europe, we [now] look for consolation in the American provinces."[152]

The memory of violent revolution in Europe notwithstanding, by the 1820s and 1830s a handful of erstwhile reactionary Catholics had turned full circle, and began to make the case that the Church owed no necessary allegiance to the absolutist principles of the *Ancien Régime*, but should make its peace with modern, democratic principles. The French priest and scholar Félicité de Lamennais (1782–1854) represents the best-known case of such an intellectual turnabout. A frequent contributor to conservative journals and the author of several weighty tomes on the dereliction of modern times, Lamennais gradually shifted his opinion, moved in large part by the actions of "legitimate" rulers against Catholics in Ireland, Belgium, and Poland. In his 1828 work *Progress and Revolution*, he argued that the church stood to benefit from complete separation from the state. In 1830, he founded the "agency for the defense of religious freedom" and the periodical, *L'Avenir* (the Future), whose contributors advocated the Church's embrace of the principles of freedom of thought, freedom of conscience, and freedom of the press. In *L'Avenir's* pages, the constitutional framework of the United States and the position of the Catholic Church in North America were invoked as examples for Europe to consider: the church there presented a true "marvel," existing not under the shadow of "thrones" but alongside "the liberty of the citizen" (*la liberté du citoyen*).[153]

Laboring under suspicions from the Vatican, Lamennais traveled to Rome in 1831 to make his case before the conservative Camaldolese monk Bartolomeo Cappelleri, who had only recently become Pope Gregory XVI (r.1831–46). While there Lamennais again called attention to religious freedom in the United States. But his meeting with the pope was brief and chilly, and it came only after a months-long wait in the Eternal City. Afterwards, Gregory issued the encyclical, *Mirari vos* (1832), which—not so subtlety alluding to Lamennais as a "wild boar" in the vineyards of the Lord—condemned religious freedom as a consequence of the error of "indifferentism," too loose an acceptance of non-Catholic paths to God. "From the shameful source of indifferentism, or rather from that insanity (*deliramentum*)," he wrote, "comes the absurd and erroneous position that claims that liberty of conscience must be maintained for everyone. It spreads ruin in sacred and civil affairs."[154] Such misguided thinking he traced back to the wanton freedoms desired by Martin Luther and championed in his own time by so many "sects" and secret societies (an allusion to freemasonry, no doubt, a mortal enemy in the eyes of the papacy). But the deeper sources derived from the very pit of hell, belching smoke to obscure the sun and locusts to blight the earth. From indifferentism comes "the transformation of minds, corruption of youth, contempt of sacred things and holy laws—in other words a pestilence more deadly to the state than any other."[155]

In harshly condemning Lamennais and religious freedom, Gregory XVI had only given voice to misgivings already present in previous popes' utterances about the French Revolution. His stance of intransigence, moreover, was assumed by subsequent popes as they encountered revolutionary movements throughout Europe and, especially the movement toward national unification (*Risorgimento*) on the Italian peninsula. As is well known, Gregory's successor, Pope Pius IX (*r.* 1846–78), first expressed some sympathy with liberal principles after assuming the papacy in 1846. But this ended abruptly when Italian nationalists and republicans sacked Rome in 1848, forcing him to flee the city in disguise. In 1859–60, *Risorgimento* leaders, sometimes invoking idealized images of the United States as a model for the future, stripped Pius IX of the Papal States as Italian nationhood was established. In his 1864 encyclical *Quanta cura*, Pius, not surprisingly and quoting Gregory XVI directly, condemned freedom of conscience as an "insanity" and freedom of speech as a recipe for "injurious babbling." In the so-called *Syllabus of Errors*, appended to this encyclical, he held it as a grave mistake for any Catholic to believe that "every man is free to embrace the religion that he shall believe true by the light of reason."[156] In 1870 the last vestiges of papal properties in Rome were forcibly annexed to the new Italian state, leaving the pope a "prisoner of the Vatican" surrounded by a liberal polity—an "odium of sacrilegious usurpation" in the words of Pius—and one often given to strident outbursts of anticlericalism.[157]

All of this history is relevant because the revolutionary tide in Europe, from 1789 to the 1870s and beyond, created a profoundly *antimodern synoptic*, an embattled and unyielding skepticism among reactionary Catholics in their views toward liberal and republican movements everywhere, including those in North America. If republicans on the Italian peninsula appealed to the United States as a model for European politics, ultramontane and "legitimist" intellectuals took it upon themselves to puncture such appeals by pointing out the putatively deleterious effects of liberalism on religious life or by arguing that the immaturity and experimental nature of the North American republic disqualified it from holding exemplary status.[158] And even more moderate Catholics, long accustomed to church establishment, marveled quizzically at the novelty of a society based on purely "voluntary" religion.

But within this skeptical frame of reference, Catholic attitudes toward America could assume several different forms. Typical charges of multiplying sectarianism and widespread dogmatic laxity were, not surprisingly, frequent and persistent. The Italian Jesuit Giovanni Antonio Grassi (the first president of "Georgetown College") captured a more widespread reaction when he observed in 1818 that

[n]othing is more striking to the Italian upon his arrival in America than the condition of religion.... Due to an article in the federal constitution every religion and every sect is fully tolerated.... Indifference [therefore]... takes on a special character in America. It does not consist of despising and abandoning all practice of religion; many people continue to speak of religion and, generally, with respect. What then? They act as if God had never manifested his will to men, never pointed out the narrow path to salvation, that is followed by a few, had never warned that there are other, broader, easier ones traveled by many whose principles seem correct but ultimately lead to perdition.... Every sect there is held as good, every road as correct, and every error as the insignificant weakness of poor mortals. In accordance with such principles, it is not surprising if America gives birth to innumerable sects which daily subdivide and multiply.[159]

In Europe, the arch-conservative Count Metternich felt that the situation described by Grassi heralded the advent of dangerous new forces, promoting "religion without a church" and "mak[ing] each man the head of his own dogma." Such a system, "independent of all authority," represented to him "an absurd idea," a blow "to the spirit of man and incompatible with the requirements of human society."[160]

But if the fissiparous nature of American Protestantism in an atmosphere of religious voluntarism disturbed many conservative observers, others espied in the situation a hopeful *reductio ad absurdum* of Protestantism and a chance for Catholic truth to shine more brightly. The French-born Sulpician Archbishop Ambrose Maréchal (1764–1828), in a report to the Prefect of the Congregation of the Faith, noted that the "Protestant sects" in America appeared to care less and less for the creeds of the sixteenth century and alongside their own proliferating divisions, there appeared to be "a manifest and general tendency toward

Socinianism [Unitarianism]" in society at large. By contrast, "the Catholic Church has vindicated herself and the Protestants turn their eyes toward her." Indeed, "there is no region in the world," he continued, "where the Catholic religion can be propagated more quickly or widely . . . [than] in the United States of America." But with opportunities came dangers. The principles of civil liberty and the popular vote reigned supreme in American society, and Protestant churches often "governed [themselves] by these same principles, and as a result they elect and dismiss their ministers at will." Presaging the "Americanist crisis" at the end of the nineteenth century, he therefore warned Catholics to avoid the temptation of championing Protestant or liberal principles within their own ecclesiastical government.[161]

For the Frenchman Camille Ferri-Pisani, who traversed the Atlantic in 1861, the American experiment in voluntary religion allowed for an epochal showdown between Protestantism and Catholicism, in which the latter would demonstrate its superiority. To fill their "monotonous existence" in the New World and to provide an outlet from their well-known absorption in "practical activities," Americans of all people desired religious succor. But absent firm episcopal oversight or a national church, Protestants in the United States were especially prone to schism and to innovation passing itself off as the genuine article. In such a climate, he reasoned, "rational" forms of faith, and above all Unitarianism, found fertile soil, and threatened to spread from New England to the rest of the country. In America, "the true spirit of Protestantism" becomes clear; it "refuses to draw a clear line between truth and error; it refuses to accept one and reject the other. Its altars are open to all—the most childish faith as well as the most unimaginable skepticism. . . . Protestantism is thus easy prey for rationalism. The latter feeds on the very substance of Protestantism." Ultimately, then, the "useless skeleton" of Protestantism would give way to "rationalism," which would then stand "face to face" with Catholicism, it alone having "survived the disappearance of all other religious sects."[162]

If Unitarianism in America intrigued some Old World onlookers, few developments aroused more curiosity and contempt than the advent and spread of Mormonism. Indeed, from its beginnings in the early nineteenth century, Mormonism elicited (and still elicits) a particular fascination for the traditionalist European imagination. *La Civiltà Cattolica*, a Jesuit publication founded in Naples in 1850, emerged as a leading organ of ultramontane opinion, often exhibiting a pointedly

anti-American slant. An article from 1860, "Mormonism in its Connections with Modern Protestantism," penned by the Cardinal Archbishop Karl August von Reisach (1800–69), provides an apt case in
point. In Reisach's interpretation, Mormonism's rise amounted to a
revealing indictment of Protestant "religious individualism," to which
the American republic had given free reign. He traced the malady of
American Protestantism back to colonial New England. Trying to govern society theocratically "in a state of total reliance on the Bible" (*stato
del tutto biblieo*), Puritans were ultimately unable to limit individuals
from interpreting the Bible for themselves and "thus the same foundational principle of the Reformation naturally and necessarily caused the
collapse of such a theocratic system and caused new sects and religious
societies to emerge." The proliferation of sects in the nineteenth century—fomented by "the absolute principle of religious liberty"—gave
rise to conditions of religious confusion and uncertainty, allowing
Mormonism fertile ground to take root and, at least for many, to pass
itself off as the one true way, a safe passage from sectarianism and individualism to a secure collective and religious certainty. But in Reisach's
view, the "pseudo-church" of Mormonism represented simply a sect
writ large, a symptom of American Protestantism, not its cure, and
thereby a powerful, inadvertent witness for the Catholic Church as the
authentic bulwark of religious truth and social cohesion. What is more,
the same principles that had given rise to Mormonism, Reisach warned,
were being diffused in Europe by liberals committed to "religious indifference" (*l'indifferenza religiosa*) and a "religious individualism set against
the divine authority of the [Catholic] church."[163]

In his article, Reisach drew freely from the scholarship of the Catholic publicist and editor Joseph Edmund Jörg (1819–1901), particularly
his two-volume *History of Modern Protestantism*. Published in Freiburg
im Breisgau in the late 1850s, this work provides a fascinating window
into mid-century reactionary Catholicism, with its strong anti-liberal,
anti-Protestant, and anti-American accents. Charting the historical arc
of Protestantism from 1517 to the present, Jörg placed great concluding
emphasis on the rise of Mormonism, a "shameless deception," in the
New World as the "natural" consequence of Protestantism; an apt subtitle for the book in fact might have been "from Wittenberg to Salt
Lake City." Unlike some observers nonplussed by Mormonism's success, Jörg insisted, ironically, that the newfangled American religion
was in fact the "crown" of Protestantism, its "logical development"

from "the atomizing divisions and hollowing-out tendencies of the sectarian spirit" in the United States.[164]

Jörg's views of Mormonism fit within a more comprehensive interpretation of American religious history. In his outlook, the Puritans in New England represented a special strand of Protestantism, in that under New World conditions they had the opportunity to develop what he labeled a "Protestant Middle Ages," a society fully saturated with Protestant principles of the most extreme sort. Based on a rigorous understanding of *Sola scriptura*, this society was not so much a theocracy as a "Bible-ocracy" (*Bibelstaat, bibliokratischen Staat*). But it soon dissolved, not from external forces but from contradictions within. Particularly, "the absolute individualism of the Bible reader" led many to run afoul of the system: at first dissenting Baptists and later Unitarians, whom he lumped together with Methodists, carriers of "the religion of pure subjectivity." And from this same toxic soil arose Mormonism, recapitulating, in Jörg's interpretation, the farce of Puritanism by attempting to establish its own "Middle Ages" in the American West, in the form of a society-dominating false church prescribing dogma to its followers, while luring Americans ever farther away from the true church.[165]

The religious freedom enshrined in the American Constitution was therefore nothing to celebrate, in Jörg's view. It represented a desperate solution to the dire problem created by the unraveling of the Puritan "Bible state." Without the possibility of granting favorite status to a single expression of the faith, and faced with "endless religious divisions," the new political union went in "the opposite extreme direction" and established a legal environment of "absolute voluntarism" (*absoluten Freiwilligkeitsprincip*) for the individual.[166] In Jörg's estimation, however, this amounted to little more than throwing fuel on a raging fire, as such freedom only exacerbated the individualism and subjectivism inherent in Protestantism, encouraging it to develop yet more bizarre forms while abetting divisions within older denominations—and, again, ultimately leading to the gangrenous but "natural" development of Mormonism. Thus, when Jörg peered across the Atlantic (he never traveled to America), what he saw was "chaos," the "systematic denial of authority" (*systematische Autoritätslosigkeit*), "barren confusion," and "the tormenting spirit of sectarianism."[167] These aspects of the new land—combined with its well-known lack of tradition, its cultural or "spiritual" vacuity, and "the breathless pursuit of the almighty dollar"—were aptly captured for him in the terms "*Yankeethum*" and "*Amerikanerthum*"[168] The sound-thinking Catholic of the Old World had every reason to reject the principles of this new land. Indeed, the spreading of these principles in Europe meant that one could not remain neutral. America "is through and through a genuinely new world," he concluded. "Compare it to the more orderly nature of the Old World, and one must say: one or the other, either this New World or the Old World is a misguided world."[169]

★★★

Reactionary Catholic misgivings about the United States not only were sustained, but grew in the late nineteenth century. In part, this represented an understandable side effect of the loss of the Papal States and the aggressive anticlericalism found in European liberal and nationalist movements, not least within the new Italian government. But it also arose from fears of a "danger within," that more and more Catholic laypeople and clergy were being swayed by liberal principles, and by the American model of religious freedom in particular. In France, where debates over "Americanism" raged with particular ferocity, the clergyman Max Leclerc, for example, regarded the United States as the true "land of liberty," where the Catholic Church would learn "to preach and teach tolerance," and eschew being an "aristocratic organization." "Rome will no longer be in Rome," he overreached, but perhaps in "Baltimore."[170] Expressions of such "Americanist" zeal led to redoubled intransigence on the part of conservatives in the late nineteenth century, expressed in a veritable tidal wave of anti-American(ist) opinion, culminating in the encyclical of Leo XIII, *Testem benevolentiae* (1899), which officially (if somewhat hedgingly) condemned the so-called heresy of "Americanism."

What exactly was meant by "Americanism" in this condemnation, and its relation to the actual society and polity of the United States, has been the subject of debate ever since the encyclical was issued. More clear perhaps were the so-called "Americanists" themselves, who included Father Isaac Hecker, the founder of the Paulist Fathers in America and the chief theoretician of the movement in the eyes of its critics; Bishop John J. Keane, the first rector of the Catholic University of America; John Ireland of St. Paul, Minnesota; and Monsignor Denis J. O'Connell, Rector of the American College in Rome. By no means did these men march in intellectual lockstep, but their outlooks

converged in greater acceptance of friendly engagement with Protestants (a practical necessity on American soil); in the belief that the
Church's future lay with the "people" and not with "princes"; in
greater emphasis placed on the "active" virtues of social outreach over
the "passive" ones of obedience and humility; in the view that certain
Old World paternalistic or "feudal" habits of thought prevented Americans—and all "moderns"—from converting to Catholicism; and, not
least, in the (often immoderately and "providentially" expressed) belief
that American society in general and American religious liberty in
particular did not pose a threat to the European Church, but in fact
offered it a blueprint for its future development.[171] That such Americanist views were gaining more and more adherents throughout Europe only compounded the displeasure of conservative critics. So-called
"americanisti" were identified in Belgium, Germany, France, Italy, and
elsewhere, and it was the welcomed task of the embattled "Romanists"
or ultramontane party to check this metastasizing problem.[172]

Yet long before Americanism was officially branded as heresy in
Testem benevolentiae, the nexus of attitudes associated with it received
strong censure from several influential sources in the late nineteenth
century. In the wake of the 1848 revolutions, two ultramontane publications were launched that regularly castigated liberal movements everywhere, often functioning as quasi-official organs of an embattled
papacy. The journal *L'Univers* was established in France in 1849 by the
Catholic layman Louis Veuillot; its essays and reviews, complained the
French liberal Montalembert, "aired daily denunciations... of rational
freedom, not only in France, but throughout Europe and America."
The previously discussed *Civiltà Cattolica* (1850), founded by the Neapolitan Jesuit Carlo Curci, played a similar role on the Italian peninsula. Moving its headquarters to Rome from Naples only six months
after its founding, the journal exhibited an especially tight connection
between the opinions on its pages and attitudes within the Roman
Curia. As the United States descended into Civil War in the 1860s, the
journal's largely Jesuit writers traced the conflict to a zeal for liberty
and disrespect for legitimate authority endemic to liberal politics, and
they relished the irony that Italian nationalists appeared bent on idealizing a republic that seemed to be in the throes of disintegration.[173]

When an extreme anticlerical faction came to power in Italy in
1876 appealing to absolute separation of church and state along the
American model, the editors of *Civiltà Cattolica* saw fit to run two

articles by the conservative Jesuit Matteo Liberatore under the title,
"Liberalism and the United States of America." The discrepancy in attitude between Liberatore's reflections and those held later by the
Americanists presaged the crisis that awaited transatlantic Catholicism
in the near future. Parrying the widespread appeals to the American
example among Italian and other European liberals, Liberatore claimed
that such appeals amounted to "specious argumentation" and "folly,"
for a close examination of American history did not vindicate liberalism, but exposed its erroneous assumptions.[174] "The absolute freedom
of conscience and worship sanctified in the Constitution" was not
based on "natural law," as some argued, but simply represented a "political necessity" among so many quarreling and divided Protestant
sects. What is more, the abominable spirit of freemasonry suffused the
entire American political experiment and that alone should make any
Catholic wary. As an "inorganic" and "artificial" construction, liberal
constitutionalism, furthermore, contained the seeds of its own undoing by giving free rein to individualism and a general spirit of divisive-
ness, the "disastrous effects" of which had been made plain for all to see
in the near "total ruin" caused by the American Civil War. The aboli-
tionists of the North—the *"radicali yankees"* as he labeled them—
charged with reconstructing the nation had little choice but to greatly
expand the powers of the state to achieve a coerced unity, thereby giving birth to a dangerous "democratic caesarism" (*cesarismo democratico*).
Such a series of unfortunate events, less than a century after the republic's founding, amounted to "a sad omen for the future of the nation"
and pointedly raised questions about the judgment of those who
would still embrace the United States as an example for the "vecchio
mondo."[175]

Qualms about the United States and its influence on European
Catholic opinion aired not only in Old World periodicals, but ema-
nated from the New World as well. Arguably, nowhere was this more
the case than at Woodstock Seminary, a Catholic institution founded
in 1869 in close proximity to Baltimore and Washington, DC, for the
purpose of stifling liberal advances within the Church and raising up
an ultramontane crop of seminarians in the New World. Largely for-
gotten today except in some Catholic circles, Woodstock served, in the
words of John Ciani, as "a cultural and intellectual European island in
the Maryland woods."[176] Its initial faculty, predominantly Jesuit, were
European political exiles who had fled liberal movements in Europe

and sought to serve as agents of transatlantic, ultramontane Roman unity in America. Camillo Mazzella, who later probably helped draft *Testem benevolentiae*, taught theology at Woodstock for eleven years after fleeing Naples before the advance of Garibaldi's troops. Father Joseph Duverney came from Switzerland after the Sonderbund War of 1847–48, and Father Charles Maldonado arrived at the seminary after Spanish liberals shut down the Grand Central Catholic Seminary in Salamanca. Father Salvatore Maria Brandi, also a Neapolitan refugee and a close associate of Mazzella, taught at Woodstock for two decades before returning to Rome in 1891 as editor and writer for *Civiltà Cattolica*, where he shaped some of the most conservative interpretations of "Americanism" and its papal condemnation.[177]

The European experience of these men united them in an embattled cause against liberalism, including that of their adopted home, which ironically provided them with the freedom and seclusion to disseminate their views. Indeed, from its Italianate architecture to its strict neo-scholastic curriculum, Woodstock functioned as a sort of self-contained citadel against modernity, a sylvan *cordon sanitaire*, where young men were to be instructed into an unyielding Old World, ultramontane worldview. Founded at the time of the First Vatican Council and during the loss of the Papal States, the seminary was congenitally marked by the "Roman Question" and a concomitant unflappable anti-modernism. The philosopher Carmelo Polino spoke for practically the entire faculty when he impressed upon his students that the *Risorgimento* had "cured him forever of any sympathy…with the republican form of government and made him a staunch defender of absolutism."[178]

At the head of Woodstock's faculty stood the redoubtable Camillo Mazzella, memorably described by one former student as a hulking "tower of orthodoxy, a kind of individualized Council of Trent."[179] Despite his eleven years in America and his US citizenship, little evidence exists that anything of democratic political values rubbed off on him. His Latin textbook *De religione et ecclesia*, defending the right of the state to promote the one true religion, went through no less than five American editions, and was widely circulated in Europe as well. "Not only individuals, but society itself, must profess the true religion," he lectured young American men. "Therefore, civil society itself must embrace religion revealed by God and must be subjected by means of infallible authority…in those things which pertain to religion."[180] Indeed,

Mazzella did not think much of American society and its institutions. At the end of Woodstock's first academic year, he assessed the general American scene in a report to his Jesuit Superior in Rome as one where "the infidel and protestant element pre-dominates immensely," where society is "full of materialism, naturalism, rationalism, indifferentism, etc., etc."Woodstock faced an uphill challenge simply "to keep our own from being infected by the air they breathe in this infected atmosphere." He continued:"Principles and doctrines undoubted in Europe [at least in ultramontane circles] here among our own appear problematic. These grave errors touch on social rights, liberty, Church-State relations.... It is not rare to find clerics... [who] do not know how to distinguish false from true in what they read.... One of Ours cannot understand why the Pope won't let Protestant churches be built in Rome. Others submit to the Syllabus [of Errors] but do not ever try to speak of it or try to make others understand it."[181]

As this quotation implies, a kind of intellectual and moral laxity, one that threatened to dilute the purity of religious orders, registered for European Catholic traditionalists as a negative consequence of American freedom. Mazzella and his colleagues would undoubtedly have resonated with the words of an earlier Jesuit Superior General, Jan Roothan, who declared that the American passion for liberty was for a religious order "like a second original sin."[182] Accordingly, general assessments of American society by Woodstock's faculty, and by kindred spirits elsewhere, focused on how liberty encouraged negligence within religious orders and among aspiring seminarians. Benedetto Sestini, an astronomer at Georgetown before transferring to Woodstock, for instance, lamented the "irregularity of religious discipline" among his American counterparts and dismissed pleas by some that "the circumstances of this country" required granting "greater freedom" than was allowed religious orders in Europe. Americans had such an inflated opinion of themselves and "a supreme scorn toward all others," he held, that they were blind to their own laxity, which included too much idle talk, too little study, and too much fraternizing with the lay public, with women, and with Protestants.[183]

Given this generally negative outlook, it should not surprise that European Jesuits who had lived in the United States often led the charge against those native-born clergy—and especially the leading "Americanists," mentioned above—who wanted to focus attention on the virtues of American society as guideposts for Old World

Catholicism. After his return to Rome in 1878, Mazzella in particular played an influential behind-the-scenes role in advising the Vatican on American matters. Supported by conservative bishops in America (the Curia-favored *intransigenti* led by Archbishop Michael Corrigan of New York), he warned key churchmen of the growth of "Americanist" sensibilities in Europe. Salvatore Brandi in the pages of the *Civiltà Cattolica*, likewise, played a significant role in keeping alive the suggestion that Americanist positions—an outgrowth of "the monstrous religious indifference" of the United States—mirrored the very currents of republicanism in Italy that had divested the Pope of his temporal authority.[184]

Conservatives such as Mazzella and Brandi gained a major victory in 1895, when Pope Leo XIII (r. 1878–1903) addressed the American Church directly in the encyclical *Longinqua oceani*, a document probably penned in large part by Brandi. The crucial passage reads:

For the Church amongst you, unopposed by the Constitution and government of your nation, fettered by no hostile legislation, protected against violence by the common laws and impartiality of the tribunals, is free to live and act without hindrance. Yet, though all this be true, it would be very erroneous to draw the conclusion that in America is to be sought the type of the most desirable status of the Church, or that it would be universally lawful or expedient for State and Church to be, as in America, separated and divorced.

Recognizing that American liberty possessed some merit, the pope nonetheless added that the Church in America would yet "bring forth more abundant fruit if, in addition to liberty, she enjoyed the favor of the laws and the patronage of the public authority."[185]

But this would not be the end of the matter. Two developments in the late 1890s brought the Americanist crisis to a head. The first concerned a book, the second a war. Shortly after Isaac Hecker's death in 1888, a member of his Paulist congregation, Father Walter Elliot, published a series of articles on Hecker's life. Compiled into a book as *The Life of Father Hecker*, the work called attention to the "saintly" life of Hecker and underscored some of his signature ideas, one of which was that the present age was witnessing the passing of churchly leadership from the "Latin" to the "Anglo-Saxon" peoples, another being the diminution of the importance of strict monastic vows in modern times. Not surprisingly, when this work was translated into French in 1897 by Felix Klein it immediately set off a storm of controversy. After all, from the ultramontane perspective, were not animus against religious vows and the exemplary character of Anglo-American institutions similar to what anticlerical liberals had offered? Under the pseudonym "Martel," the French traditionalist Charles Maignen wrote a series of scathing reviews of Elliot's biography, soon publishing his attacks in book form as *Le Père Hecker, est-il un saint?* (1898). Maignen disavowed that the "crypto-Protestant" Hecker merited any saintly consideration, and viewed his Americanist outlook ("the greatest danger menacing the Church") a close cousin to the ideology of the French Third Republic, which had launched a frontal assault against the social influence of the Church.[186]

These transatlantic scholarly polemics were aggravated by geopolitical realities in the form of the Spanish–American war (1899), which pitted a traditional Catholic "Latin" empire in decline against an emerging "Anglo-Saxon" one. It did not help matters that many of the priests in the United States associated with Americanism audibly supported the American cause as a tell-tale sign of the decline of the Latin, feudal world and of the promising, youthful vigor of the United States. From the ultramontane side, the forced divestment of ecclesiastical properties in the Spanish Philippines was compared, not unreasonably, to the rapacious confiscation of church property during Italian unification. And thus as the United States won the war, the Americanists fell from grace in Rome. Indeed, the combined one-two punch of Maignen's book—widely read by the highest Vatican officials—and the war tipped the balance powerfully in favor of the ultramontane cause and led in short order to the official condemnation of Americanism in *Testem benevolentiae* (1899).[187]

While the text of this encyclical reflects far more discretion than Maignen's broadsides, its underlying point comes across strongly. In it, Leo XIII distinguished between "political Americanism" and "religious Americanism," granting limited acceptance to the former so long as it meant simply a benign love of one's country. Echoing sentiments in *Longinqua oceani*, however, the pope forbade "religious Americanism" in no uncertain terms. This teaching, he wrote, "involves a greater danger and is more hostile to Catholic doctrine and discipline, inasmuch as the followers of these novelties judge that a certain liberty ought to be introduced into the Church, so that, limiting the exercise and vigilance of its powers, each one of the faithful may act more freely in pursuance of his own natural bent and capacity." This represented a sharp blow to the principle of religious liberty and liberty of conscience, not only within the church, but also within individual nations. "Hence from all we have hitherto said," the pope concluded, "it is clear . . . that we cannot approve the opinions which some comprise under the heading of Americanism. . . . For it raises the suspicion that there are some among you who conceive of and desire a church in America different from that which is in the rest of the world," one "in unity" and one "rightly called Roman."[188]

While liberals tried to put the best possible face on the condemnation or question whether the "heresy" in question actually existed,[189] conservatives read Leo's letter as a clear vindication of their views. Many went even further, likening Americanism to Pelagianism and other ancient heresies that had beset the church. The Frenchman Abbé Henri Delassus of Lille penned *L'Américanisme et la conjuration anti-chrétienne* (1899), extolling Leo XIII for exposing this perfidious conspiracy within the church and practically equating Americanism with the degenerate spirit of modern times itself. Americanism, he explained, comprised a lethal mix of Protestantizing tendencies, Freemasonry and its Jewish supporters, and the familiar, pestilential liberalism of 1789. Were it to run its course, the Bride of Christ would be left in ruins.[190] Publications such as *L'Univers, La Civiltà Cattolica*, and *Historisch-politische Blätter für das katholische Deutschland* aired conservative glosses on the encyclical, often tacking on additional denunciations. Speaking with the authority of someone who had lived in the United States, Salvatore Brandi insisted that Americanism was, finally, not a "specter" (*fantasma*) of European reaction, as some insisted, but a genuine export from the New World; "its origin is fully American and was there first adopted to designate the 'new idea' which must rejuvenate the Church, and particularly the 'new crusade' which must fight against the intransigence of Catholics of the 'old belief' (*vecchio credo*)." While speaking high-mindedly about the people of the United States, he made clear that only under the republican conditions of American freedom could such a "restless and noisy" minority have made such inroads within the Church. The Pope had no choice but to condemn this "sad reality" and reaffirm the timeless teachings of the church. "The practical teaching all must draw from the letter of Leo," Brandi wrote, "is that Catholic principles do not change, neither with the role of years, nor the changing of countries. . . . Whoever accepts them in all their fullness and rigidity is Catholic. Who wavers...[or] makes compromises may call himself whatever he wants, but before God and the Church he is a rebel and a traitor."[191]

A postscript to the Americanist saga came when Pope Pius X (r. 1903–14) linked Americanism with Modernism, which he condemned in his 1907 encyclical, *Pascendi dominici gregis*. Motivated particularly by worries that Catholic scholars and educators were succumbing to previously condemned errors (e.g., rationalism, liberalism, and indifferentism) in their work, Pius sought to define the boundaries of orthodox Catholic intellectual life. Among the many problematic trends identified and rebuked in the encyclical, one held that the Modernists "with regard to morals...adopt the principles of the Americanists, that the active virtues are more important than the passive, both in the estimation in which they must be held and in the exercise of them."[192] While the mention was brief, the evocation of Americanism in the context of the many blanket condemnations issued in *Pascendi* only heightened, according to Gerald Fogarty, lingering suspicions about the Church in America: "[T]he juxtaposition of them [Americanism and Modernism] in the reactionary days of Pius X had its effect on the American Church. Regardless of its denials, the Church in the United States was under suspicion."[193]

This suspicion would persist until the time of Vatican II (1962–65), and even beyond. It was in this climate that Jacques Maritain, as we shall see, reflected on the United States and modern religious freedom. But the climate not only shaped conservative Catholic views of the American Church, it also colored general European perceptions of American culture and religion. If an institution as venerable and durable as the Catholic Church could be subject to such alleged distortions and errors on American soil, what of the rest of the society? This reactionary synoptic confirmed for many America as fecund ecology for theological misjudgment—a place at once deeply pious, infamously torn by (Protestant) sectarianism, but finally defenseless against a theological liberalism that dissipated all dogmatic fixities. In his book *Religion in the Society of the United States* (1902), for example, the Frenchman Henry Bargy—citing both the Americanists and their European critics—argued that despite the existence of many sects and confessions in the United States, one was justified in speaking of "la religion américane." "Religion is the most original thing in the United States," he argued; it is "a daughter of the soil." On this soil, "all denominations, from their different points of view, are gradually becoming merged in a cult of human virtue and progress." American Christianity "does not protest against anything," he added, "because it is sprung from a soil where nothing grew before it. The name 'Protestantism' recalls controversies too strongly to fit it.... American liberalism has its roots in American history rather than in the reform of Luther." One might think of it not even as a species of Christianity at all, he opined, but as "a religion of humanity grafted on to Christianity."[194] In a review of this book, Charles Maignen, the French conservative who helped instigate the Americanist controversy, observed that Bargy's book exhibits "a clear and penetrating mind and may serve . . . to further the cause of Roman orthodoxy against the pretensions and the fascinating spell of the Liberal [i.e., Americanist] school in both hemispheres."[195]

Finally, the French-born, English Catholic traditionalist Hilaire Belloc published in 1924 *The Contrast*, a book richly illustrative of the mood of post-*Testem*, post-*Pascendi* European ultramontanism. The book's title aptly suggests the point: America was an utterly foreign and disturbing place to the conservative European imagination. "Like all modern men," Belloc confessed, "I had not escaped the effluvium of this modern disease where America was concerned." But his intrigue had turned to shock and sheer bewilderment upon actually arriving on America's shores; a conviction of the sheer "separateness of America" gripped him, of the strangeness of "that completely New World beyond the immensity of the Atlantic." "My thesis is that the New World is wholly alien to the Old," he bluntly asserted, adding that superficial cultural and linguistic similarities only mask "the essential division between America and *all* Europe."[196]

What was true of the whole was acutely true in religious matters. The United States presented unprecedentedly problematic conditions for religious life. In aggregate, these conditions suggested to Belloc a near complete antithesis to Old World Christianity in general and Roman Catholicism in particular. Even anticlericalism in Europe posed less of an opposition, he believed, because with it one at least had a clear and definable adversary, and its exponents evinced a dogmatic certainty and a general manner of being which made them products if not partisans of a traditional culture. In America, however, the utterly new conditions, the vacuum of history and tradition, produced a kind of soupy, *laisser-aller* mentality; not hostility to religion per se, but a general indifference and blurring of older divisions, the bewitching demise of all authority and dogma. This attitude, as benign in appearance as pernicious in effect, posed among the greatest threats for traditional Catholicism as Belloc conceived of it. "The new and separate spirit," he summed up,

which has made America, which creates a spiritual condition peculiar to that Continent...tends to produce some quite unique experiment in the religious field....I cannot but think that the future holds some rapid, and to us of Europe startlingly new, American growth...in the domain of religion. Not an isolated, fractional experiment, but a great new national or cultural invention. A new Religion. Should such a transformation come, then the conflict with Catholicism of which I have spoken must arise immediately and in its severest form.[197]

3

The Secularist Critique: "A Certain Backwardness of Thought"

North America is pre-eminently the country of religiosity....But since the existence of religion is the existence of a defect (*Mangel*), the source of this defect must be sought in the *nature* of the state itself.

—Karl Marx, "The Jewish Question" (1843)

[How] can one find in one population the most acute practical sense...and material and mechanical advances at their highest point of development, coexisting with childlike credulity, illogicality, and hopeless unreason?

—Jules Huret, *En amérique* (1904)

Introduction

In a letter dated 31 December 1892, Friedrich Engels wrote Friedrich Adolph Sorge, a German socialist living in the United States: "Here in old Europe, things are livelier than in your 'youthful' land, which still doesn't seem to want to outgrow its fledgling years. It is noteworthy, but quite natural in a young land, which has never known feudalism and has grown up from the beginning on a bourgeois foundation, that bourgeois prejudices should [remain] so firmly planted." This had contributed to "a certain backwardness of thought," Engels felt, that frustrated the expected pattern of socialist development. Without an *Ancien Régime* on their own soil, Americans clung tenaciously to "the

traditions connected with the foundation of the new nationality";
chief among these were "Puritanism," which had become a "traditional heirloom," and a general spirit of "religion and sectarianism."
These elements of society would likely persist, Engels shrugged, until
the coming of full socialist emancipation, at which time they, finally,
would be unmasked as "false consciousness" and peter out.[1]

Engels' analysis evinces a variant of what I have designated as the
European Leftist or secularist critique of the United States. If the traditionalist critique emphasized the ungainly or scattered forms of religion produced by popular democracy and religious disestablishment,
the secularist critique focused on the general vitality and omnipres-
ence of religious credulity—as telling signs of socio-political backwardness and/or of the peculiarities of the American historical situation
when compared to that of Europe. In classical Marxist terms, of course,
religion—"the sigh of the oppressed creature,...the opium of the
people"—was understood to be part of society's ideological "superstructure," useful for oppressors (feudal and bourgeois alike) to deflect
social energy from class conflict and working-class emancipation. Its
very presence signified repression and inadequate enlightenment.

But we should not regard Marxist conceptions of religion in isolation. It is more helpful to see them as reflecting a more pervasive historical framework, a master narrative of "the modern," which came
into its own during the Enlightenment and the French Revolution, and
has since, *mutatis mutandis*, colored practically all variants of Leftist historical and political thought. In his much-discussed book *Provincializing
Europe*, Dipesh Chakrabarty describes this as a large-scale "transition
narrative," a "stadial" or "developmental" view of historical progress,
which, though embedded in specifically European assumptions about
time and change, asserted a "universally" valid standard for assessing
human achievements, one predisposed to decry the absurdity of strong
religious belief ("superstition,""fanaticism") and regard its "persistence"
as a "survival" from a deservedly receding era.[2] Put differently, a widely
shared benchmark of historical progress for eighteenth-century *philosophes*, post-1789 republicans, and socialists alike (the nascent Left) was
the attenuation or even evisceration of dogmatic religiosity and the
institutions serving it, or else its transmutation into a less rigid, humani-
tarian ethos. Throughout the nineteenth century, Robert Stuart re-
minds us, many of Europe's most progressive minds devoted themselves
to the view "that humanity would not be free until religion had been

extirpated, while entire political movements founded themselves upon a ferocious anticlericalism."[3] "The social revolution of the nineteenth century," in Marx's own formulation, was of a piece with "the stripp[ing] off of all superstition in regard to the past."[4]

This chapter will highlight several significant branches of this secularist, stadial conception of progress, in an effort to better understand post-1789 Leftist historical thought in general and its implications for interpreting the United States and American religious dynamics in particular. The first branch is the early tradition of French social or "sociological" thought as seen in the writings of the Marquis de Condorcet, Saint-Simon and his followers, Proudhon, and Auguste Comte.

The second is the influential trajectory of thought from Hegel to Marx and, in turn, to various Marxist-inspired interpretations of the United States. Along with the legacy of "the French Revolution, Hegelianism and Marxism form the matrix of [Leftist] political ideologies in Europe," the political theorist Manfred Henningsen has argued, "and anti-Americanism is in part a by-product of these ideologies."[5] We shall keep in mind Henningsen's thesis, paying special attention to the religious vitality and pluralism in the United States as seen through Hegelian–Marxist lenses.

The third branch might be described as the republican anticlerical tradition, i.e., left-leaning Continental liberals who did not necessarily want to transcend the "bourgeois" French Revolution in the name of a higher "socialist" development, but who nonetheless felt that realizing the Revolution's full potential entailed a relentless assault on ecclesiastical influence. Many leading figures in this camp were inclined to smile upon the United States during the post-1815 reactionary milieu. But once their political hopes were dashed by the failure of the revolutions of 1848, forcing many to flee across the Atlantic for refuge, their image of the New World frequently soured, as they were taken aback by the religious dynamism and churchly influence in the *actual* United States. The aftermath of 1848, we might say, prompted an early dramatic encounter between the Continental republican traditions of *laïcité*/anticlericalism and the American voluntarist tradition of religious pluralism—an encounter holding significant portent for the future. At first mediated by many radical German-speaking "1848ers" who had fled abroad in the 1850s, the drama of this encounter lived on and manifested itself particularly clearly in commentary on America arising during the pointedly anticlerical French Third Republic (1871–1940).

Many of the aforementioned figures and developments helped prepare the ideological soil, from which grew in the twentieth century the so-called "secularization thesis." We shall, finally, consider the contours of this thesis, both as an organizing principle "inextricably linked" to the rise of modern social science and, concomitantly, as a monopolizing master narrative about modernity, a "background" assumption, embedded in the general Left–European social imaginary.[6] We shall, moreover, probe its reliability, asking whether it harbors the unwarranted belief that the European experience of modernity offers predictive insight into modernization processes generally. Observing how the United States regularly must be cast as an "anomaly" in secularization theory will serve as our starting point.

Admittedly, the secularist intellectual trajectories sketched above do not bear witness to a monolithic phenomenon; they contain internal tensions and evince external differences. Nevertheless, several core assumptions warrant locating them in the same intellectual family tree. First, their various exponents, virtually to a person, took it for granted that the French Revolution was *the* touchstone event of modernity: a new dawn for freedom and reason, according to Hegel. The American Revolution, if considered at all, was viewed either as a precursor to 1789 or, more dismissively, as little more than the self-interested insurgency of a colonial people across a distant ocean. Second, past forms of "religion" (still a fairly new abstraction in the nineteenth century) were routinely associated with its most unsavory manifestations in the European *Ancien Régime*—clerical privileges, religious wars, abstruse theology, "Jesuitism," the Inquisition, and so forth—and therefore something that humanity required liberating *from*, not providing freedom *for*. Third, the presumed emancipatory course of European history occupied a vanguard and benchmark status, a model to which other parts of the globe, in the fullness of time, should attempt to "catch up."

The combination of these patterns of thought helped shape a tradition of interpretation or a critical synoptic (sometimes oddly dovetailing with that of the European Right), which routinely situated the historical particularities of the United States within a discernable European historical explanatory framework. Within this framework, the United States was not regarded as a historical constellation of distinctive provenance, but more often as the absence of specifically European conditions—and a puzzling laggard by comparison, a kind of oafish, pious misfit swimming against the (secularizing) tide of history. This synoptic or framework has exerted immense influence, in Europe and elsewhere. A thinker as otherwise perspicacious as the philosopher Charles Taylor reflects it when he writes that the United States often appears as a "curious throw-back to an earlier epoch," adding that "the great enigma of secularization... remains the United States. Why does this society so flagrantly stand out from other Atlantic countries?"[7]

America and Early French Social Thought: From Condorcet to Comte

> Our French genius withheld itself from the Reformation so as to preserve itself for the Revolution.
>
> —Jean Jaurés

In 1905, the year of France's epochal laws separating church and state, the French scholar of religion Jean Réville published an essay on "Anticlericalism in France" in the *American Journal of Theology*. In it, he sought to explain to an English-speaking readership the "deep and ancient" roots of Continental anticlericalism, especially in his own country. "[F]or those who take care to inquire into the history of France since the Revolution, the [present] anticlerical movement appears as the final act in a long evolution." Réville also offered observations relevant to understanding the early French tradition of social thought expressed in the writings of Condorcet, Saint-Simon, Proudhon, and Comte. When such men leave the Catholic Church, they rarely stop "at the middle station of Protestantism," but more often "go straight to free thought." They "do not easily understand Protestantism," he continued, with its "great variety of... denominations." "From their age-old Catholic education, they have preserved the conviction that there is but one... church, and that there cannot be another one"—even when they feel that the Catholic Church was false or, at best, superannuated in the modern age.[8]

Anyone perusing the lengthy tomes of these early French "sociologists" cannot help but notice the quizzical attitude toward Protestantism that Réville refers to, and also a lingering "Catholic," and perhaps even more aptly "Gallican," sensibility despite a resolute repugnance toward traditional clericalism. While this tendency is arguably less marked in the case of the idiosyncratic Proudhon, one sees it with special force in Saint-Simon's "new Christianity" and in Comte's "religion of humanity," and also in Condorcet's progressive, grandiose scheme of history, which pulsates with a residual eschatological longing. Indeed, each thinker, one might say, pays unwitting, backhanded respect to the universalizing aspects of Catholicism, as evinced in impulses to provide a (post-Christian) totalizing account of history for a revolutionary age, a mandate for progress, and a prescription for cultural cohesion and meaning.

These impulses carried implications for sizing up the United States. When these thinkers and their followers glanced across the Atlantic, they found things to admire, to be sure, but they also found much to question and contemn: a society rife with Protestant "fanaticism" and a polity legally incapacitated from providing any overarching cultural direction or unity. Every person in this New World appeared truly out for themselves, shifty and adrift in a huge wilderness lacking requisite institutions for education and progress. Society often appeared to be splintering according to the desires of the (untutored) many, not progressing according to historical laws recognized by the (enlightened) few. What is more, in comparison to the French Revolution, the American Revolution appeared at once noble but misbegotten, insufficiently breaking with the past and therefore saddling society with a number of congenital shortcomings, not least anachronistic religious ones. Without the galvanizing threat of throne-and-altar restoration, furthermore, society in the New World appeared too easily satisfied with half measures and compromises; Americans lacked sufficient awareness of the "immense horizon" of progress acutely felt by enlightened Europeans who had endured "centuries of slavery and misery" under the tutelage of priests and kings.[9]

Like Voltaire, Diderot, and other *philosophes*, the Marquis de Condorcet possessed impeccable bona fides with respect to anticlericalism. Before the Revolution, he regarded France, along with much of the rest of Europe, as "deluded by priests," suffering "under the yoke of superstition."[10] As the clock wound down on the *Ancien Régime*, he wrote admiringly of the American example. In *Lettres d'un citoyen des États-Unis à un Français sur les affaires présentes*, published anonymously in 1788, he assumed the voice of an American citizen urging reforms for freedom and against "tyranny and superstition" in France. In a 1790 eulogy to Benjamin Franklin (every *philosophe's* favorite American), he admired this "new man" of American democracy and the free, merito-cratic society that had given him a prominent voice. A few years ear-lier, he had penned *De l'influence de la Révolution d'Amérique sur l'Europe* (1786), in which he extolled the American Declaration of Independ-ence and opined, cautiously, that the American example would serve as "a useful brake on ministers [in Europe] who might be tempted to govern badly."[11]

Nevertheless, the American Revolution had its limits and defects, which in Condorcet's mind, finally, set the French Revolution apart as the more exemplary path to modernity. Already in 1786, he had lamented the Protestant "fanaticism" in the New England colonies which had made them resistant "to yield to the first efforts of philoso-phy." "Remnants of English prejudice," moreover, compromised the entire New World political experiment. These realities, combined with the fact that "America is separated from the people of Europe by a vast ocean," made the American Revolution, if a noteworthy and helpful goad toward change, not necessarily a template for Europe's own future.[12]

In Condorcet's famous *Sketch of a Historical Picture of the Progress of the Human Race* (1793), the French Revolution took center stage; the American Revolution was reassigned the status of precursor. The pe-nultimate "ninth stage" of history in his famous ten-stage scheme is labeled "from Descartes to the foundation of the French Republic," in which Descartes symbolized the birth of rational philosophy and the French Revolution its triumph in the realm of politics. In this (truly grand) narrative, in which "superstition" and "fanaticism" are tram-pled down by reason's inexorable advance, the American Revolution comes across as an estimable, but partial measure. While he still ad-mired the young New World republic, he felt that the French Revolu-tion had battled more successfully against religious prejudice and ecclesiastical influence. Lacking a full-blown national "system of intolerance to destroy," Americans remained "tainted with the preju-dices that [they]...had imbibed in their youth." Proponents of En-lightenment and Revolution in Europe, therefore, ought to prefer the French model, which had "more successfully escaped every kind of prejudice." "In France...the revolution...was to embrace the entire economy of society, change every social relation, and find its way down to the furthest links of the political chain." Its underlying principles, therefore, "were purer, more precise, and more profound than those that guided the Americans." In short, "the revolution in France was more far-reaching than that in America."[13]

An enthusiastic admirer of Condorcet, Henri de Saint-Simon (1760–1825) felt that the French Revolution represented the greatest cataclysmic shift in human consciousness since the advent of Christianity. He also welcomed the American Revolution as signaling "major progress for civilization in general." As a young man, in fact, he spent two months in North America as a soldier helping the thirteen colonies in their cause, and this heady experience certainly played a role in shaping his later views. In a list of noteworthy features about American society drawn up in 1817, he mentioned religion first: "[N]o religious dogma [was] regarded as the dogma of the state. There were many different religions, all of which were permitted, and everyone was free to invent new ones and seek converts. Within each religion . . . every kind of controversy was permitted."[14]

But after 1789, Europe absorbed the lion's share of Saint-Simon's attention, particularly the need to re-order society and politics after the Revolution. The grand intellectual system—"Saint-Simonianism"—associated with his name assumed from the outset several features structurally incompatible with the developing social and religious dynamics of the American republic. Saint-Simon himself did not evince great hostility to the United States, although he once observed that Europe and America were "essentially different" and that "civilization would not follow the same course in the two hemispheres."[15]

Intellectual modesty would describe neither Saint-Simon nor his key followers—figures such as Olinde Rodrigues, Amand Bazard and Barthélemy-Prosper Enfantin. Indeed, these men were subscribers to historical–philosophical "systems" of the grandest sort and dedicated enthusiasts of human progress. While the French Revolution constituted for each an epochal watershed, it was primarily one of destruction, a violent, necessary sweeping away of the old order, but leaving chaos and confusion in its wake. Dissatisfied with revolutionary-era liberalism, the Saint-Simonian circle believed that they possessed the insights necessary to reconstruct society on a socialist–technocratic model, guided by knowledgeable elites. If aristocrats had dominated the old order, men of science and learning would dominate the new. Industry, technology, education, progress, and, not least, socialism became Saint-Simonian watchwords. Democracy and pluralism did not.

Equally critical of the feudal economic order of the *Ancien Régime* and the emergence of free enterprise, Saint-Simonians desired the abolition of private property and the institution of economic centralism, in which scientific savants would coordinate the economy according to the dictates of merit and rational planning. What is more, European nations were enjoined not to compete with one another, either economically or militarily; but all should work in concert toward a grand European federal state, superintended by a European parliament and central bank. In a real sense, Saint-Simonianism represents a harbinger of the European Union today—an ideal already sketched in Saint-Simon's *De la réorganisation de la sociéte européenne* (1814).[16]

Religion played a major role in Saint-Simonian social theory. In the scope and significance accorded to it one can readily detect a residually Old-Regime-establishmentarian dimension in the new socialist movement. Advocates of religious freedom, according to Saint-Simon, failed to understand the necessity of unified religious sentiment, and that any durable social structure required an agreed-upon religious–ethical underpinning. The medieval world had understood this. The turbulent, post-revolutionary age, by contrast, stood in dire need of a common religious vision to overcome fragmentation and promote solidarity. In *Nouveau christianisme* (1825), Saint-Simon sought to supply this vision himself—a vision built upon by his followers to the point of establishing, under Barthélemy-Prosper Enfantin, an official secular religion, a "Saint-Simonian Church," complete with priests, rituals, and catechesis.

According to the doctrine of Saint-Simon, "the Catholic system was in contradiction with the system of sciences and modern industry. Hence, its collapse was inevitable." He even had the chutzpah to label Catholicism a Christian "heresy," one that only could "maintain itself by trickery." Protestantism offered cold comfort, for it encouraged "vulgarized Christian sentiments" and "[democratic] political desires contrary to the public good." Protestantism had also given a "false direction to philanthropic feelings," as every sect felt the need to take care of its own, instead of contributing to the general (Saint-Simonian) socialist–technocratic commonweal.[17]

What was needed, therefore, was a "New Christianity," a superseding of traditional, supernatural Christianity, even if one carried out under the banner of some of the latter's highest ethical ideals. The new Saint-Simonian religion dedicated itself to promoting socialism, industry, and scientific progress; but progress was to serve a central aspect of New Testament morality: encouraging fraternal love among humankind and improving the situation of the poor. Its central tenet enjoined "the whole of society ... [to] work to improve the moral and physical existence of the poorest class; it should organize itself in the way most suited to allow it to achieve this great end."[18] Far from seeing such a vision in conflict with past forms of Christianity, Saint-Simonians regarded it as *the* organic, culminating religious vision of Western society, one that judiciously appropriated the best in the past and placed religion in a harmonious relationship with modern science and industry.

Because of its impulses toward unity and synthesis, Saint-Simonians often felt their vision actually shared more in common with premodern Christendom than with revolutionary-era liberalism and pluralism. As Georg Iggers has written, "Incapable of admitting a pluralism of views, they considered the lack of unanimity [in post-1789 Europe] as symptomatic of the crisis. Like Catholic Restoration thinkers, they saw the Revolution as the political aftermath of the forces unleashed by the Protestant Reformation and the subsequent intellectual revolution which gave birth to the skeptical spirit of eighteenth-century philosophy." However, unlike Restoration thinkers, or in dialectical counterpoint to them, they did not want to restore throne and altar, even as they sought a "common spiritual direction" for all of society. Saint-Simonianism, Iggers concludes, "marked the most radical rejection of liberal and democratic institutions by any of the reform or revolutionary movements of the 'Left' in the nineteenth century, not excluding Marxism."[19]

The Saint-Simonian philosophy in general and its religious aspect in particular shaped perceptions among its adherents when they peered or traveled across the Atlantic. Some, like Saint-Simon himself, harbored generally mild attitudes toward the United States, welcoming the young nation's industrial potential. But from the late 1820s onward, a decidedly skeptical attitude toward the New World gained currency within Saint-Simonian literature.[20] An example appeared in a six-page essay, "Notes sur les États-Unis," appended to the second edition (1832) of Saint-Simon's *Catéchisme politique des industriels* (1823–24).[21] The document contains charges that North America did not make a clean break from "feudalism"; that property was not dealt with there in a "philosophical" manner; that the legal system demonstrated that the country lacked a mature conception of "public interest"; and that its "new people are more ambitious about wealth than knowledge." What is more, because of the "vast immensity of their territory," no impetus for political science existed—a science intimately connected to the practical question of how a sizable population might exist in a limited geographical space. The new country, in short, evinced many problems that one might expect from a political fledgling, and therefore held negligible interest for Europe's future.[22]

Some of the principal organs of Saint-Simonian thought during this period—such as the *Revue encyclopédique*, *Le Producteur*, and *Le Globe*—began to air regular criticisms of the United States, a number touching on the religious conditions and the wanting "spiritual" environment of the new land. A writer in *Le Globe*, for instance, charged that the United States existed in a dreadful state, ruled by a vain and selfish bourgeoisie without social ties or social sympathy in any organic sense. Amand Bazard remarked, similarly, that America completely lacked a unifying and coherent social doctrine; the new society was little more than a chaotic tangle of individuals in search of gain and property. A despotic "reign of utility," commented another, dominated American life, retarding the development of art and literature.[23] Partly to blame for this state of things was a "puritan austerity" (*rigorisme puritain*) that permeated the entire republic. Indeed, a writer in the *Revue encyclopédique* commented, "Christianity [in America] preserves with obstinacy the petty refinements of its decrepit devotions," making it difficult for the higher life of positive science and culture to find a home in the New World.[24]

A revealing example of a leading Saint-Simonian figure sizing up American religious life comes in the travelogue of Michel Chevalier (1806–79), one-time editor of *Le Globe*. In 1833, at the behest of the French Minister of the Interior Adolphe Thiers, Chevalier traveled to the United States to study its industry and public works. Like many Saint-Simonians, Chevalier esteemed "Anglo-Saxon" skills in industry and regarded the United States as the site of major technological progress. But perhaps precisely for this reason, the religious physiognomy of the new land frequently took him aback. In France, he averred, political authority held the nation together; in America religion served this function: "[To] the principle of political authority, which has always been most vigorously established among us—under all forms of government, whether monarchy, empire, or republic—corresponds the austere reserve of American morals... [and] the religious severity (*la rigidité religieuse*) which exists here alongside the multiplicity of sects."[25] Despite official church disestablishment, he noted, "There is in America [a] religious authority, which never closes its eyes."[26]

But this, of course, was not the progressive Saint-Simonian religion; it was the old-fashioned, dogmatic—and mostly Protestant—sort, transplanted from the Old World and unleashed into the New with uncomely, if often socially useful, effects. Chevalier even wondered if Americans lacked the notion that religion could progress; the dominant role that personal engagement with the Bible played in American society suggested to him instead a regressive religious spirit. "[T]he Yankees," he wrote,

have carried [a] retrograde tendency to the greatest extreme; they have, except in some few points, relapsed into Judaism.... They appeal with preference to the formulas of the Old Testament; they borrow their names from it, and among the peculiarities that strike a Frenchman in New England, one of the strangest is the great prevalence of Jewish names, such as Phineas, Ebenezer, Judah, Hiram, Obadiah, [and] Ezra.... As the religion of a people regulates their general sentiments and character, the Yankees, having thus fallen back into Judaism, possess, like the Jews, that exclusive spirit which was already inherent in their insular origin.[27]

This "Jewish"–Puritan spirit, in Chevalier's interpretation, had willy-nilly taken the lead in shaping the ethos of the nation as a whole. The "extreme Protestants" (*les ultras du protestantisme*), as he called the Puritan settlers, not only exercised a lingering, controlling influence over all other sects and denominations, but their unremitting work ethic had left a legacy of great economic activity and industrial growth. As a proponent of industry, Chevalier admired this aspect, even if he looked askance at the same "puritanical fanaticism" that led to crusades against amusements, such as theater and billiards, and rigid adherence to Sabbath restrictions or so-called "blue laws." "Any where else this rigorous attitude [against amusements] would be called intolerance, inquisition; here it is submitted to without a murmur, and few people are really annoyed by it." After spending a number of Sundays in America, he sighed that "nothing is... more melancholy than the seventh day in this country; after such a Sunday, the labor of Monday is a delightful past-time."[28]

Nonetheless, as someone shaped by Saint-Simonianism, Chevalier insisted that the importance of religion for social progress could not be discounted. Religion needed to be "transformed," however, or "recast" to meet the challenges and intellectual conditions of the present. In this respect, the Old World in general and France in particular pointed in a higher direction. In America, religion had contributed to the commonweal and often to social progress. This much Chevalier did not deny. But under New World conditions it had also been compromised, not only by the aforementioned "retrograde" tendencies, but also by a republican "spirit of individuality." In the United States, he averred, "individuals stand apart from one another, or if they are associated together, they have formed only limited connections, which have no common bond of union." This social reality was acquired in imitation of the "diverse sects" in America, all of them "independent of each other...and most of them tend[ing] to splinter infinitely into completely detached fragments."[29]

The true religion of the future would not lead to fragmentation but to "association and unity"—goals and yearnings which the legacy of Catholicism had deposited in the heart of every Frenchman. Indeed, the high degree of confessional unity in France during the *Ancien Régime* had served, fortuitously and unwittingly, as the chrysalis of the new religion, one of progress and humanity, one that would eschew theological dogma for social ethics, and thereby foster "the brotherhood of nations" and "the unity of the whole human family." An inkling of this new religion had reared its head after 1789: the "principles of the French Revolution were only the precepts of the Christian religion practiced by persons who were no longer Christians, and the revolutionary actors themselves gave to Christ the title of *sans-culottes*, in their eyes a title of honor."[30] The religio-political task at hand was to harness this new, often turbulent spirit and effect a "moral remodeling of society." For this, the American example possessed limited usefulness, because in the final analysis the new land had hitched its social doctrine to anachronistic manifestations of Christianity—ones typified by "the sect" and not more generously focused on "humanity."

Finally, Chevalier felt that the same American religious practices that generated a strong work ethic and economic success also strained transatlantic solidarity. "[W]ithout those...religious notions which imperiously repress all passions, except those of working, producing, and earning, can any one suppose that the Americans would have achieved their great industrial prowess?" But this prowess, however impressive, had also produced a dour and uninteresting people, who

"appeared destitute of the sense of pleasure." "It must be admitted,"
Chevalier concluded, "that this ardent and exclusive preoccupation
with business gives this nation a strange hue (*nuance étrange*) in the eyes
of a European. And this explains the fact that the Americans have
found so little favor with most foreigners who have visited this country."[31] For Chevalier, the Europe of his desired future would combine
industrial output with high-minded spiritual or ideal sensibilities. Unfortunately, "The American . . . has become impoverished in the realm
of ideals (*appauvri en idéalité*) in proportion as he has become rich in
material wealth."[32] Europe, he believed, could do better.

The theme of America as a place of material abundance and "spiritual" or intellectual impoverishment, an *idée fixe* among traditionalist
thinkers, also emerged as a commonplace among many leftist and
secularist thinkers in the middle decades of the nineteenth century. A
number of figures could be marshaled to support this claim. The idiosyncratic, bitterly anticlerical socialist Pierre-Joseph Proudhon (1809–
65) provides an apt case in point. Although he, like others, was more
absorbed with European affairs and a product of the revolutionary
tradition in France, he occasionally turned his gaze across the Atlantic.
When he did, conventional charges of intellectual want, vulgarity, and
material excess flowed freely from his pen:

The spiritual poverty of the Americans [is] evident . . . What, in fact, is American
society? It is composed of commoners who have suddenly acquired wealth.
Now fortune, far from civilizing men, most often brings them to vulgarity. . . . Have the Americans thought about the enormous problems of economics that are being hatched by our century? No, far from it. The Americans
are perhaps more bent on gain than any other nation. . . . While one half of the
nation, with Bible in hand, cultivates slavery, the other is already creating a
proletariat. In short, the Americans are by tradition strangers to the moral,
political and philosophical developments of the Old World. They are kept at
a distance from it by their way of life. . . . It seems to be that the Americans
neglect these things [of the Old World] too much and this is the reason why,
in spite of their dollars and their pride, they rank last among the civilized
nations.[33]

The American Revolution, Proudhon insisted, owed its success almost
exclusively to the inspiration of French ideas and French military assistance. The new polity and society that had come into being, however, rendered past French efforts hardly worth the effort. What were
"American" ideas, he asked? "Truly a jumble of principles, a monu-

ment to intolerance, to exclusiveness and arbitrariness,... Anglo-Saxon individualism projected into an immense territory." Were it not for that "negative liberty which resulted from a small population and land of amazing fertility, it would be better to live under the despotism of Louis XIV or Napoleon than in the American republic."[34]

Proudhon's contemporary Auguste Comte (1798–1857) shared a similarly hostile view of the United States. Along with Proudhon, the Saint-Simonians, and others, Comte took the singular significance of the French Revolution and the historical primacy of Europe for granted. As Raymond Aron has observed, Comte "regarded the history of Europe as the history of the human race."[35] For Comte, the French Revolution represented the cataclysmic purgation of the Old Regime, a "salutary explosion" (*salutaire explosion*) in his own words, the culminating point of a whole process of decay and criticism that the old order had been quietly undergoing for centuries.[36]

At the same time, in its general appeals to "humanity" and in its fumbling efforts to establish a post-Christian *cultus*, the French Revolution had adumbrated a newer, more progressive "universality." Not unlike his erstwhile employer Saint-Simon,[37] Comte regarded the task of the future as building on this "universality" to reestablish a durable and cohesive social order. The French Revolution thus signaled for him both an ending and a beginning.[38] On positive and negative grounds, Comte concluded, France was destined to lead the final revolutionary movement, to occupy "the definitive center of a universal movement."[39] Toward these ends, Comte laid down his fundamental laws of historical evolution, or his so-called "law of the three phases" of history. First, humankind existed in a "theological" phase, the state of the world prior to the modern era, during which supernatural explanations of phenomena predominated. The second or "metaphysical" phase brought into focus the discovery of human rights and the beginning of philosophical questioning and inquiry. The final "scientific" or "positive" phase released humankind altogether from the "théologico–métaphysique," as he sometimes abbreviated the pre-positivist phase. This final phase, guided by the all-encompassing discipline of "sociologie" (his neologism), would witness the application of the methodology of the natural sciences to every domain of human thought. "Positivism" in the intellectual realm would be complemented by "altruism" toward "humanity" in the ethical realm to restore a newer and higher social unity—the old premodern religious unity having been dissolved forever during the revolutionary period.

Not surprisingly, and here, too, not unlike Saint-Simon, Comte retained abiding respect for Catholicism, or at least for the notion of a well-ordered confessional state. With Restoration thinkers, he admired France's Bishop Bossuet (1627–1704) in particular, who had supported the revocation of the Edict of Nantes under Louis XIV and had penned both a powerful indictment of Protestantism and a sweeping providentialist vision of "universal history."[40] Indeed, Comte numbered Bossuet, alongside eighteenth-century secular visionaries such as Condorcet, among his intellectual predecessors. "It is surely to our great Bossuet that we shall ever be indebted for the first important attempt of the human mind to contemplate from a sufficiently elevated perspective the whole history of society." Comte described his own task as "the rational coordination of the fundamental sequence of the various events of human history *according to a single design*, at once more real and more extensive than that conceived by Bossuet."[41] What Bossuet had attempted under a theological–metaphysical aegis, we might say, Comte sought to do for a secular–positivist one. "Essentially," as Michael Burleigh has summarized, "Comte sought a new unifying social doctrine to replace theology and the church."[42] Or, as Henri de Lubac once observed, Comte wanted to transpose the rhetoric of (Catholic) universalism, if not its theological substance, as a vehicle for his utopian project.[43]

Historical forces that promoted diversity were routinely castigated in Comte's writings. He derided as pathological and destructive all doctrines of liberalism and laissez-faire economics. Every form of Protestantism received his censure. Churches stemming from the Reformation were at once anachronistically "theological"—and hence fundamentally at odds with his progressive scheme of history—and seedbeds of liberalism and social disorder—and hence an abiding impediment to the type of post-Christian social cohesion and universality that he sought to advance. Protestants, he once wrote, are intoxicated with "theological–metaphysical" ideas; they represent "the spontaneous enemies of positivism"; their hearts are ordinarily depraved; and they are at bottom "intellectually backward."

Protestantism, as R. L. Hawkins concluded, presented to Comte "the chief obstacle to a decisive intellectual and moral renovation."[44]

Comte never forgave the United States for its formative ties to Protestantism. Indeed, the *novus ordo seclorum* typified for him a loathsomely regressive society, a misbegotten counter-example to practically everything he desired for the future of Europe, of humanity. While still a secretary for Saint-Simon, he complained that America was the country "where the spiritual disorganization" (*désorganisation spirituelle*) of humanity "had been infinitely more pronounced than everywhere else."[45] The "radically discordant" and "tyrannical" sectarian environment of North America held much of the blame; it kept society divided and mired in a theological–metaphysical stage, rendering higher development toward positivism extremely difficult. America had thus achieved scant liberation from the past; the "the philosophical tremblings" (*l'ébranlement philosophique*) that had awakened Europe in 1789 had hardly been felt across the Atlantic.[46]

While the French Revolution, negatively, assailed the *Ancien Régime*, it also, positively, pointed to a new "universality." By contrast, the American Revolution in Comte's eyes was simply an expression of Protestant rebellion and anarchy—"l'insurrection américaine" as he once labeled it.[47] He interpreted events in the New World after 1776 as an unhappy extension of two other major "Protestant" developments of the early modern era: the Netherlands' revolt from Spain and the English Revolution of 1688. The American Revolution, in this view, represented little more than the flight from established unity and authority into spiritual and intellectual confusion, minus the liberating spirit of modern philosophy. It merits quoting Comte's rather convoluted prose at some length on this point:

The American revolution was as purely Protestant as the others.... In its origin, it reproduced in new forms the Dutch revolution; in its final development, it prolonged the English revolution, which it realizes as far as Protestantism will allow. There is nothing to be said for its success as a decisive social enterprise; for it has developed to excess the inconveniences of the critical doctrine. It sanctions more emphatically than any other society the political supremacy of metaphysicians and jurists, among a people who pay, through their innumerable incoherent modes of worship (*innombrables cultes incohérents*) that lack any genuine social purpose, a tribute more costly by far than the treasury of any existing Catholic clergy. Thus this universal colony, despite the eminent temporal advantages of its present position, must in fact be regarded in all important respects as more remote from a true social reorganization than the [European] nations from which it is derived, and to which it will owe, in the course of time, its final regeneration. The philosophical induction into that ultimate state [positivism] is not to be looked for in America—whatever may be the existing illusions about the political superiority of a society in which the elements of modern civilization are...most imperfectly developed.[48]

To those who insisted that the American Revolution paved the way for the French Revolution, Comte responded that salutary influences flowed mostly from the Old World to the New, not vice versa. "The revolution [in America] was regarded as a crisis in which the whole civilized world had a direct interest," he admitted. But "when it is said that France gained much by that event, it should be understood that the benefit to her was simply in the opportunity afforded for the manifestation of her [own] impulses and tendencies; and that *she gave more than she received* by planting down among a people benumbed by Protestantism (*engourdies par le protestantisme*) the germs of a future philosophical emancipation. While all indications thus pointed to a regeneration, there was no doctrine [in America] by which to bring it about."[49] In other words, insofar as America could partake in Comte's positivist vision, it was due to the intellectual stimulus of France and a new European universality, coming to consummate expression in Comte's own writings, but already hinted at in "la grande révolution française."[50]

But even if "philosophical emancipation" might one day come to the United States, the prospects of this happening in Comte's lifetime appeared unlikely. In the final analysis, Comte's America was congenitally ill-suited for higher development, maintaining a "childish restriction to the primitive things of the spirit." Overrun with "Protestant insurgents" and other "innumerable and incoherent" religious sects—including those "miserable anarchists," the Mormons—the United States represented the country where the building "anarchy of the West" (*l'anarchie occidentale*) had reached its most repugnant display.[51] Lacking a full-scale purgative explosion comparable to the French Revolution, moreover, the deficiencies of the new land appeared to have a fecund environment in which to spread. To be sure, the "stagist" laws of history would eventually catch up with America, Comte held; the inexorable spread of positivism to all of humanity could not be stopped. But in this case, Comte would probably agree with Edmund Burke: the march of the human mind is slow.

Hegel, Marx, Religion, and America

Every July 14, according to some of his contemporaries, the German philosopher Hegel drank a toast to the French Revolution. Like many who had lived through the turbulent 1790s, Hegel felt that the Revolution had, at times, careened into excess. Nonetheless, it remained for him a magnificent event, the intellectual gateway to the modern world. Because of the Revolution, he wrote, "the idea of Right asserted its authority all at once, and the old framework of injustice could offer no resistance to its onslaught.... Never since the sun had stood in the firmament and the planets revolved around it had it been perceived that man's existence centers in his head, in thought.... [The Revolution] was accordingly a gloriously mental dawn."[52] At Jena in 1806, as he completed his *Phenomenology of Spirit*, Hegel famously referred to Napoleon as "the world spirit on horseback," transmitting the ideals of the Revolution to the rest of Europe. Not once, in his voluminous reflections on freedom, did Hegel seriously wrestle with the meaning of the American Revolution.

But he did comment on American social conditions. The society taking shape across the Atlantic in the early nineteenth century cut squarely across the grain of Hegel's political and "spiritual" sensibilities. Although in one brief passage he indicated that America might represent "the land of the future," most of his remarks on the *actual* state of American society were highly derisive and critical. The United States represented for him an expansive, virtually stateless oddity, in the grip of individualistic liberalism and allowing for the most anachronistic and fissiparous forms of religious life. It languished across the Atlantic as an undeveloped social field, a worrisome question mark before the cunning power of reason that he sought to express in his philosophy and help advance in the Prussian state, which in 1817 had granted him a prestigious chair at its premiere university in Berlin.

While the French Revolution had brought reason, freedom, and progress to the fore of human consciousness, these ideals could only be realized and regulated with a powerful centralized state. Accordingly, the ethical agency of the state stands at the center of Hegel's political philosophy. The expansive role of the state in Hegel's thought and in German idealist philosophy in general, as is commonly observed, separates Continental political thought during this period from Anglo-American, Lockean currents, in which the state is granted a much more restrictive role.[53] By contrast, Hegel regarded the state as the embodiment of humankind's highest moral aspirations and the proper superintendent of the "spiritual" life of the nation. "All the worth the human being possesses—all spiritual reality he possesses only through the state," he wrote in his *Philosophy of History*.[54] "The march of God in the world, that is what the state is," as he put it in his *Philosophy of Right*.[55] Remarkably then, as the United States stood in the throes of free-church revivalism and as the self-reliant frontiersman Davy Crockett emerged as an American icon, Europe's leading philosopher was busy explaining why a state official (*Beamte*) constituted the highest human vocation.

Despite holding religious views critical of traditional orthodoxy (more on this below), Hegel accepted the Prussian state–church system, and felt that it was among the state's leading tasks to mold the cultural and religious life of the nation. Scholars of the period frequently speak of a "tutelary state" (*Erziehungsstaat*) or "culture state" (*Kulturstaat*) to describe the role of the state as theorized among German idealists and as implemented (at least to a degree) during the reform of Prussia after its humiliating defeat by Napoleon in 1806.[56] Prussia's *Kultusministerium* or Ministry of Culture, which oversaw universities and churches, bore the lengthier title of "the ministry of ecclesiastical (*geistlichen*), educational, and medical affairs." Hegel maintained a close relationship with this ministry until his death in 1831. For Hegel, granting greater autonomy to church bodies, as a handful of free-church enthusiasts and liberals desired, was a regressive measure, a sure recipe for obscurantism and social disorder. But he also did not think the state should provide succor to creedal Lutheranism— hence he cannot be easily placed in the traditionalist camp. Rather, the state—through the agency of the Ministry of Culture—should seek to "enlighten" religion and bring it, even if incrementally, into greater conformity with the dictates of modern reason and philosophy. In a real sense, churches for him were superfluous entities in the modern era; their tutelary function might appropriately be absorbed by the state. Few expressed this better than the Hegelian theologian Richard Rothe (1799–1867). "The moral community, the modern state," Rothe reasoned, "has done more to bring man to a condition befitting the will of Christ than all the churches of Jerusalem or Rome or Wittenberg or Geneva."[57] The prevalence of similar sentiments among idealist thinkers led Hajo Holborn to conclude that "German idealism changed the sphere of ethical and spiritual action in human history.... Hegel is a typical example. For Hegel the state was the realization not only of law, but also of morality. If this is the case, the church loses any vital role it had in history.... German idealism did not have any great place for the church in its intellectual house."[58]

Not unlike Saint-Simon and Comte, Hegel saw himself as upgrading and improving upon traditional, orthodox formulations of the Christian faith, even as—through the subsequent writings of the so-called Left Hegelians—he paved the way for arguably the most devastating criticism of Christianity and religion in modern history.[59] For Hegel, the biblical narratives and early creedal statements of Christian belief were not necessarily false; they had simply been expressed in premodern subjective, representational forms (*Vorstellungen*)—forms that emphasized pictorial thinking, metaphor, and sensuous experience. They lacked the maturity of reason and the benefit of modern philosophical concepts (*Begriffe*). The theological task of the future, Hegel made clear, was to elevate Christianity from the "representational" to the "conceptual" realm, to release the kernel of truth embedded in biblical stories and creedal expressions and grant them the surer substance of modern philosophical reason. The state, the guarantor and locus of reason in history, played a crucial role in this process. While ecclesiastical bodies possessed only a "subjective conviction" with respect to religious truth, "the state is the one that knows" (*das Wissende*), the one more open to philosophy.[60] Accordingly, the state alone possessed the final paternalistic responsibility to guide the spiritual life of the nation as a whole: to prod it along from "representational" adolescence to "conceptual" adulthood.

In light of all of this, it is not difficult to see why the American experiment in "voluntary" religion and limited government could hardly stand more at odds with Hegel's general outlook. American society of the nineteenth century spawned a kind of organic, grass-roots anti-Hegelianism, one might even quip. Insofar as Hegel considered the United States at all, he therefore reduced it to a realm of historical primitivism or immaturity—an "incapacity for world history," as one scholar has summed up, even a site of barbarism.[61] A passage in Hegel's *Philosophy of Right* describing "barbaric" conditions, in fact, is not too distant from the description of the United States offered in his *Philosophy of History*. In the former work, Hegel averred that "under conditions of barbarism, all forms of spiritual life had their seat only in the church, while the state was a mere mundane rule of force, caprice, and passion. At such times it was the abstract opposition of state and church, which was the main underlying principle of history."[62]

While his primary reference here was to the Middle Ages, the description resonates with his characterization of the United States during the time of the Second Great Awakening—a characterization bereft of any first-hand knowledge. The state in America he regarded as a "caprice," a rudderless non-entity in comparison to the enlightened bureaucracy of Prussia. "As for the political situation in North America," he wrote, "its general goal has not yet been settled upon as something fixed. There is as yet no firm coherence in the political structure." A true state existed only when a people lived together from necessity; but in America the lure of western lands meant "a constant stream of settlers into the plains of the Mississippi," which for the foreseeable future assured a condition of political infantilism. Under present conditions, he put it bluntly, America simply did not possess a "genuine state and genuine government." He dismissed "[the] basic character of society [in America] as marked by the private person's striving for acquisition and profit and by the predominance of a private interest which devotes itself to the community only for personal benefit."[63]

The religious sphere in North America bore out in spades the general social deficiency. Absent a full-fledged tutelary state, absent a forward-looking Ministry of Culture, geographically remote from currents of enlightened philosophy, the United States had cast religion to the whims of everyman. This ill-conceived experiment had predictably resulted in obscurantism and confusion. In the United States, as Hegel memorably wrote,

every person may have his own worldview ... [and] his own religion. This explains the proliferation of sects, to the point of sheer insanity (*Verrücktheit*). ... This total arbitrariness is such that the various communities hire and fire ministers as they please: the church is not something that subsists enduringly ... [as] an external establishment; instead, religious matters are handled according to the particular view of the congregation. In North America the wildest freedom of imagination prevails. What is missing is the religious unity found in European states, where deviations are limited to a few confessions.[64]

Compounding matters, Hegel was a late subscriber to the "degeneracy thesis" about the New World, so perhaps it should not surprise that such a distasteful and alarming religious scene played out on a continent that, prior to European settlement, he regarded as "physically and spiritually impotent" (*physisch und geistig ohnmächtig*), peopled with "irrational children," who appeared "remote from higher thoughts and purposes."[65] His triadic division of world history, moreover, only included Europe, Asia, and Africa, and made no place for the entire Western hemisphere![66]

In light of the New World's manifold shortcomings and incapacities, the United States, finally, held little interest for the student of world history, from a Hegelian standpoint. Again, Hegel did speculate that America might have some distant, future world-historical meaning. But in the present (the 1820s), it held virtually no significance. At best, it constituted a repository for Europe's ambitious and shifty "surplus population"—a "land of longing for all those who are weary of the historic arsenal that is old Europe." Insofar as the philosophy of history concerned itself with charting the path of rationality through time, the United States of his day could be summarily dismissed. As Hegel instructed students who streamed from across Europe for a coveted place before his lectern:

America [is] separate ... from the ground upon which the world's history has taken place until now. What has taken place in America so far is a mere echo of the Old World, and the expression of a strange vitality (*fremder Lebendigkeit*). As a land of the future it does not concern us here: for in the historical perspective we are concerned with what has been and with what is; and in regard to philosophy our concern is neither with what was nor with what is yet to be, but with what *is* as eternal Reason—and that is enough to keep us occupied. Let us therefore set the New World aside, along with its associated dreams, and return to the Old World, the theater of world history.[67]

The political theorist Manfred Hennigsen has observed that this passage represents a classic example of Hegel's "suppression" (*Verdrängung*) of America, a dismissive, trivializing interpretation of it with the trajectory of European history and the French Revolution serving implicitly as the assumed markers of historical reason. "After more than 200 years of North American history and a revolutionary process attaining a new level at the time of Hegel's lectures in Berlin," Hennigsen sums up, Hegel insisted that "America still had to wait on a future."[68] Hegel's America was at once "immature and impotent," in Antonelli Gerbi's formulation, religiously backward and confused to the point of "sheer insanity" and "total arbitrariness," hardly within earshot of Reason's pathways.[69]

★★★

Hegel's stance toward the Revolution and his interpretation of Christianity generated enormous interest during his lifetime and shortly after his death. The so-called "Hegelian Right" felt that the views of "the Master" were reconcilable with traditional orthodoxy and with the outlook of the Prussian monarchy. But this conservative following, though sizable, has been vastly eclipsed in history by the better-known Young Hegelians or "Hegelian Left," those critics who felt that Hegel, as masterfully as unwittingly, had instigated an epochal dismantling of a traditional–theological worldview and paved that the way for a purely immanent, anthropocentric humanism and social criticism, which, as hindsight reveals, would go to reach its most consequential expression in the writings of Karl Marx, Friedrich Engels and their innumerable epigones.[70]

Indeed, the rise of social theory "from Hegel to Marx" (via left-wing Hegelians such as David Friedrich Strauss and Ludwig Feuerbach) obtained a quasi-mythological status in the outlook of socialists and Marxist intellectuals of the twentieth century—a veritable campfire tale of the far Left, told and retold to new generations, at once an inspirational narrative of origins and a powerful means of intellectual legitimation.[71] In this story, there are some familiar markers. Hegel had pursued an admirable synthesis, attempting to forge a link between traditional, supernatural Christianity and modern (read: Hegelian) philosophy. But the latter ultimately introduced categories of thought and tools of criticism that devoured the former. The appearance of David Friedrich Strauss's *The Life of Jesus* in 1835 signaled the beginning of the end for the "old faith." This work reduced many of Christianity's central claims about the person of Christ to the mythological—and, by implication, delusional—messianic outlook of the early Christian community. From Strauss's criticism, it was but a short step to Ludwig Feuerbach's *The Essence of Christianity* (1841), in which Feuerbach argued that the idea of God, in the final analysis, was a purely human construction and did not refer to a transcendent reality. True reality was a purely human, immanent reality, and the idea of God, rightly understood, only bore witness to the dignity of humankind and human thought. To advance an immanent understanding of human dignity in the modern world, therefore, supernatural forms of Christianity, the spiritual spine of the Restoration order, ought to be exposed as anachronistic and discarded.

Early Marxism took shape in the critical atmosphere prepared by the Hegelian Left. "[T]here is no other road...to truth and freedom," wrote the young Marx, "except that leading through the fiery brook," a play on Feuerbach's name which literally means a fiery stream or brook.[72] "The criticism of religion is the premise of all criticism," Marx famously wrote, following Feuerbach; "The criticism of religion ends with the teaching that man is the highest essence of man, hence the absolute imperative to overthrow all relations in which man is debased, enslaved, [and] abandoned."[73]

Even as Marx's well-known "materialist conception of history" was indebted to Feuerbach, it also went beyond the "fiery brook," just as his views on the French Revolution—and modern revolution generally—at once owed a debt to and transcended those of Hegel. Marx's views on religion and revolution, in turn, bore significantly on his interpretation of the United States, and they have also bequeathed, it hardly needs stating, a truly massive legacy for the intellectual and political Left since the nineteenth century—not only in Europe, but also in the United States, and around the globe.

Marx's criticism of religion, in brief, is comprised of two main aspects. Marx followed Feuerbach in regarding religion as an example of alienated consciousness, the "externalization" or "projection" onto the idea of God of humankind's own inner capacities and worth: "Religion is the self-consciousness and self-feeling of man who has either not yet found himself or has already lost himself again." But Marx added another tenet, in which religion was seen as a fundamentally false ideological consciousness, arising from unjust and repressive socioeconomic conditions. Marx felt that the "Young Hegelians" had remained theologians or idealists at heart, because they still gave to religious consciousness a causative role in the human condition of alienation. They had not gone far enough in their criticism. As is well known, Marx concluded that economic alienation was the ultimate cause of both political and religious alienation. Religion, in this view, was utterly epiphenomenal, a part of society's "superstructure," which mirrored the perverted and repressive underlying conditions of society at large. In short, Marx reduced religion to the symptom of an unwholesome situation, "the pus of a sick world" as one critic has pithily summed up; attacking it frontally might be intellectually

therapeutic for the critic, but its decisive escort from human consciousness depended on the overthrow of existing socioeconomic structures
through proletarian revolution.[74]

The coming revolution, in Marx's analysis, had been heralded by the
French Revolution. Following Hegel, Marx regarded the Revolution in
France as an event of superlative world historical importance, the introduction of critical philosophy into the fabric of human history, the death-
knell of the *Ancien Régime*, and a powerful catalyst for the development of
working-class consciousness. Of course, 1789 did not signal the proletarian–socialist revolution of Marx's projections, but rather an exclusively
political and liberal–bourgeois revolution. Yet if it was not the final revolution, which would obtain freedom and equality for all people and not
merely the bourgeoisie, it was a necessary and salutary step in the right
direction. The French Revolution, in Hegelian language, served for Marx
the "cunning of Reason" and advanced the spirit of history, for it had
felled the aristocracy as a class and paved the way for the epic, culminating
class conflict between the bourgeoisie and the proletariat. The impend-
ing revolution, therefore, would complete the French Revolution's quest
for freedom and equality, but introduce it to all people through a classless
society and the termination of social conflict. And somewhere in the
process, the need for religion would become a relic of a bygone era.

These all-too-succinct summaries of Marx on religion and revolution constitute some of the basic elements of a synoptic through which
generations of European socialists have perceived and interpreted the
United States. For Marx himself, and for many followers, the United
States always presented something of a hard case, theoretically intriguing but hard to pin down. Consequently, his views on America are
often ambiguous. On the one hand, he wanted to press the American
Revolution into the mold of the French Revolution and regard the
United States as an essentially bourgeois society, even the site of liberalism and capitalism's highest development. But on the other hand, the
United States presented too many "exceptional" features—greater
economic opportunities for workers, religious disestablishment, streams
of Old World emigrants, the absence of a feudal past, a boundless frontier rich in land and resources. Therefore, Marx, with Engels, frequently resorted to characterizing the United States as a puzzle or
peculiarity in light of their putatively "scientific" laws of history.
America would comply with these laws in the long term, they felt
confident, but in the present, the new land—like Ptolemy's solar sys-

tem—was replete with "retrograde motions" that frustrated theoretical precision. And as in Hegel's outlook, the European experience and the revolutionary trajectory since 1789 often comprised the unspoken benchmarks.[75]

A "Ptolemaic" retrograde motion par excellence in the new republic was the prevalence and vitality of religious belief. The young Marx felt so strongly that religion constituted a sign of social malignancy that he held up the well-documented religiosity of the United States as proof-positive that emancipation in strictly bourgeois–political, instead of socioeconomic, terms did not adequately advance human flourishing. It did so because "bourgeois" emancipation failed to remedy the deeper cause of false consciousness (religion), but merely proclaimed the doctrine of "religious freedom." "North America," he wrote in "The Jewish Question" (1843),

is pre-eminently the country of religiosity, as Beaumont, Tocqueville and the Englishman Hamilton, assure us in unison. However, the states of North America only serve as an example. The question is: what is the relation between *complete* political emancipation and religion? If we find in the country which has attained full political emancipation, that religion not only continues to *exist* but is *fresh* and *vigorous*, this is proof that the existence of religion is not at all opposed to the perfection of the state. But since the existence of religion is the existence of a defect (*Mangel*), the source of this defect must be sought in the *nature* of the state itself.[76]

The "fresh and vigorous" religious life of the United States, in short, revealed a "defect" within the bourgeois–liberal order typified by the United States. This was the case simply because by this point in Marx's intellectual development, religion as an indicator of insidious social conditions had emerged as an unassailable a priori commitment.

Even though Americans were "free citizens," Marx elaborated, they were still characterized by "religious narrowness" (*religiöse Beschränktheit*). But unlike some European anticlericals, Marx felt that the American case revealed the futility of polemicizing against religion. One should rather concentrate on "human emancipation," overthrowing bourgeois–liberal conditions, and religion, or "superstition," would simply evaporate as liberal political structures were swept away by the tide of socialist revolution:

History has for long enough been resolved (*aufgelöst*) into superstition; but we now resolve superstition into history. The question of the relation between *political emancipation and religion* becomes for us a question of the *relation between political emancipation and human emancipation.* We criticize the religious failings of the political state by criticizing the political state in its secular form, disregarding its religious failings.[77]

For a period, Marx felt that the American Civil War was hastening the revolution as the industrializing North emerged victorious over the more agricultural South. But since the revolution failed to materialize, Marx and Engels kept revising their expectations about America in light of its many "peculiar" features.[78] They had high hopes, too, that the streams of European emigrants, especially the German ones, would foment greater working-class consciousness in America. They were continually taken aback, therefore, when emigrant communities seemed more interested in taking advantage of the economic opportunities offered by the United States and remaining in comfortable linguistic and religious enclaves with a "sectarian, ghettoized consciousness."[79]

Neither Marx nor Engels were surprised that Protestantism constituted the dominant form of religious expression in North America. In keeping with their theory, that religion always expressed the underlying socioeconomic order of things, Protestantism was viewed as the bourgeois religion par excellence. As Marx wrote in *Das Kapital*, "The religious world is but the reflex of the real world. And for a society based upon the production of commodities, in which the producers in general enter into social relations with one another by treating their products as commodities and values, whereby they reduce their individual private labor to the standard homogenous human labor—for such a society, Christianity with its cultus of abstract man, more especially its bourgeois developments, Protestantism . . . is the most fitting form of religion."[80]

The mixing of business and religion in America, a frequent critique from the Right, also has its place in Marxist analysis. Indeed, an insistence to show that all things "spiritual" (religion, culture, art) only reflected the juggernaut of capitalist production and sinister profit motives have emerged as commonplace Leftist critiques of the United States and capitalist societies everywhere. Marx himself, revealingly drawing from the aristocratic Frenchman Gustave de Beaumont (Tocqueville's traveling companion), formulated the general template:

In North America, indeed, the effective domination of the Christian world by Judaism[81] has come to be manifested in a common and unambiguous form; the *preaching of the Gospel* itself, Christian preaching, has become an article of commerce, and the bankrupt trader in the church behaves like the prosperous clergyman in business. "This man whom you see at the head of a respectable congregation began as a trader; his business having failed he has become a minister. This other began as a priest, but as soon as he had accumulated some money he abandoned the priesthood for trade. In the eyes of many people the religious ministry is a veritable industrial career."[82]

While, again, aristocratic voices offered similar critiques, theirs more often arose from a desire to demonstrate the ignobility of religion outside the guardianship of an established church. Marxists critiques, by contrast, owed their motivation to the theoretical need of demonstrating that religion itself, always and everywhere, was a hapless chameleon of the regnant social system. Functionally, however, the two lines of critiques, Right and Left, look a lot alike.

In Marxist perspective, the social and religious conditions of North America appeared to retard both working-class consciousness and the maturation of socialist theory. Marx himself offhandedly suggested an explanation for this in his well-known essay, "The Eighteenth Brumaire of Louis Bonaparte" (1852). Unlike conditions in Europe, where he felt a critical intellectual consciousness had made great strides, the United States, despite its high-degree of bourgeois development, still displayed a "conservative form of life" more compatible with premodern Europe. The coincidence of a liberal revolution and the vast geographical expanse of economic opportunity, Marx believed, helped account for this, and in particular for why Americans appeared mired in a (premodern) religious consciousness instead of developing a secularist, class-oriented one. A more progressive, critical outlook would come in due course, Marx maintained until his death; "superstition" must be "stripped off" for rational analysis to emerge. But for the time being "the feverishly youthful movement of material production, that has a new world to make its own, had left neither the time nor the opportunity for abolishing the old religious world."[83] Americans, in short, were temporarily burdened with too much bounty and opportunity to desire revolution and irreligiosity.

To European socialists with a transatlantic vision, the fact that socialism did not appear to be gaining a stronger foothold in America (as, according to theory, it should) became an exasperating problem by the late nineteenth century—a problem immortalized in the "salon-Marxist" Werner Sombart's famous volume of 1906, *Why is there no Socialism in the United States?* —a title that implies a (normative) comparative matrix in which America is judged deficient.[84] In keeping with Marxist theory, religion was rarely accorded a major or causative role in analyses of America, even as its persistence necessarily signified an indictment of the social order. Engels did a lot of hand-wringing about America toward the end of his life, as he increasingly resigned himself to the erratic nature of American development. In his letters from the 1880s and 1890s, he frequently bemoaned the "backwardness" encouraged by American conditions of life. Self-satisfied and intellectually deficient, infected with "religion and sectarianism," Americans of all classes displayed a worrisome "contempt for theory," he held, that did not bode well for working-class consciousness and socialist revolution. In that "God-fearing country," he wrote his friend Sorge, Americans remained "in swaddling cloths in theory—that's how they are, nor can it be otherwise. But it is a land without tradition (except for the religious), which has begun with the democratic republic, and a people full of energy as no other. The course of the [revolutionary] movement will by no means follow the classic straight line, but travel in tremendous zigzags and seem to be moving backward at times."[85]

Other socialist Ptolemaists would follow suit. The standard-bearer of the German Social Democratic Party (SPD) in the late nineteenth century, Karl Kautsky (1854–1938) voiced opinions similar to Engels's. While he too regarded the United States as among the most bourgeois and economically energetic of lands, he noted that it had been founded largely by religious refugees who had dragged with them (*mitschleppen*) their ideological outlooks to the new world. These "ideological leftovers" (*ideologische Überlieferungen*) combined with the want of an intelligentsia versed in historical materialism had left American workers with little guidance as to the nature of their true interests or instruction of their high destiny as a class. Despite many positive indicators, therefore, the prospects of revolution in America appeared for Kautsky "very unfavorable" and the land itself appeared to be overrun with "demagogues and fools."[86]

By the early twentieth century, some socialists positively despaired of the situation in the United States. Again, while religion often does not stand at the forefront of such commentary, it is the "dog that did not bark," the sign of illness hastily passed over in search of deeper (socioeconomic) causes. Issues of property, taxes, wages, labor rights, and unions came first in socialist writing—as one would expect given the theoretical framework. But the same framework invariably casts religion as the tell-tale indicator of backward and peculiar circum-

stances. What is more, with the flexing of America's geopolitical mus-
cle at this time and its involvement in World War I, the image of the
United States, as in much European conservative commentary, mutates
significantly. Through socialist lenses, it goes from being a worrisome,
distant hard case to a threatening counterexample of Europe's historical path, which according to many on the Left had received new illu-
mination with the Russian Revolution of 1917 and the smaller-scale
communist revolutions in Bavaria and Hungary at the end of the war.
These dramatic developments and the swelling of socialist parties in
Europe prior to the war made the United States appear all the more
refractory and irregular. Structurally ill-fit for a "normal" revolution, proliferating capitalism's cruelties and insecurities with apparent impunity, the new power elicited both fear and pity. Given
conditions of exploitation, competition, relentless striving for
wealth, and the lust for world markets, it should not surprise, according to socialist critics of America, that this emergent power
harbored religion in its bosom, a comforting balm for a restless and
alienated people.[87]

In 1910 the German radical socialist Karl Liebknecht (1871–1919)
embarked on an "agitation tour" (*Agitationstour*) of the United States
to analyze the situation first-hand and attempt to stir up working-
class consciousness. He was at a loss to understand why many workers in Europe looked to America as "the praised promised land"
when from his outlook the country was a site of "tyranny," a "witches'
Sabbath of high capital." Nonplussed by the power of religion across
the Atlantic, he complained of the "ubiquity" of "American pastors"
and the "famous Puritanical morality." Despite the disestablishment
of religion along liberal–bourgeois lines, he warned that the "the
church in America . . . is a much more a dangerous power than in Old
Europe."[88] Earlier, the English socialist Edward Eveling (with his
consort Eleanore Marx, the daughter of Karl Marx) had made a similar trip to America and arrived at comparable judgments. The workers he found reduced to "machines," the average American he
regarded as "indescribably unpleasant" and the whole country languished under the spirit of a "deformed Puritanism."[89] "The industrial worker in imperial Germany is as a socialist an outspoken critic
of the church," another observer wondered, in America "workers,
artisans, and the lower middle classes [place] an unusually high value
on ecclesiastical organization. Amid America's surging economic life,

amid the pursuit there of gain and pleasure, this well-behaved church-liness (*wohlanständige Kirchlichkeit*) appears utterly bizarre."[90]

As was the case for the European Right, the 1920s represent a high-water mark of America-loathing for the socialist Left. Numerous works could be marshaled to substantiate this claim.[91] The English socialist W. T. Colyer's *Americanism: A World Menace* (1922) is indicative of the larger literature, both in its assessment of the waxing threat represented by the United States and by its specific derision of American religious life. "[The] power of America," he warned, "is being exerted to draw the world into a universal Industrial Feudalism as an alternate to universal Communism." Europe required a bracing wake-up call, because "the forces which have crystallized into Americanism are at work in the Old World, too," often having an "unrecognized influence." The possibilities of debasement and historical regression were immense, for America "standardises human beings" according to its own social stage which is "markedly below the levels attained by the average civilised humanity elsewhere."[92]

With respect to religion, Colyer's criticisms mirrored others on the Left in that the line between Marxist analysis and a kind of aristocratic hauteur toward the New World is often blurred. Embracing the view that all religion equals "superstition," an illusion to ease social malaise, he nonetheless evinced some nostalgia for established religion: "Severed from the moving traditions of Anglicanism...American Christianity did not take long to develop forms as unlovely as superstition ever assumed on this planet." Christianity in North America, he felt, had devolved back into a "primitive religion," an elemental anxiety of uncertain existential conditions, arising from the natural fears of an immense wilderness and the man-made fears of industrial capitalism. The spirit of capitalism, especially, had imprinted itself on American Christianity as churches displayed the same "commercial rivalry" that was pervasive in American society at large. Beholden to "theatricality" to draw in crowds, some forms of faith appeared to be "openly competing with the circus." European culture, by contrast, appeared more aligned with the trajectory of the modern world, incrementally sloughing off bygone "ideologies" through historical criticism and science. Americans, too, could have participated in an emancipation from religion, but "in cutting loose" from Europe, their orbit had drifted away from many salutary, modernizing intellectual developments. A self-satisfied obscurantism then, a reflection of social disharmony, contributed to "the intellectual and spiritual poverty of the United States."[93]

Coyler's line of criticism, along with his general disposition of Marxist conviction spiced with aristocratic hauteur, has enjoyed a long life in the twentieth century. Left-leaning scholars—following the English and unflappably Marxist historians Eric Hobsbawm and E. P. Thompson, for instance—have tended to dismiss the whole Second Great Awakening in America and the rise of transatlantic Methodism in general as little more than a "chiliasm of despair," an atavistic, uncritical response by the uncouth masses to the rise of industrial capitalism.[94] The religious sensibilities or "puritanismo" of the *petit bourgeoisie* in America, Antonio Gramsci and his many epigones have assumed, helps underwrite the "cultural hegemony" of Americanism.[95] The French Marxist-influenced social critic and postmodern guru Jean Baudrillard, moreover, has wryly described the United States as the "only remaining primitive society" in the modern West. Its cultural dynamics, "born of a rift with the Old World," manifest themselves quintessentially in "pompous Mormon symmetry," "evangelical marketing," "Puritan obsessiveness," "religion as special effects." Elaborating on the transatlantic divide and the entrenched religiosity in American life, Baudrillard opined:

[Europe's] social and philosophical nineteenth century did not cross the Atlantic.... [T]he fact is simply that in their collective consciousness [Americans] are closer to [earlier] models of thought...than to those that were to be imposed by the French Revolution, which were ideological and revolutionary. Why are the sects so powerful and dynamic [in America]?...In a sense, it is their micro-model which has been extended to the whole of America.... It is as though America as a whole had espoused this sect-like destiny...with its immediate demand for beatification, its material efficacy, its compulsion for justification, and doubtless also its madness and frenzy.[96]

Two things in particular have not crossed the Atlantic to America, Baudrillard once quipped: fine wine and Marxism.

The Spirit of 1848: Republican Anticlericalism and America

The unsuccessful revolutions of 1848–49 mark a turning point in the religious history of modern Europe. For a brief period, following the "February Revolution" in France, many Old World republicans felt that fundamental political change was finally at hand; the post-1815 Restoration was spent; a new dawn of political freedoms, religious liberty, and constitutional government had arrived. That this moment did not last, and that established church bodies throughout the Continent played a significant role in shaping a new reactionary milieu in the 1850s and 1860s, pushed many liberals over the edge into vitriolic anticlericalism, increasingly tied to a materialist outlook stemming from the contemporaneous ascendancy of positivism and the natural sciences. Of course, anticlericalism had remained a simmering force since the French Revolution, but after the "failure of 1848" it reasserted itself with a crusading vigor. "*Le cléricalisme, voilà, l'ennemi!*" the French Third-Republic politician Léon Gambetta (1838–82) famously proclaimed in 1877, capturing the hostile mood of a new generation of "red" republicans inclined to aggressively secularist politics.[97]

This facet of secularist thought contributed, too, to misgivings about the United States, but it did so often in unexpected ways and from a standpoint distinct from that of the socialist critiques previously discussed. By definition, republicans and liberals subscribed neither to Marxist ideas about the abolition of private property nor to utopian views of a completely classless society. But they did widely conclude, especially after 1848, that religious forces in general and the Catholic Church in particular constituted among the most intractable obstacles to enduring political and social progress. The "Voltairean bourgeoisie," as they have sometimes been called, played an influential role in the revolutionary agitations that swept the Continent at this time. Many positively esteemed the United States and the religious freedoms guaranteed by its laws. But all too often, they assumed that the American constitutional landscape entailed the deflation of religion as a vital social force. When the Continental revolutions collapsed, forcing many "forty-eighters" to seek refuge in the United States, they were thus frequently unsettled by the extent of religious belief and institution-building in the young republic, and many took it upon themselves to tutor the new country on religion's reactionary, contaminating potential.

In rounding out the leftist critique of America, therefore, we will look at some of the commentary on American religious life by refugee republican "1848ers" from central Europe. Relatedly, we will glance at attitudes toward America by some of leading secularist lights in France's Third Republic (1870–1914), which witnessed major clashes between (monarchist) clerical and (republican) anticlerical forces, with the latter achieving a decisive upper hand in the epochal legislation of 1905: a victory of a type of church–state separation, an "assertive secularism" as one scholar has called it, quite at odds with America's tradition of "passive secularism," of religious voluntarism and pluralism.[98]

While the revolutionary spirit of 1848 began in Paris, it spread rapidly into Central Europe, destabilizing the monarchies of Prussia and Austria. Throughout 1848 and into 1849, historic developments took place, including efforts in Frankfurt am Main to establish German nationhood and a liberal constitution, and the near disintegration of the multiethnic Habsburg Empire. Yet the powers of the past prevailed. In the summer of 1848 Austria's generals checked Hungarian, Czech, and Piedmontese movements of independence. These efforts made clear the vulnerability of the revolutionaries and inspired forces of reaction everywhere. Combined with disunity among revolutionaries themselves, these forces ensured the failure of the parliament at Frankfurt. Refusing to recognize the constitution drafted there, the Prussian king Friedrich Wilhelm IV (r. 1840–61) disbanded the parliament. Republican holdouts, who had fled to the south German state of Baden, were routed by the Prussian army in the summer of 1849, ending the revolutionary movement.[99]

The artist Friedrich Schroeder famously captured this turn-of-events in an 1849 illustration, "The Victory of Reaction in Europe," which depicted outsized monarchs of Prussia and Austria astride a map of Europe, sweeping (quite literally) revolutionaries off the continent. Religious imagery is prominent in the picture: both rulers are adorned with large crosses, symbolizing the reassertion of the alliance of throne and altar. On the left side of the illustration a small band of revolutionaries boards a boat in the Atlantic, indicating the considerable number of forty-eighters who fled Europe for political asylum in the United States.

While these refugees wound up in many places, some of the most vocal concentrations settled in the urban Midwest—in Milwaukee, Cincinnati, Louisville, and St. Louis in particular. Often having idealized the American Revolution as a model for Europe, they were delivered a "severe jolt" when they realized the extent of religious belief and ecclesiastical influence in the United States.[100] "Typically," one scholar has written, "the Forty-eighter was an uprooted intellectual who underwent bitter disillusionment in the United States" and found "the naiveté of their simpler countrymen hard to bear.... As liberals [1848ers] were militant critics of America's many religious sects, organized churches, and the established clergy."[101] "Having found the established hierarchies in close alliance with the enemies of reform abroad,...[they] continued in America their fight against the churches."[102] Or, as the young Friedrich Nietzsche described them: "Naturally they are terribly disappointed (*schrecklich enttäuscht*) in America and cannot criticize and mock enough the Sunday services, church-going, the number of houses of God, Bible- and missionary societies, or the moral training of their new compatriots."[103]

To be sure, America had shown the world political freedom, many forty-eighters reasoned; and for this gratitude was owed. Nonetheless, the new land still lacked intellectual freedom and secular emancipation in the fullest sense, and this basic deficiency cried out for remedy. Many rationalist and freethinking 1848ers concluded that bringing this higher "intellectual enlightenment" (*geistige Aufklärung*) and "cultural progress" (*Kulturfortschritt*) to the United States constituted their special calling. Toward this end, they founded numerous freethinking societies, newspapers, and journals dedicated to promoting rationalism, humanism, and irreligion.[104] Some founded schools devoid of religious content or based on deistic humanitarianism; others waged war on what was sometimes called the "Bible spirit" of the United States. "We must rid ourselves of all religious nonsense and superstition," summed up Eduard Schröter in the Milwaukee-based *Humanist*; "Christianity is a religion of the rude masses." As the title of the journal suggests, humanism untainted with religion constituted for Schröter "the strongest bulwark against priestcraft and religious sects" found in the United States.[105]

1848ers looked favorably on the founding era of the United States, but often they understood and appropriated it in selective terms. The Puritan legacy in New England ("Protestant Jesuitism" as it was dubbed by some) was almost universally disparaged and held to be the source of many present-day ills. Thomas Jefferson, Benjamin Franklin, and especially Thomas Paine, by contrast, were regarded as the true heroes of the earlier period. Freethinking societies and congregations regularly established holidays venerating the legacy of Paine. At one banquet of the Wisconsin Freeman's League *(Bund freier Menschen)* honoring Paine, the following revealing toast was given: "D'Alembert, Rousseau, Voltaire, Diderot, Hume, Shelley, Lessing, Kant, and Feuerbach. These fought for the same cause as Paine—for the emancipation of *Reason* from intellectual and political oppression."[106]

A "Paine-Feuerbachian spirit," we might say, was pitted against the "sect spirit," "Puritanism" or the "Bible mentality" that prevented America from realizing a more decisive emancipation from the past. Particularly reprehensible, many 1848ers held, was the allowance of tax exemption for church properties, Sabbath laws, the temperance movement, and even the Thanksgiving holiday. A group of 1848ers in New Jersey, to provide one example, saw their crusade against Newark's Sabbath laws as part of a larger, epic historical struggle—an attitude nicely captured in the title of an 1879 article from the *New Jersey Freie Zeitung*: "The Struggle against Unreason and Hypocrisy. The Sabbath Laws as an Inheritance from the Puritans, an Evil of Social Life of the City. The Restless Struggle of Free Reason that [has] Lasted over Two Centuries and still is Raging Today." This article represented the latest installment of a conflict between Newark's City Council and a group of outspoken forty-eighters who in 1853 had first petitioned the city to repeal Sabbath and temperance laws. In the same year, this group founded the *Verein des Fortschritts* (The Club of Progress), the goals of which, not surprisingly, included fighting for the elimination of Sabbath laws and against the "temperance plague."[107]

But the stuggle against "Puritanism" was not limited to Sabbath practices and temperance laws. Practically every aspect of American life drew criticism from forty-eighters where strong religious influences persisted. In the sphere of education, for example, the line of attack was twofold. On the one hand, they lambasted any whiff of positive religion in the public schools and accordingly decried the common practice of daily readings from the King James Bible. On the other hand, they agitated for and helped set up a smattering of private schools committed to free-thought, humanism and irreligion. "Irreligion has the same right as religion," proclaimed Christian Esselen of Wisconsin; a school system committed to undermining the latter would not stop at the half-measure of "religious toleration," but lead on to "the necessity of unbelief." "We propose to replace the church by the free school," he elaborated elsewhere; "Priests and religious sects cannot be gainsaid, but they can be made superfluous." And this required "the foundation of a school system free from all religion and the compulsory laws of all religious sects."[108] The pedagogical institute set up by Friedrich Knapp in Baltimore exemplified the general trend. Its most famous American alumnus, H. L. Mencken, would doubtlessly have pleased many an 1848er in the satiric contempt that he hurled at homebred American religiosity.[109]

If the legacy of American Protestantism worried 1848ers, fears of the spread of Catholicism in the new land practically unhinged them. In theory, they admired the First Amendment with its guarantees of the expression of religious belief apart from all coercion. But in actuality, many worried that it also allowed "priestcraft" and "Jesuitism" an unhindered field in which to advance, and that Americans in their naiveté did not understand the mortal threat to liberty and reason posed by the Catholic Church. Their European experience, many reasoned, had taught them this indispensable lesson and qualified them as abler guides in the matter. In battling Catholicism, 1848ers contributed significantly to (nativist and Protestant) currents of Anti-Catholicism that manifested themselves during this period in the infamous popularity of the Know-Nothing political party.[110]

In Europe, Pope Pius IX's root-and-branch rejection of the revolutions of 1848–49, as we have seen, made clear the profound enmity between the Catholic Church and political liberalism. The apostate monk and friend of the Italian revolutionary Giuseppe Garibaldi, Alessandro Gavazzi (1809–89), came to the United States on a speaking tour after the tide of revolution on the Italian peninsula had been checked. Roman Catholicism posed a permanent threat to the republican system of the United States, he proclaimed, and he took it upon himself to awaken Americans to the danger. The rising number of Catholic emigrants crossing the Atlantic ought to cause grave concern, he remarked, warning that a yet more insidious threat came in the growing number of European-born Jesuits eager to make converts in the New World. "[T]o be silent on the Popish system is no longer a duty, indeed it is a crime," he concluded. Granting such elements of society sanctuary under the banner of religious freedom was simply naïve and underestimated the extent of their threat. The "Popish system" should not be tolerated, but extirpated.[111]

The Hungarian revolutionary Louis Kossuth (1802–94) expounded a similar message. In his famous tour of the United States in 1851–52 after the revolution against the Habsburg monarchy had collapsed, he warned against a worldwide effort of European reactionary forces united against liberty and republican forms of government everywhere. Americans could no longer rest content in isolation, he explained, but needed to step up support for the forces of liberty and revolution in Europe. To demonstrate that the poison of reaction had reached the American heartland, he pointed to the proselytizing activities of the Jesuits in the western states and territories as a sign of this order's "historical ambition...to rule the world."[112] Harsh measures were needed to combat such a threat; simply invoking religious freedom missed the point.

Other German-speaking 1848ers held similar views. In St. Louis, Heinrich Börnstein edited the *Anzeiger des Westens*, among the most widely circulated papers in Missouri and the most anticlerical. Börnstein's personal disdain for organized religion in general and the Catholic Church in particular recognized few bounds. In 1851 he published an anti-Catholic novel, *The Mysteries of St. Louis*. The villains of the novel included decadent, scheming priests from the newly founded St. Louis University and the many Swiss Jesuits who had fled Fribourg in 1847 to make their home in the United States.[113] In the journal *Atlantis*, to provide another example, the publicist Christian Esselen worried that the American system, in allowing the Catholic church to accumulate lands, put itself at great risk: "We fully justify [therefore] the opposition of our American citizens to Catholicism. A thousand years of experience has show that in their principles the Catholic hierarchy are the enemies of civil liberty, of enlightenment, and of civilization. In America...enormous wealth is gathered together by the bishops, which in this land where the dollar is almighty, gives them undue influence."[114] Similarly, the so-called Louisville Platform, a statement of broad political principles by forty-eighters, made clear that religious liberty in the United State too easily served "as a pretext and instrument for organizations...to create States within the State." "Popish officers in this country," operating under a "foreign potentate" (i.e., the pope) constituted a prime example. "Democracy is anti-Catholic" the Platform therefore proclaimed, and recommended "that the order of Jesuits be treated as a declared enemy of the republic." What is more, the Platform indicated that the promise of the United States could not be fulfilled so long as "a republican people" felt they could be in "open league with the darkest of all powers, the deadly enemy of all liberty, the power of the Popes and the Jesuits."[115] The Milwaukee-based *Volksfreund* went so far as to declare that all Jesuits should be hanged as traitors to the republic.[116]

1848ers from German-speaking lands reserved particular contempt for their more pious kinsmen, i.e., those who saw the United
States, not as a site of social emancipation, but as a place to protect
and seclude their transported Old World beliefs. German religious
communities—whether made up of Anabaptists, Pietists, or conservative Lutheran emigrants—were regularly disparaged by forty-
eighters, even if special scorn, not surprisingly, was reserved for
ultramontane German Catholics. When a movement arose to form
a union of foreigners against the powerful nativist currents running
through the American body politic in the 1850s, many forty-eighters, revealingly, sided with the Nativists, arguably even against their
own self-interest. The unwashed Catholic masses coming from
Europe, in particular, threw a wrench in their collective *Amerikabild*,
their image of America's progressive promise. As one Bernhard
Domschke responded bluntly when confronted with the request by
older German immigrants to form a foreign league against American Nativism:

[T]he idea of forming a union of foreigners against Nativism is wholly wrong
and destroys the possibility of any influence on our part; it would drive us into
a union with Irishmen, those American Croats. In our struggle we are not
concerned with nationality, but with principles; we are for liberty, and against
union with Irishmen who stand nearer barbarism and brutality than civilization and humanity. The Irish are our natural enemy...because they are the
truest guards of Popery.[117]

To be sure, the America of the Nativists' imagination itself remained
imperfectly conceived according to most Continental forty-eighters.
The legacy of conservative Protestantism, revivalism, and sectarianism
had arrested America's historical development, rendering large swaths
of the population "totally untouched [by reason] and unenlightened."[118]
But here is where forty-eighters saw a role for themselves: as guides and
tutors along the path of an improved-upon modernity. Exchanging the
spirit of Jonathan Edwards for that of Thomas Paine, trading in the revivals of Francis Asbury for the materialism of their own Ludwig Feuerbach, forty-eighters sought in earnest to create a more perfect union.
As a writer in the journal *Atlantis* nicely summed up:

We [forty-eighters] are the yeast of the fermenting process of the modern
age....We stand on the foundation of our modern philosophy of life. We
must replace [American] religion by our *Wissenschaft*, slavery by freedom, and

nationalism by cosmopolitanism. In this manner we will foster true Americanism, which is republican, free, universal, and cosmopolitan.[119]

Without the progressive uplift that forty-eighters offered, another opined, America risked stagnating as a "primeval forest of churches and dogma."[120]

★★★

While forces of reaction drove many 1848ers to America, these same forces, though ascendant for a period, did not endure in Europe in the late nineteenth century. In fact they helped galvanize a powerful anticlerical and secularist backlash that dominated academic discussions and politics in practically all western European countries. The rationalism of the eighteenth-century Enlightenment paled in comparison, one scholar has averred, to the "great tidal wave" that swelled up within Europe at this time, "menacing the very bases of Christianity, and of all supernatural and revealed religion." This was an age among intellectual and political elites, after all, that often witnessed polarizing, public struggles between proponents of "theology" and "science," between voices ready to preside over "God's Funeral" and those convinced that rumors of God's death had been greatly exaggerated.[121]

In politics, France bore out in spades the general tensions and conflicts of the period: "the war of the two Frances," it has been called.[122] The early Third Republic (1870–1940), in particular, witnessed dramatic conflicts between "clericals" and "anticlericals," between an embattled Catholic Church and her rightist allies who wanted to roll back the Voltairean ethos of the Revolution and those on the Left convinced that "clericalism" constituted France's—and, by extension, the modern world's—most implacable enemy. Robert Stuart speaks of the French Left's "anticlerical and anti-religious obsession": half measures were not an option.[123] Through the efforts of *républicain* political figures such as Jean Macé, Jules Ferry, and Léon Gambetta, the party of "secularism" (*laïcité*) triumphed in the so-called "laic" laws of the 1880s and, more extensively, in the church–state separation laws of 1905—a major program and a concomitant *esprit* of statist secularism, which, though unique to the French revolutionary tradition in some respects, harkened back to the Continent-wide "ethos of 1848" and has since exerted a broad influence over many sectors of Western European intellectual and political life.[124]

The American example was not lost on French policy makers during the Third Republic. But often it was taken to be largely besides the point, bearing witness to an incommensurate (Protestant) historical experience in some formulations, or signifying, in others, a worrisome compromise with the New World's well-known clashing, sectarian forces. But whatever the case, the churning religious vitality in the American republic elicited a largely skeptical response from proponents of *laïcité* who bothered to turn their gaze across the Atlantic. Damning America with faint praise, blistering it with ridicule, or simply sighing in puzzlement at the apparent religious cacophony "over there" served to highlight the fact that France had set out on a more high-mindedly "Voltairean" historical course.

An example of ridicule came quickly in the form of a popular play, *L'Oncle Sam*, a violent satire of American life, written by Victorien Sardou, arguably Paris's leading dramatist in the 1870s. Its contents were so controversial that Adolphe Thiers, acting as provisional head of the government in the wake of the Paris Commune of 1870, at first prohibited the play from being performed, citing that it "would keenly wound a sister nation."[125] It was finally staged, however, on November 6, 1873, and to great acclaim. The comedy lashed out at practically every American institution, indicting American business dealings as fraudulent, its democracy as farcical, and its society as a seedbed for ne'er-do-wells. "You must stop that maddening habit of offering us *you* as a model!" the play's French heroine pointedly instructs the Americans in the play. Not surprisingly, it portrays Americans' religious life as rife with charlatans and misfits. The shady character of one clergyman "Jedidiah Buxton"—equally con artist, ignoramus, and seducer—is served up as an example. American revivals and camp meetings are characterized as erratic outbursts of the new nation's nervous spiritual energy where young women were preyed upon to confess all.[126]

When Léon Gambetta proclaimed "that there is no way to compare America with France" on the floor of the Champer of Deputies in 1875, the stage was set for a fresh wave of leftist anti-Americanism.[127] On the front lines of this new wave stood the journalist, author and social critic Frédéric Gaillardet (1808–82), an ardent 1848 republican and anti-socialist with neo-Jacobin tendencies. While adopting firmly pro-American stances during the Second Empire (1852–70), he abruptly changed his mind during the republican period and published his opinions in *Aristocratie en Amérique* (1883), an attempt to put Americanophilia to rest among French republicans and point out the wide chasm between the French and American revolutionary traditions.

The book's title of course recalls Tocqueville's work, the thesis of which Gaillardet sought to undermine. Far from being the prototype of modern democracies, as Tocqueville had believed, Gaillardet argued that the United States was fatally compromised by all sorts of social aristocracies and petty tyrannies. In fact, he held that America had never experienced a genuine and fully democratic revolution in the European sense of the term. The aspiration toward social democracy inherent in the spirit of 1792, which the Third Republic had put back on the agenda, had revealed America as a phony republic—a nation of slavery, religious fanaticism, conquest, and plutocracy. The ideals of democracy and progress did not hold the nation together; it was rather "the Monroe Doctrine," the desire to create a colonial empire, beginning in the Western hemisphere. Perhaps this doctrine did not seem that threatening when America had only recently emerged from being "an obscure satellite" of the Old World, but after the Civil War, the resurgent, industrializing nation "now aspires to nothing less than to drawing all of humanity into its orbit."[128]

Looming Yankee imperialism constituted a special misfortune for world history, because in Gaillardet's eyes the country was essentially backward. Lacking the egalitarian and progressive impulses of France in the 1790s, American society remained "medieval" in many respects, not least in the religious sphere. While in France "religious rigidity" had enjoyed an inverse relationship with political freedom, this did not hold true for the United States, where "a naïve credulity and an unconscionable hypocrisy" held sway. The confessional age, to which the eighteenth-century Enlightenment had dealt a deathblow in Europe, continued seemingly unabated in the United States, as Protestants despised Catholics, and the daily multiplying Protestant sects, if superficially tolerant, loathed one another while competing for new recruits.[129] In many parts of the United States "one meets only fanatics," he opined; "the warring sects of Protestant America tear into one another, never to be united except in their common denunciation of the Catholics."[130]

Like German 1848ers, Gaillardet reserved special ire for customs and laws pertaining to the Sabbath and the temperance movement. He deplored the "oppressive" legislation that restricted the sale of wine and other spirits—laws that had forced many "sick" people, he claimed, to the pharmacy to buy their alcohol. On Sundays, "infidels" were regularly exposed, he averred, because the question "where did you go to church?" constituted "the sole subject of conversation." "In France, Italy, and Spain, Sunday is a day of repose,... but repose for us does not exclude diversion." In America, the contrary prevails; there "repose means a solemn reverence (*recueillement*) and the absence of diversion." While the land might be open to limitless political discussion, Gaillardet concluded, genuine "social liberty" faced "numerous restrictions." Indeed, the American republic actually constituted a "despotism" with respect to morals.[131]

Gaillardet offered the rise of Mormonism as the clinching argument for American backwardness. Like many Europeans, whether of the Right or Left, the story of Joseph Smith and the westward trek of his followers to Utah captured the imagination like few other episodes in American history. For Gaillardet, the sheer audacity of Smith to found a new religion—an "intellectual curiosity" based on "simple-minded credulity"—gave expression to a fundamental dereliction in "the American character." Astoundingly, he reasoned, while the French Third Republic and other European nations were progressively sloughing off clericalism and superstition, American society had generated its own newfangled "mahométisme," as Gaillardet labeled the Mormon belief system.[132]

Gaillardet found a kindred spirit in Urbain Gohier (1862–1951), a fierce anticlerical and critic of American civilization. In 1903, he believed that he saw the writing on the wall, and wondered what would befall Europe confronted with America's "desire to dominate the world in the twentieth century." No friend of Catholicism, he nonetheless found his encounters with American Protestantism so nauseating that he quipped of wanting to return to the Catholic fold. In Chicago, after hearing the sermon of a young preacher, he wrote: "After just getting out of bed, this 'boy' came to dispense advice with ludicrous gravity, talking about conscience, virtue, and the meaning of life to five hundred persons who should have pulled his ears, but who meekly listened to him. Catholic Priests who do this at least disguise themselves as beings of a different species." Were this a local incident, Gohier might have felt less need to fret, but he complained that such events in fact occurred "everywhere" in America.[133]

Similar opinions were arrived at by Jules Huret (1864–1915), a like-minded anticlerical given to misgivings about the United States—that "ogre" across the Atlantic as he phrased it. The religious practices of the "Puritan race" in New England had contributed to an "abnormal mentality" (*mentalité anormale*), he opined.[134] Like Gohier, Huret too visited Chicago and while there went to hear a popular charismatic preacher, John Alexander Dowie. Huret's reflections on this experience aptly capture a broader French Third Republic anticlerical—and, more broadly, Continental secularist—characterization of America as industrially advanced yet, puzzlingly, spiritually backward or "medieval." In Huret's formulation:

When hearing about this fabulous exploitation of human gullibility [by such preachers], don't you ask yourself whether we are not living in the Middle Ages or dealing with some tribe of Sudan.... Surely the sociologists will have to understand, before they can generalize, [how] one can find in one population the most acute practical sense, the most ruthless and concrete realism, and material and mechanical advances at their highest point of development, coexisting with childlike credulity, illogicality, and hopeless unreason.[135]

Only in America.

The "Secularization" Ethos and the Spirit of European History

In 1912, the great French social theorist Émile Durkheim published *The Elementary Forms of Religious Life*. A foundational work in shaping the sociology of religion, the book also reflects the life and times of its author. Descending from a long line of rabbis in Alsace, Durkheim abandoned his ancestral Jewish faith, persuaded by the likes of Comte and Feuerbach that religion could be accounted for strictly on the basis of its social function.[136] What is more, an invested "anticlerical" in the debates of the Third Republic, Durkheim was eager to delegitimize the authority of the Catholic Church by demonstrating that Christianity's capacity for creating social cohesion had been permanently crippled by various forces afoot in the modern world. The book's principal focus, aboriginal religion in Australia, carried with it the implication that "primitive" or "totemic" forms of religious life stood closer to some "true essence" of religion, and that religion's entanglement in the modern world invariably divested it of its social function and heralded its decline. "If there is one truth that history teaches beyond a doubt," Durkheim wrote, "it is that religion tends to embrace a smaller and smaller portion of social life."[137] Only nostalgics and reactionaries would try to resurrect the "old faiths." Any future social cohesion—an abiding desideratum for Durkheim—would have to come from a general civic morality derived from modern republican traditions and a secular political consensus. Durkheim himself has been called "the high priest and the theologian of the civil religion [*laïcité*] of the Third Republic."[138]

In 1910, at the height of Durkheim's career, the Edinburgh World Missionary Conference took place—a landmark event marking the explosion of global Christian missions in the modern era and laying the groundwork for the modern ecumenical movement. What is more, Durkheim wrote at a time when religious movements such as Pentecostalism, Mormonism, along with myriad strands of "evangelicalism," many reflecting American provenance, were poised to become among the most consequential global forces shaping modern history.[139] And this is to say nothing of the modernity-weathering capacities of Catholicism, Eastern Orthodoxy, Judaism, Islam, Buddhism, Hinduism, etc.[140] At the end of the twentieth century, one may fairly speak of a "worldwide resurgence of religion," Peter Berger has remarked.[141] "God is Back," editors of *The Economist* agree; a "global revival of faith," too often under-recognized by scholars, has been quietly "changing the world."[142]

The incongruence between Durkheim's declensionist prognostications about religion and the subsequent trajectory of vast sectors of modern world history underscores what many revisionist scholars have begun to decry as the European blinkeredness of the "secularization thesis," i.e., the idea, long dominant in sociology and many other social sciences, that processes of modernization ineluctably entail the diminution of religion as a social force and bring about its evacuation both from social institutions and individual consciousness.[143]

Durkheim of course was not alone, even if his immediate political context in the French Third Republic helps crystallize the ideological commitments and longings implicated in early secularization theorizing. Many of the figures discussed in this chapter—Condorcet, Saint-Simon, Comte, Feuerbach, Marx, and Engels, and of course Max Weber too (although for reasons evident earlier I chose to discuss him in chapter two)—are central to understanding the intellectual foundations of the secularization thesis, its basis in the European experience of modernity, and its broadly leftist associations with a stadial, emancipatory "logic" of modern history. The European-educated American sociologist, Talcott Parsons, a follower of Durkheim and Weber, gave the idea quintessential expression when he wrote that "the world was [once] filled with the sacred—in thought, practice, and institutional form.... [T]he forces of modernization swept across the globe and secularization, *a corollary historical process*, loosened the dominance of the sacred. In due course, the sacred shall disappear altogether."[144]

But, again, the very notion of secularization, as Jeffery Hadden has pointed out, has always had a questionable relationship with empirical reality. Its actual origins, Hadden avers, also rested on a "prescriptive assertion," based on European intellectuals' protracted struggles against reactionary religious forces in the nineteenth century. Equating the secular as a necessary corollary of the modern, Hadden asserts, derives from a "European heritage" that witnessed "a struggle over status and power" between social scientists and clergy over which group would emerge as the principal definers and molders of social reality. "The founding generation of sociologists were hardly value-free armchair scholars, sitting back and objectively analyzing these developments. They passionately believed that science was ushering in a new era which would crush the superstitions and oppressive structures which the Church had promoted for so many centuries. Indeed, they were all essentially in agreement that traditional forms of religion would soon be a phenomenon of the past."[145] Long embedded in this outlook, moreover, was the assumption, that Europe's "secularizing" path to modernity possessed something of a vanguard status, a route all modernizing nations ought and, indeed, eventually would take. This assumption has led David Martin, another of the earliest critics of secularization theory, to suggest that an assumed European frame of reference was virtually codified into the sinews of modern social science and had given birth to "unilateralist history," an "unwillingness to look at history apart from the heuristic devices employed to make its superabundant data manageable."[146] Secularization theory was "essentially mistaken," Peter Berger has added; it was "an extrapolation of the European experience to the rest of the world." For Berger, the more interesting question for social theory is not explaining "why America is different," as the question has come down with ritualistic predictability, but in accounting for the exceptional secularity of Europe, or what Berger calls "Eurosecularity," in a world that today appears as insistently and complexly religious as ever.[147]

Despite the criticisms of scholars such as Hadden, Martin, Berger, and others, the general idea of secularization, it ought not to surprise, remains alive and well. It has been vigorously reasserted by leading sociologists, parrying revisionist critics and developing ever more sophisticated—and elastic—models of the theory.[148] Apart from sociology, the philosophical and political necessity of "the secular" in various guises has been forcefully defended by a range of European intellectuals in recent decades. Leaving aside attention-grabbing science-versus-religion, popularizing works by figures such as Christopher Hitchens and Richard Dawkins, the weightier contributions of Hans Blumenberg, Jürgen Habermas, and Marcel Gauchet deserve mention.[149] And this is to say nothing of the religious policies and legal environment of the European Union, which, despite the EU's origins in postwar Christian democracy and Catholic social thought, have been described by Jean-Paul Willaime as an attempt in recent years to "consecrate" the ethos of *laïcité* and transform it into a European-wide reality.[150]

But more important for our purposes perhaps is how, within educated circles, the general narrative structure of modern history—the "background landscape" *to*, the "big story" *about* modern times—has been thoroughly inflected by the language and assumptions of secularization. Despite manifold incongruities with empirical reality, Jeffrey Cox has written, the accretion of longstanding assertions of the inevitability of secularization, beginning in the nineteenth century, have transformed a falsifiable social scientific theory among a limited group of scholars into to what Cox calls a diffuse "controlling master narrative," widely popular in the press, the academy, and in the general "social imaginary." In fact, he believes that (*pace* revisionist critics) it really has no rivals. "The master narrative of secularization is causal, invocatory, comprehensive, and partly hidden; it is also uncontested.... The secularization story is the only master narrative of religion in modern history."[151] The reality sketched by Cox has produced what José Casanova identifies as an historically unprecedented abundance of "unreflexive secular identities and secularist self-understandings" in Western Europe. "In this respect," Casanova adds, "theories of secularization in Europe have functioned as self-fulfilling prophecies to the extent to which a majority of the population in Europe came to accept the premises of those theories as a depiction of the normal state of affairs and as a projection of future developments."[152]

The normative, quasi-teleological status attributed to the secularization narrative carries with it, of course, extensive implications for perceiving and interpreting the United States. The divergent historical experiences of North America and Western European countries with respect to religion are often elided, and the United States is viewed as a "peculiar" case, a "deviation" from the expected historical pattern. In light of the dominance of the secularization paradigm, David Martin has observed, that educated Europeans tend to view the United States not in light of its distinctive historical conditions and pathways, but as a case of "arrested development" when compared to European standards and benchmarks.[153] With respect to religiosity, Rainer Prätorius has written, Europeans are inclined to see an "American irregular path" that they find hard to make sense of and instinctively ridicule.[154] From the standpoint of "secular Europe," John Micklethewait and Adrian Woolridge humorously add, the United States often comes across as "an evolutionary freak—the sociological equivalent of the duck-billed platypus."[155]

As should be clear from the material in this chapter, such views and judgments did not originate recently, but have a much longer history. They reflect something structural, not episodic. Indeed, criticism of American religious life from the Left goes much deeper than is often suspected, even if criticism from the Right, as discussed in the previous chapter, goes deeper still—the former discourse about America is historically sedimented on top of the latter. Whether from the Left or Right, therefore, such criticism cannot be pegged to a particular historical phenomenon or development in recent years nor to a particular US administration or particular policies. Such criticism, instead, locates cultural deficiencies and abnormalities in the earliest chapters of American history, posits their continuity until the present, and enframes them within habits of interpretation and historical expectation derived from European experience along with the (secularization) theories and narratives that have sought to make sense of this experience. The accretion of such lines criticisms over long stretches of time—often advanced by influential intellectuals and endorsed by powerful institutions—have contributed to a prism of understanding or a critical synoptic about America, which tends to construe genuine transatlantic differences in the religious field as an example American defectiveness or strangeness—"the sheer weirdness of the American citizenry" as Salman Rushdie once summarized the British Left's conception of middle America.[156] This embedded hermeneutical proclivity, in turn, sustains a simmering cultural *ressentiment*, which can be aggravated by contemporary events and trends in American society,

even as it significantly predates them. The "transatlantic rift" in recent
years, to quote Casanova again, "has important religious undercurrents
that [have] exacerbate[d] an unprecedented wave of anti-Americanism
spreading across Europe."[157]

Finally, and perhaps most ironically of all, because of the influence
of the social sciences derived from European models of interpretation,
combined with longstanding, internalized patterns of deference and
self-assessment before the bar of Old World "high culture," many educated Americans have come to rue America's enduring religious vitality and look instead to the secular modernity of Western Europe as a
preferable alternative, indeed as a more "normal" one. Edward Shils,
for instance, once observed "the utopian function of Europe for American intellectuals," and a widespread tendency to pit the more secular
milieus of "the European metropolis" against "the puritanical attitude"
prevalent in the United States.[158] "The American who...wants to be
modern," Max Weber once observed, "gets increasingly embarrassed
when, in conversation with Europeans, the ecclesiastical character of
his country is discussed."[159] Or, as Christian Smith has noted, "America's activist secularizers" in the formative stages of American social
science and modern university development were inclined to adopt
the Western European Enlightenment and its revolutionary skeptical
heritage as their own, often after protracted study sojourns abroad.
Smith elaborates:

> The historical evidence is clear that our American secularizing activists [in the
> early twentieth century] drew most of their inspiration, ideas, and models
> from European carriers of Enlightenment culture. Secular movement ideol-
> ogy was almost entirely imported from Europe—particularly from England,
> France, Germany, and Austria—where Enlightenment battles against estab-
> lishment churches had spawned hard-line anticlerical movements more radi-
> cal than any ever seen in the United States. In the world system of
> knowledge-production during this era, Western Europe was the core and the
> United States was the periphery. As these dynamics typically work, the pro-
> duction of knowledge on the periphery was developed according to the con-
> cerns and interests of knowledge elites at the core.[160]

Talcott Parsons, mentioned above, might serve as an illustrative case of
this more general trend.

Not surprisingly, ever since, American knowledge classes—or at
least influential sectors thereof—have been among the most receptive
to and/or misled by the plausibility claims of secularization theory and

the types of "social imaginaries" about modernity that it has generated.[161] They have been less inclined, accordingly, to regard America's relatively high levels of religious belief and practice as a dynamic and integral expression of the American experience, but rather as a home-grown riddle, a case of abnormal historical development, an inability to measure up.

But thus is the power of description, of the presence of the past, and of how narratives about social reality can well-nigh become constitutive of social reality itself. In another context, the poet Wallace Stevens once wrote, "And what [was] said of it / became a part of what it is."[162]

4

Philip Schaff: Herr Doktor Professor in the American Frontier

The United States has indeed opened a new chapter in church history, which differs widely from the...[ancient] persecution of the Church by the State, from the mediaeval Roman Catholic dominion of the State by the Church, and from the modern European Protestant subjection of the Church to the State....[T]his point should be placed in its proper light and carefully guarded against frequent misrepresentations of European writers, who can see nothing but culpable indifferentism...in any attempt to emancipate the State from the Church and the Church from the State.

—Philip Schaff,"Christianity in America" (1857)

Introduction

If one put down this book after reading the preceding chapters, one might conclude that virtually no European ever had anything positive to say about American religion and culture. But of course this would present an incomplete picture. I should reiterate then that my aim in these chapters has been to shed light on recurring attitudes and frameworks of interpretation at the far sides of the Right–Left religio-political spectrum. By no means does this add up to a monolithic European image of America—even if many of the previously-discussed figures have exerted, in some quarters, perdurable influence on knowledge formations and assumptions about historical processes, which often negatively enframe perceptions of the United States.

The larger historical picture reveals that philo-Americanism was not hard to come by in the nineteenth century. Some political cultures with affinities to the United States positively seemed to nuture it: those of Switzerland and the Netherlands immediately come to mind, along with Great Britain's (and particularly Scotland's) strong free church tradition.[1] It was especially prevalent among the lower classes, moreover, among whom were those who regretted the paucity of land and opportunity in the Old World and rued the entrenched social stratification. Not surprisingly, it was also strong among religious minorities, not least among Jews, who well into the nineteenth century faced mistreatment in their home countries despite the incremental growth of practices of toleration.[2] One is even tempted to formulate the rule that the less stake one held in the Old World status quo, politically or religiously, the higher one's chances of holding a favorable opinion of the United States. Conversely, a negative view was more likely if a) one felt an abiding attachment to the throne-and-altar conservatism of the post-1815 reaction or, in counterpoint, b) one rued that status quo, but associated progress and modernity (as I argued in chapter three) with aggressive anticlericalism and/or the secularization of society. In both cases—Right or Left, traditionalist or secularist—the American pattern of early disestablishment, religious vitality, revivalism, and a churning pluralism cut squarely across one's ideological grain. Extremes oddly meet, as I have been arguing.

Yet, as we know from Alexis de Tocqueville, one need not have been a pauper or religiously marginalized to hold a generous view of religious freedom in the United States; numerous educated liberals and even "aristocratic liberals" such as Tocqueville expressed admiration too. Indeed, let me go ahead and sneak in the confession that Tocqueville's *Democracy in America* does remain, in many respects, unrivaled in its engaged, sympathetic (albeit far from adulatory) treatment of American religious life, even if, as I have also argued, the sheer frequency of its invocation often crowds out others figures, whether negative or positive, from the historian's field of vision.[3] Other notable, high-minded treatments of American religious life might include the Austrian Francis Grund's *The Americans in their Moral, Social, and Political Relations* (1837) and the Englishwoman Harriet Martineau's *Society in America* (1837). Subsequently published works—such as James Bryce's two-volume *The American Commonwealth* (1888), Hugo Münsterberg's *The Americans* (1904), and André Siegfried's *America Comes of Age* (1927)—also stand out as achievements of constructive, probing inquiry. And there are yet other examples.[4]

In the following chapters, I sketch portraits of two lesser known, sympathetic commentators on the American religious scene: the Swiss–German, Reformed church historian Philip Schaff and the French Catholic philosopher Jacques Maritain, the combined careers of which run from the mid-nineteenth through the mid-twentieth century. Even though they are recognized within specific disciplines (Schaff among various church history guilds and Maritain among Catholic, particularly Thomist, philosophers), I want to propose that they have a much broader relevance for modern intellectual and religious history, generally, and for the history of European–American transatlantic exchanges, in particular. Indeed, they both represent what I earlier called *transatlantic personalities*, each being familiar with the religious and political dynamics on both sides of the Atlantic. Schaff moved to the United States permanently at the age of twenty-five, although he returned to Europe frequently, often to lecture on American society and institutions, while Maritain spent nearly two decades living in the United States.

As indicated in the introduction, this might seem an odd pairing, given the national, confessional, and generational differences between Schaff and Maritain. But, again, this can be construed as much a virtue as a liability—given that they offer different vantage points of perception. However, the commonalities between the two are striking, with respect to initial misgivings about the "New World," and, more saliently, in their respective efforts to understand, explain, and, indeed, esteem the religious (and religio-political) dynamics of the United States, which both men concluded differed profoundly from European patterns and too often had been subjected to misapprehension and caricature. Fathoming and explaining the "transatlantic religious divide," and redressing the European caricatures, emerged as a notable aspect of each man's intellectual vocation, even if their contrasting personal backgrounds, theological commitments, and historical moments meant that they went about doing this in different, if not contradictory, ways.

Young Man Schaff and America's "Deplorable Confusion"

Who was Philip Schaff? Why did he come to the United States? And what were his early impressions of the religious situation in what became his adopted country? As mentioned, Schaff is generally recognized among church historians, especially in the United States.[5] As a founding member of the Society of Biblical Literature and Exegesis (1880) and the founder and first president of the American Society of Church History (1888), as well as the author, editor, and translator of numerous works on theology, biblical interpretation, and church history, Schaff left a legacy that cuts in diverse directions. Countless American theologians and historians of Christianity owe an often unknown debt to this industrious Swiss–German émigré.[6]

A scholar of the past, Schaff was also an insightful commentator on contemporary affairs, whether of those in the United States or Europe. Taking up permanent residence in the United States in 1844, he traveled back to Europe fourteen times—a remarkable and time-consuming feat for his time. Aware of his unusual vantage point, Schaff came to see himself as a bridge maker, an "international theological nuncio," seeking to explain America to Europe and Europe to America in an era, not unlike more recent times, often marked by mutual suspicion and misunderstanding.[7] His contemporaries at the University of Berlin dubbed him "the Theological Mediator between the East and the West."[8]

In his "Autobiographical Reminiscences," written toward the end of his life, Schaff referred to himself as Swiss by birth, German by education, and American by adoption.[9] He hailed from the city of Chur in the confessionally and linguistically complex Canton of Graubünden.[10] "Born and bred in poverty and obscurity," as he later put it, Schaff nonetheless demonstrated exceptional academic promise in his early studies and, in 1834, allowance was made for him to attend a boys' academy in Kornthal, Württemberg, and subsequently a prestigious *Gymnasium* in Stuttgart. He never forgot his Alpine childhood. Grateful especially for Helvetic traditions of republican and local government, he once confided that these perhaps helped him "feel [more] at home in this country [the United States] than emigrants from imperial Germany, who are apt...to retain a preference for a more centralized form of government."[11]

Schaff continued his studies, in church history and theology, at some of the most prestigious German universities: Tübingen, Halle, and, finally, Berlin, Prussia's flagship university. In these distinguished institutions, he came into contact with many of the leading theological and historical minds of the nineteenth century, including Ferdinand Christian Baur, August Tholuck, Isaak August Dorner, Julius Müller, and August Neander, among others. The broadly Hegelian emphasis on progressive historical development (*Entwicklung*), pervasive in German intellectual life at this time, left a lasting impression on Schaff and played an important role, as we shall see, in his interpretation of the United States and its religious conditions.

Throughout his life Schaff remained grateful for the German university system in general, despite expressing a few reservations about the spirit of excessive criticism (*Kritik*) that it sometimes fostered and the heavy-handed state(s) that administered it.[12] In 1857 he published a book, *Germany; its Universities, Theology, and Religion*, in which he sought to convey to an English-speaking audience the depth and riches of German scholarship and academic theology and thereby "bring the German and American mind into closer union." "The German universities," he wrote,

are regarded by competent judges as the first among the learned institutions of the world....[N]o active branch of Protestantism can keep entirely aloof from its contact without injuring its own interests.[13]

While one would not describe Schaff as a theological radical, he was also no reactionary. Deeply shaped by the pietist awakening (*Erweck-ungsbewegung*) of the early nineteenth century in Württemburg, Schaff never evinced the anti-intellectual tendencies sometimes associated with this form of heartfelt piety. Instead, he eagerly embraced the importance of first-rate scholarship (*Wissenschaft*) for the vocation of the theologian and historian of Christianity. Often he is depicted as a representative of *Vermittlungstheologie*, or "mediating theology," a centrist theological position of the mid-nineteenth century, inclined to intra-Protestant ecumenism, which sought to harmonize what many regarded as a growing incommensurability between the claims of modern scientific inquiry and those of traditional Christian confessions.

Upon becoming a *Privatdozent*, or beginning lecturer, Schaff was preparing himself for an academic career at a German (or Swiss) university when outside factors intervened. In 1843, he received a call from the German Reformed Church in America to come and teach at its newly founded and rather isolated seminary in Mercersburg, Pennsylvania.[14] Vacillating at first, he nonetheless accepted and later traveled to the United States, resolved, as he put it, to serve as a "missionary of science" to the scattered peoples of German descent on the American frontier.[15] He would teach at Mercersburg for nearly two decades, establishing an especially close friendship and scholarly alliance with the theologian John Williamson Nevin (1803–86), his colleague at the seminary and a notable intellectual force in his own right.[16] In 1863, Schaff accepted a post at Union Theological Seminary in New York City, where he finished his career in 1893, the year of his death.[17] But, again, through frequent travel as well as indefatigable letter-writing, he maintained lasting ties to Europe, in general, and to German-speaking academic and ecclesiastical circles, in particular.

Schaff's early impressions of the United States appear in his sermon of ordination, delivered upon accepting the call to go abroad, and again in his inaugural lecture in the United States (delivered in Reading, Pennsylvania) and subsequently published as *The Principle of Protestantism* (1845). Both the sermon and the address broadly reflect the traditionalist disquiet about the United States, as discussed in chapter two, as well as an (often overweening) eagerness to instruct the new nation and serve as a bridge builder between the Old World and the New.

Schaff's ordination sermon took place on April 12, 1844, on the eve of his departure to America, at the Protestant Reformed Church in Elberfeld in the Rhineland. Dependent exclusively on second- and third-hand reports of the spiritual conditions in North America, his picture of the United States was far from favorable. "I was overpowered by anxiety and fear" about traveling to America, he confessed, but believed, finally, that the will of the Lord would be served by it. In contrast to the theological profundity and intellectual high culture of Germany, America seemed to him a site of utter destitution, populated by a "conflux of beggars, adventurers, liberty dreamers, culprits, and often blasphemers of religion." The land stood "free from restraint," stricken with "spiritual wants" of all kinds. German-speaking peoples there appeared to be losing touch with their Old World roots, dissipating into a vast frontier, and standing on the brink of what he called "the threefold abyss": "heathenism" (an ebbing of churchly sensibilities altogether), "Romanism" (falling prey to the proselytizing efforts of frontier Catholic missionaries), and "sectarianism" (hiving off into various factions or joining up with revivalist groups such as the Methodists or Baptists).[18]

The so-called "third foe," sectarianism, especially unnerved Schaff, who had been ordained in the Prussian Union Church—an early nineteenth-century measure that served, with partial success, to merge the Calvinist and Lutheran branches of Protestantism within the Prussian territorial church.[19] In the United States, by contrast, no forces for religious cohesion appeared to exist. "Deplorable confusion" reigned supreme in this "sect-bewildered country." "Every fanatic," he did not mince words, "in whose brain is engendered of…some new conceit builds the next day a new chapel and baptizes it with his own name, as a legacy for future generations."[20] Schaff understood his own "Macedonian call" (cf. Acts 16:8–10) as helping to arrest this descent into religious chaos or at least trying to protect the small German Reformed community from its ravages.[21]

Crossing the Atlantic for the first time in the summer of 1844,[22] Schaff brought his misgivings about the New World with him, and he made clear, early on, that he came as a tutor to the new country, not a learner. His inaugural address, "The Principle of Protestantism," delivered in Reading, Pennsylvania, stands out as a notable event in nineteenth-century American religious history.[23] In it, Schaff sought to identify two dangerous tendencies within Protestantism: rationalism and sectarianism. The former pertained more to Germany (with its advanced culture of learning), the latter to the United States (with its wide-open freedoms and possibilities). Focusing his listeners attention on the sixteenth century, Schaff insisted that an abiding catholicity and reverence for church tradition (including that of the Middle Ages) had been present at the time of the Protestant Reformation. These features had subsequently been eclipsed, most egregiously in the United States, by a highly individualistic and presentist approach to the faith. The resulting "sect plague" in America undermined the possibility of church unity by fomenting continuous discord and divisions among Christians.[24] What is more, many of the divisions were not even dignified by serious theological disagreement, as they were in Germany, but had developed over social, ethnic, and other "practical" matters. This came as no surprise to Schaff, for America, the "land of practicality," was made up predominantly of Anglo-Saxon peoples who, lacking the German profundity that Schaff sought to supply, approached the world in an overly matter-of-fact manner.

Moreover, Schaff placed extensive blame for this situation on the enduring influence of Puritanism in American culture. In his interpretation, the early Puritan settlers—representatives of an "extreme, naked Protestantism"—had demonstrated "a zeal for God, but not according to knowledge."[25] Their purely "congregational" approach to church organization laid the basis of a more general religious "atomism" that had spread from New England to permeate the religious ethos of the nation generally. The "puritanization" of American religion, we might say, combined with the unprecedented legal separation of church and state effected by the First Amendment in the US Bill of Rights presented to the young Schaff a religious environment of unrelieved chaos and confusion. Lacking the "hierarchic bond" of Catholicism and the "civil supremacy" of Anglicanism or Lutheranism, the church in America lacked a principle of authority and a mechanism toward unity and thus seemed to him destined for a career of fissiparous, obscurantist ignomy. "Tendencies, which had found no political room to unfold themselves in other lands," he wrote, "wrought here without restraint. Thus we have come gradually to have a host of sects which is no longer easy to number, and that still continues to swell from year to year. Where the process of separation is destined to end, no human calculation can foretell."

Schaff was especially dismayed by self-declared prophets and revivalist preachers, who, throwing tradition and concern for church unity to the wind, arrogated to themselves power and influence by appealing directly to the Bible. Such individuals, he lamented, are "not ashamed to appeal continually to the Scriptures, as having been sealed entirely...to the understanding of eighteen centuries...till now at last God has been pleased to kindle the true light in an obscure corner of the New World!" Worry about such religious mavericks led Schaff, in an unmistakably traditionalist register, to memorably sum up the United States as "a variegated sampler of all conceivable religious chimeras and dreams....Every theological vagabond and peddler may drive here his bungling trade, without passport or license and sell his false ware at pleasure. What is to come of such confusion is not now to be seen."[26]

A Changing Outlook

While Schaff maintained an insistently and fairly lonely "catholic" understanding of Protestantism throughout his life, and a concomitant lament of church divisions, his general outlook toward the United States and its religious freedoms began to mellow almost immediately after his arrival. Mostly critical musings about the New World's want-ing conditions soon gave way to more sanguine assessments, which in turn increasingly became tied to critiques of "Europe's state-church system."

To the published version of *The Principle of Protestantism*, Schaff ap-pended 112 so-called "Theses for the Times," in which he sought to address various and sundry religious and cultural concerns. In these, one already observes a slightly more ambivalent attitude toward Amer-ica. On the one hand, he judged the United States of the 1840s as largely unimportant with respect to the history of Christianity: "Amer-ica...has produced nothing original, no new fact in the history of the church as a whole." On the other hand, he felt that his adopted coun-try nourished tremendous possibilities; it constituted the fermenting of a new social and political order, where, in Hegelian language, the "thesis" of the Old World's faith(s) would meet the "antithesis" of un-precedented social and political freedoms and a seemingly endless geo-graphical expanse to effect a hitherto unknown "synthesis" in the religious history of the West. "Nowhere else," he wrote, "is there at present the same favorable room for further development, since in no country of the Old World does the church enjoy such freedom, or the same power to renovate itself from within."[27] Thus, while American freedoms seemed necessarily to engender church divisions, Schaff also admitted, even at this early juncture of his American career, that these same freedoms also bequeathed to the church a novel, post-Constantinian moment: the opportunity to be guided and help guide society by its own lights—by what Maritain would later call "the things that are not Caesar's."[28] This remained difficult in most German-speaking lands, Schaff felt, where the state continued to exercise a firm grip on the direction of ecclesiastical development and practice.[29]

Schaff's esteem for American religious freedom increased as he es-tablished his career at Mercersburg Seminary in the 1840s and 1850s: disparaging notions of a "sect-bewildered land" gave way to yet greater reflection on his actual experience and on new vistas of historical ob-servation and reflection that American life presented to him. "Think of America as one may," he wrote friends in Germany in 1845, "there is here more personal piety and practical church activity than anywhere in the Old World," and he even speculated that America might repre-sent "the future of Protestantism, the cradle of a new and splendid reformation."[30] Writing in 1847, he began to weigh the strengths and weaknesses of church–state models on both sides of the Atlantic. "An American," he wrote, "cannot submit to the theory of dependence in which the church stands to the state in Europe. But the church's independence of the state does not necessarily carry with it true freedom. There is also the danger, when religion is left absolutely to the choice of the people, that the masses will go astray, who, under the European system, might remain in some connection with the church." Nonetheless, the weaknesses of the Old World outshone the strengths: Protestantism in Europe, in particular, had made "[the] mistake of binding itself so closely to the worldly power and in transferring its episcopal rights to princes and kings." A people "of enterprise, energy, and tireless industry," Americans could not accept this yoke.[31]

In 1848 and 1849, Schaff published a series of articles under the title "Introduction to the Church History of the United States" in the *German Reformed Messenger*, the principal English-language organ of the German Reformed Church. While his censure of sectarianism remained firm, one notices a growing positive evaluation of the political and social conditions of Christianity in America. "All the [religious] elements of the old world," he wrote, "meet [here] in renewed strength, possessing civil rights altogether equal and full of ardent hopes, engage in conflict with each other, the final issue of which cannot by any means now be foreseen." While the separation of church and state had allowed "sectarianism with all its evils...to obtain formal sanction," it had also allowed religion, voluntarily embraced, to shape individuals and society in ways neither possible nor conceivable under the conditions of European "state-churchism"—his usual English phrasing of the German *Staatskirchentum*. The stark contrast between voluntary religion in America and established religion in Europe prompted Schaff to conclude that Europeans simply lived too far away "[to] obtain a clear view of the peculiar conditions of the new world." And he even wondered if "there are yet many things that the mother [Europe] might then learn of the daughter [America] heretofore rather superciliously regarded."[32]

By 1850, Schaff had also concluded that it was folly for German emigrants in America to isolate themselves in cultural and linguistic enclaves, as was often the case.[33] The promise of the *novus ordo seclorum* should rather elicit a spirit of engagement, not seclusion. Leading by example, Schaff began at this time to lecture and publish more in English: "German ideas cannot take root in...American soil unless they are freely reproduced in the English language and adapted to the practical wants of a free church in a free state." "The German has a great mission in America," he proclaimed, "[but] he will not fulfill it in any adequate manner by rigidly and stiffly secluding himself from the Anglo-Americans." Rather, he should "in a cosmopolitan spirit, energetically appropriate the Anglo-American nature and its excellences and, as far as possible, penetrate it with the wealth of his own German temper and life."[34] Seclusion led to "ossification"; a more appropriate path entailed entering "into a vital sympathy with American life and keep[ing] up with its development."[35]

Schaff's America

By the mid-1850s, Schaff was indeed convinced that the "daughter" (America) did in fact have something to teach the "mother" (Europe). Schaff himself sought to play the role of the instructing child when in 1854 he was granted a year-long leave of absence to travel back to Europe and, among other things, give several invited lectures on American civilization. Speaking in Berlin, Frankfurt am Main, and elsewhere, Schaff shifted his attention from America's religious imperfections to its religious liberty and historical promise, offering a much more optimistic interpretation of his adopted country and seeking to correct what he now regarded as blinkered Old World prejudices against the United States. His lectures were soon published and quickly translated into English as *America: A Sketch of the Political, Social, and Religious Character of the United States of North America*.[36]

This would not be the only time Schaff sought to explain America abroad. Equally sanguine, if not uncritical, accounts came in later publications, often derived from speaking tours in Europe. Passing over numerous minor writings, these include *Der Bürgerkrieg und das christliche Leben in Nord-Amerika* (1865), inspired by European interest in the American Civil War; *Christianity in the United States of America* (1879); and *Church and State in the United States, or the Idea of Religious Liberty and its Practical Effects* (1888).[37] Together, these publications, or at least significant portions of them, deserve ranking as among the most informative and searching analyses of the United States by a foreigner in the nineteenth century.

Commentators on these works, however, regularly go astray in two ways. First, in light of Schaff's generally favorable attitude toward the

United States, especially when compared to his earlier *Principle of Protestantism*, scholars tend to see these texts as an index of Schaff's "Americanization"—his personal "identification" with the "idealized image" of his adopted country, according to one critic.[38] Second, Schaff's providentialist assessment of the United States—i.e., the view, sometimes expressed, that America possessed an indispensable historical vocation for the development of "the Kingdom of God" in the modern world[39]—is dismissed as imposing a theological interpretation on historical facts. Both of these analyses are by no means beside the point. One would be hard pressed to deny that Schaff became "Americanized" to a degree during his long residence in the United States, and anyone looking for a Rankean-objectivist historian of the strict observance is certain to raise eyebrows at some of Schaff's theologically inspired remarks about past and present events.[40] He was trained, after all, as a church historian and understood his field, finally, as a branch of theology, not as a free-standing secular discipline.

But if valid in certain respects, these criticisms deflect attention from something more noteworthy about Schaff's perspective: Schaff was among the first European interpreters of American religion to grasp and convey with esteem the radical novelty of historical conditions affecting the Old World faith—"circumstances and conditions altogether peculiar," as he would write.[41] In doing so, Schaff anticipated lines of inquiry that one might fruitfully compare to Frederick Jackson Turner's well-known "frontier thesis" about the United States. In 1893 Turner famously argued that the abundance of "free lands and the consciousness of working out their own social destiny" had indelibly affected Americans' habit of being with vast ramifications for a host of social, cultural, and political institutions. "The frontier ... furnish[ed] a new field of opportunity, a gate of escape from the bondage of the past; and freshness and confidence, and scorn of older society, impatience of its restraints and ideas."[42] These conditions did not simply produce license and social disintegration—as many Europeans had assumed about the fate of religion in the New World[43]—but they also, according to Turner, imparted to individuals and communities alike an inner drive and resourcefulness "to preserve order" apart from direct governmental mediation; unleashed tremendous social energy oriented to the future, fueled by pragmatic confidence; and placed a premium on direct–democratic over distant–bureaucratic forms of social organization. Although Turner did not concentrate extensively on religion, he did, in a pregnant aside, once remark that the "expansive tendency . . . of a moving frontier must have [had] . . . important results on the character of religious organization in the United States."[44]

Anticipating Turner's line of analysis, but addressing the religious aspect directly, Schaff came to the conclusion, after residing in remote Pennsylvania (truly a frontier experience) for over a decade, that the noteworthy thing about American religious life was not how far it fell short of European conditions or assumptions, but how its turbulent dynamism, replete with problem and promise, illuminated constraints and prejudices in the European political–religious order itself and, concomitantly, in commonplace European assessments of America. At the very least, Schaff reasoned, European scholars could no longer simply ignore the nexus of religion and liberty in the United States as a fact of historical importance. On this score especially, America was far more than "a feeble echo of Europe," as he felt many foreign analyses insinuated.[45] In an 1852 review of a book by the German theologian Richard Rothe, Schaff complained that "it seems for many European scholars that the world and church historical fact of North America does not exist at all."[46] Later, he would criticize Hegel for "ignor[ing] America altogether in his philosophy of history, although he teaches that the history of the world is the idea of liberty."[47]

Indeed, settled habits of thought and judgment long shaped by "European state-churchism," Schaff came to believe, afforded no stable perch to assess the United States and its transformative potential for religion and society generally. The separation of church and state in America did not lead inexorably to chaos and degeneracy, as he, reflecting common opinion, had once believed; rather it had cast religion into the domain of human freedom, individual initiative, and private philanthropy. And there it had witnessed a momentous resurgence, generating the virtue of benevolence or "liberality"; nourishing all kinds of voluntary social reform energies, even among those far down on the socioeconomic ladder; and exercising an enduring, if diffuse, moral and democratizing influence on the nation as a whole. The habit of generosity formed by private giving, in particular, seemed to Schaff to hold significant consequence for America's social and religious life; "it makes the laity feel their responsibility, calls forth a vast amount of liberality, and attaches them to the church in proportion to the amount of labor and money they have invested in it."[48] In short, then, the American frontier ethos joined with a polity grounded in

radical religious disestablishment was, willy-nilly, charting its own conceptions of human flourishing and freedom, often in marked and un-
predictable contrast to how those terms might be understood from a
milieu of long-standing church–state symbiosis. "Schaff [thus] found
himself," as Perry Miller has observed, "as the European intellectual in
America obliged to revaluate the fundamental terms of European
social discourse [about America]."[49]

Ever cognizant of his own humble origins, Schaff was particularly
troubled by the contempt for American institutions and religious life
among Europe's aristocratic circles, including the "mandarin" aristocracy of the German universities, whom he otherwise admired. A major
purpose in taking on the subject of "America" in his 1854 lectures, he
made clear, was to countermand "false impressions and strong prejudices, which are widely spread in the higher circles of Europe, concerning the United States."[50] Often he managed to do this in a spirit
of gentleness and with an irenic search for mutual understanding. But
sometimes a more curt tone prevailed, as when he expressed dismay
that "there are respectable people, professedly of the highest culture...who have a real antipathy to America, speak of it with the
greatest contempt of indignation, and see in it nothing but a grand
bedlam, a rendezvous of European scamps and vagabonds.... Such
notions it is unnecessary to refute."[51] Occasionally he seasoned his
message with a little humor. He warned readers, for instance, "against
the ridiculous caricatures of American Christianity which abound in
European works," citing as an example the Catholic Encyclopedia edited by Heinrich Wetzer and Benedikt Welte, whose article on America
gave credence to the existence of a number of non-existent sects, including one group alleged to require its members to pluck out their
right eye in a literal understanding of the biblical passage in Matthew
5:29.[52] Not only did these sects (and other concocted ones) not exist,
Schaff insisted, but the authors' discussion of them on the same pages
with more established Protestant denominations betrayed an anti-
American, and, in this case, a conservative European Catholic, prejudice to cast the United States simply as the "grand bedlam" of the
modern world, the *reductio ad absurdum* of Protestant principles.[53]

Nonetheless, the European critique of American sectarianism Schaff
continued to take seriously, seeing ecclesiastical division as an obstacle
to the Christian unity that he felt the New Testament called for. But his
more positive embrace of American voluntarism led him to revise his

understanding of church divisions. Increasingly, he distinguished between historic "denominations" (larger historic bodies such as Presbyterians and Methodists) and smaller, breakaway "sects"; he valued the
former as legitimate transmitters of Protestant verities while regretting
the latter as a testimony to the pride and vanity of schismatic individuals.[54] What is more, he emphasized that sectarianism could not be regarded as a distinctly American phenomenon, but rather as one intrinsic
to Protestantism. Many of the sects in America, he reminded his readers,
stemmed from European emigration, and hence "by pointing out kindred evils in Europe" he felt he could "forestall an immoderate condemnation of America."[55] "Sectarianism," he summed up,

is by no means a specifically American malady, as often represented; it is deeply
seated in Protestantism itself.... America in fact draws all its life originally
from Europe. It is not a land of new sects; for those which have originated
there... [do not] determine the religious character of the people. It is only the
rendezvous of all European churches and sects, which existed long before,
either as establishments or as dissenting bodies.[56]

More fundamentally, Schaff began to regard church divisions as a necessary stage toward a higher, integrative level of historical and religious
development—a robust, dynamic *unity*, where differences of past development were esteemed, not a mere *uniformity*, where all differences
were denied. Here one glimpses evidence of his indebtedness to the
German, "Hegelian" academic milieu of the early nineteenth century,
where notions of "historical development" reigned supreme. In his
interpretation, the religious freedom allowed by American law and
society represented a major improvement upon European state–chur-
chism: "America may be an improved continuation of Europe;... [A]
new age of humanity and church is to be expected by all."[57] The dis-
integrative cultural forces unleashed by religious voluntarism, while
certainly worrisome from a theological–ecumenical standpoint, nonetheless could lay claim to a legitimate (indeed, in his view, divinely
sanctioned) place in a progressive historical drama in which the United
States played a key role. In Schaff's own formulation:

[W]e must regard the present distraction and fermentings of Protestantism as
the necessary transition state to a far higher and better condition, a free unity
in spirit and in truth, embracing the greatest variety of Christian life. But first
the religious subjectivity and individuality of the sect system, with all its
accompanying infirmities, must freely and fully develop themselves.... Now

America tends toward this consistent carrying out the religious and political principle of Protestantism; that is, the practical application of the universal priesthood and kingship of Christians.[58]

Although the exact shape of the future remained ultimately unknown (and Schaff often pointed beyond temporal events to the mysterious hand of providence), the United States nonetheless possessed superlative significance in his view for the unfolding of events in sacred history. His adopted land held "extraordinary prospective importance for church history" as the site where "the ultimate fate of the Reformation will be decided."[59]

It followed that the absence of religious voluntarism constituted a stage in history in need of supersession. While Schaff regarded unity as a necessary goal for Christians, this must be a "free unity" enacted by free people, and not a coerced unity achieved under what he once humorously called "the cold step-motherly arm of the nominally Christian state."[60] While in his 1854 lectures he conceded that, theoretically, a Christian state could be a positive force, it was nonetheless "very hazardous for the church to expect too much of that union, and to put her trust in the temporal arm."[61] In subsequent publications, his rejection of "the evils of state-churchism" and "the despotism of a state church" became more pronounced.[62] In an article, "The State Church System in Europe" (1857), he stated the matter bluntly:

The glory of America is free Christianity, independent of the secular government and supported by the voluntary contributions of a free people. This is one of the greatest facts of modern history. Its significance can only be fully estimated by a careful comparison with State-churches of Europe, over which it makes gigantic progress. Whatever be the defects and inconveniences of the separation of Church and State, they are less numerous and serious than the troubles and difficulties which continually grow out of their union, to both parties.... [O]n the Continent generally, it [Protestantism] is almost entirely supported and ruled by the State, and this has a natural tendency to secularize religion as much as possible and to convert it into a sort of moral police.[63]

Assessments of American religious dynamics from the standpoint of adherence to established state churches, it followed, begged questions for Schaff; these represented for him a superseded stage of historical development, unwarrantedly self-confident, attempting to pass judgment on a more progressive one.

Interwoven with the issue of historical development was that of transatlantic difference: Schaff felt that the New World's different

historical terrain conditioned the nature of the new developments taking place. He therefore felt it necessary to emphasize just how novel
conditions were in America when compared to Europe, particularly
those affecting religious dynamics but in other areas as well. His remarks on this topic are numerous, but several themes merit underscoring. Like Tocqueville before him, he repeatedly called attention to the
fact that North America never possessed an hereditary aristocracy nor
an established church at the national level.[64] This reality fundamentally
separated the historical currents affecting the United States in the
nineteenth century from those present in Europe and betokened further possible divergences in the future. As suggested earlier, the frontier too, "the vast and still uncultivated tracts of the most fertile soil,"
played a prominent role in Schaff's imagination; the lure and promise
of the western land elicited "the boldest enterprise and the most untir-
ing energy" from the American people.[65] On this point, he sought to
question a commonplace European tendency to dismiss enterprising
Americans as wealth-obsessed upstarts, religiously hypocritical in their
pursuit of Mammon. Some were perhaps, to be sure. But Schaff argued
that many Americans (often descending from impecunious European
backgrounds) were only trying to make good on one of the oldest
injunctions of Christian wisdom, St. Benedict's admonition to pray
and work, *ora et labora*. "The good old advice: Pray and work," he
wrote, "is nowhere more to the point than in the United States. The
genuine American despises nothing more than idleness and stagnation;
he regards not enjoyment, but labor, not comfortable repose, but busy
unrest, as the proper earthly lot of man; and this has unspeakable importance for him, and a most salutary influence on the moral life of the
nation."[66] Put in broader historical terms, while in Europe, the bourgeois classes too often ending up aspiring "upward" toward the lei-
surely world of the declining aristocracy, in America "bourgeois
virtues" (thrift, work, frugality, self-betterment, etc.) could be more
firmly and durably established in the general social consciousness: the
democratization of *ora et labora*, we might say.[67]

Since Europeans of a conservative cast of mind often associated the
ideas of democracy and religious freedom with the radicalism and irreligion of the French Revolution, Schaff felt it necessary to insist that
the "ideas of 1776" and the "ideas of 1789" should not be conflated.
"The American revolution of 1776," he wrote, "was entirely different
in principle, character, and tendency from all the revolutions of the

European continent since 1789; and it is of the greatest importance to keep this difference in view, if we would duly understand and appreciate [the United States] and its prevailing idea of freedom."[68] In fact, the word "revolution" hardly applied to the establishment of the United States, he felt; what happened after 1776 was more an "emancipation," one which he compared to the uprising of the German states against the Napoleonic yoke and the efforts of the Greeks to achieve freedom from the Ottoman Empire. With respect to religion in particular, the American separation of church and state allowed for the robust flourishing of religious life (removed from state tutelage) and should thus be sharply distinguished from the anticlerical and dechristianizing measures of the French Revolution in its radical stages. Religion was disestablished in America so that it could thrive, not exiled so that it could perish. Despite "the apparent excess of freedom" when viewed from Europe, "deep reverence for Christianity" and a "conservative spirit" persisted on the other shore.[69] By contrast, the aggressively secular and anticlerical impulses that had reared their heads in France in the 1790s threatened to grow in the Old World, Schaff believed, if European nations maintained the dead hand of the past in the form of state churches. Politically and religiously, "Europe rests upon a volcano," he often remarked, evidenced by the growing cleft between reactionary and radical forces. American conditions, conversely, had allowed society to be "at once conservative and liberal."[70]

The conservative, religion-friendly cast of American liberalism, Schaff observed, often confounded progressive Europeans, who, fleeing the monarchies of Europe, expected to find in the United States a congenial abode. To the contrary, they were just as often disillusioned, especially by America's abiding religiosity. This was borne out, Schaff pointed out, by the many who left Europe for America after the abortive revolutions of 1848. Having esteemed the United States as a model for European development in matters political and religious, they quite often found themselves "exceedingly uncomfortable" in America, as Schaff observed and as we have seen in chapter three; revolutionaries "would fain come back again to kindle revolutions in Europe which they cannot kindle in America."[71] "The American idea of religious liberty," he opined elsewhere, "differs in *toto coelo* from the [Continental] red-republican idea, as faith differs from infidelity, and as consitutional liberty differs from antinomian license."[72] While 1848ers regularly saw church bodies as the "back bone of all political despotism," American liberals generally regarded churchly involvement and religious sentiment as both the motor behind and stabilizer of American freedom.[73] Divergences on this issue, Schaff concluded, could not be more "completely different."[74]

★★★

The combination of his academic training in church history and the amount of time he spent on both sides of the Atlantic makes Schaff, if not an altogether *sui generis* figure, an extremely rare one in the nineteenth century. This, of course, does not mean that his views were invariably accurate or insightful, but it does mean that they ought to command abiding attention and respect. His general neglect by students of transatlantic history is therefore all the more regrettable.

Schaff's awareness of a "transatlantic religious divide" in his lifetime should be clear from much of the foregoing. His insistence that the United States represented a new departure in the religious history of the West should also be evident. But this latter point perhaps merits underscoring once again in light of Schaff's prodigious learning in church history. In essence, Schaff felt that the withdrawal of state support for churches in the United States amounted to an abrupt, unprecedented rolling back of historical forces, first set in motion by Emperor Constantine, who enabled Christianity's transition from persecuted sect to the eventual established religion of the Roman Empire. Developments in the Roman Empire after Constantine served, *mutatis mutandis*, as the prototypes for forms of official establishment in Europe from the Middle Ages up through the Peace of Westphalia and beyond. The general desirability and taken-for-granted status of this arrangement, although not without critics, had become such an embedded aspect of European political realities and assumptions about the social order that thinking "outside" of it—even for those who adamantly opposed it—had become virtually impossible. "Ah Constantine!", Schaff quoted Dante, "of how much ill was mother / not thy conversion, but that marriage-dower / which the first wealthy pope received of thee."[75]

The American experiment, in Schaff's interpretation, had not only brought Constantinianism and its numerous successor arrangements to an abrupt terminus, but it had done so under conditions historically and geographically remote from the seething reservoirs of oppositional hostility—whether "red-republican" or socialist—that it had acquired in revolutionary-era Europe. What is more, North America did not possess a "Constantinian" faction, i.e., embittered traditionalists eager to reunite throne and altar, state and church. In the United States, Schaff maintained, Christianity had become "throughout self-maintaining and self-governing (*selbsterhaltend und selbstregierend*), just as in the first three centuries [before Constantine]." On the desirability of this arrangement, he offered the authority of early Christian authors such as Justin Martyr, Tertullian, and Lactantius.[76]

But there is more. While the America situation lacked a "Constantine," it also lacked a "Diocletian"; the church was neither established nor persecuted. A "friendly separation" had taken place between the two powers, church and state, and precisely this, Schaff tirelessly averred, was the glaring *novum*, "a new chapter in the history of Christianity," which both piqued Old World curiosity while often frustrating full comprehension. Unlike the persecuted church of antiquity, the church in America "has the advantage that it is protected in its possession and other rights by the state just like any other legal corporation."[77] Accordingly, he summed up, "The United States furnishes the first example in history of a government deliberately depriving itself of all legislative control over religion, which was . . . regarded as by all older governments as the chief support of public morality, order, peace, and prosperity." While not without some harbingers, "the American relationship of church and state differs from all previous relations."[78] For Schaff, this situation was as discontinuous with the past as it was salutary for the future; for "civil liberty," he believed, "requires religious liberty, and cannot prosper without it."[79]

A child of the Reformation, Schaff regarded the American religio-political outcome as an unmistakable expression of Protestantism. But he understood this both in a negative and positive register. Negatively, the Reformation had produced not only irreconcilable divisions between Catholics and Protestants, but deep divisions within Protestantism itself. The numerous religious communities that had wound up in America, sometimes fleeing persecution at home, meant that by the time of national independence too much diversity existed to make the creation of a single established church a viable idea. All groups feared their religious competitors gaining monopoly status more than they desired it for themselves. The many religious groups, as Schaff sized up the situation, "which sprang directly or indirectly from the great

Protestant movement of the sixteenth century, and which were forced
in part, by persecution, to seek common asylum in this western world,
is the historical condition without which the bond of union between
Church and State would probably never have been broken." North
American religious freedom, he concluded, ought to be considered as
"the sweet fruit" of bitter European experience traceable to the sixteenth-century split.[80] At one level, then, the American outcome was
simply a matter of expedience.[81]

But it was more than just that. Although necessitated by messy historical circumstances, the American experiment in religious liberty also
bore witness in Schaff's view to important prior Protestant developments and verities. With numerous others, Schaff regarded "the prevailing religious character" of the United States as "primarily a continuation
of European Protestantism," especially in its Calvinist manifestations
and refracted through the turbulent English political experience of the
seventeenth century.[82] More to the point, the Reformation's recovery
of the role of the laity, the dignity of non-clerical vocations—i.e., the
"priesthood of all believers"—constituted for him the signal theological accent that had shaped the American experiment and its core assumptions. Self-government of the sort promoted in the American
Constitution, in Schaff's judgment, amounted to "a transferring to the
civil sphere the idea of the universal priesthood of Christians, which
was first clearly and emphatically emphasized by the Reformers."[83]
Often citing Luther on the inviolability of conscience, Schaff felt that
the "Americans have made the first bold attempt to carry out to its last
consequences the Protestant principle of religious subjectivity and toleration and to make it the basis of a civil and political freedom."[84] Freedom, progress, and conscience, then—all hallmarks of the Reformation
in Schaff's view—had been swept across the Atlantic; and from these
Protestant principles, and the mingling of so many diverse Old World
elements, "something wholly new" would arise.[85]

But what of Catholicism? If America was the land of Protestantism
par excellence, and the seat of the unfinished Reformation, how did
Schaff regard the fate of Roman Catholics in this new land? In light of
the ensuing discussion of Jacques Maritain, this question takes on
pointed significance here.

In many respects, Schaff held views typical of his time and Protestant
milieu. As Christianity has superseded Judaism, he felt, so Protestantism
had superseded Catholicism. While divisions among Protestants

troubled Schaff until his last breath, he opined confidently that "history never moves backward, and the open Bible and Protestant freedom are making faster and deeper progress [in America] than Romanism."[86] Developments in Catholicism from the time of the Council of Trent and the founding of the Jesuits especially vexed Schaff. "It was then that the mediaeval Catholicism was consolidated into Romanism in opposition to the evangelical doctrines of the Reformers." Under the colonial tutelage of such "Romanism," South and Central America presented to Schaff's eyes "the gloomy picture of an almost hopeless stagnation," whereas (Protestant) North American "offered the very embodiment of life and progress."[87]

Nonetheless, Schaff did not indulge in the extreme ridicule of "Popery" common among the majority of his Protestant coreligionists in the United States, and he deplored the shrill tone and menacing tactics of the anti-Catholic Know-Nothing political party. The presence of Roman Catholics in North America, in fact, placed a salutary check on the atomistic and anti-churchly elements afoot in revivalist Protestantism, he insisted, adding that "what is true and great and good and beautiful in the hoary but still vigorous Catholic church, should, must, and will be preserved."[88]

Furthermore, Schaff felt that the historical necessity of having to work out its destiny in America before watchful Protestant eyes and in an atmosphere of religious liberty would effect momentous change within the Catholic Church itself. At several junctures in his writings he even proclaimed that a "glorious future" awaited Catholicism in the United States. An island in a Protestant ocean, the Catholic Church's first Episcopal See at Baltimore, Schaff was keen to point out, had early on affirmed the "fullest religious liberty"—something completely unthinkable, he held, in predominantly Catholic Spain or Italy. "Catholicism, therefore, must in the process of time assume a more liberal character in America than in Europe."[89]

While Schaff did not live to see the Vatican's condemnation of "Americanism" in 1899, the strain that this condemnation produced between Rome and America was something that Jacques Maritain would be forced to confront. As we shall see, Maritain, too, felt that the American experiment offered Catholicism what Schaff elsewhere had called "a more liberal track." Distinguishing *this* liberal track, however, from the more aggressive, anticlerical track that had roiled European Catholicism, from the time of the French Revolution and the Italian

Risorgimento, presented a formidable challenge. But Maritain embraced it, insisting even—in a register of thought quite foreign to Schaff's—that Catholic theology possessed untapped insights that would not only help make sense of the American experiment in religious liberty, but also (and, here, contravening many of his more conservative, European coreligionists) for heartily affirming it.

5

Jacques Maritain: A French Thomist and the New World

A European who comes to America is struck by the fact that the expression "separation between Church and State"... does not have the same meaning here and in Europe.

—Jacques Maritain, *Man and the State* (1951)

America is promise.

—Jacques Maritain, *Reflections on America* (1958)

Introduction

In 1882, as Philip Schaff toiled away at Union Theological Seminary in New York, Jacques Maritain was born in Paris. The grandson of the renowned freethinker and Third Republic politician Jules Favre (1809–80), brought up in the fin-de-siècle cosmopolitan environment of the French capital, Maritain would appear far removed from the nineteenth-century, German Protestant milieu that had shaped Schaff.

In turns a socialist, agnostic, Bergsonian idealist, Catholic convert, and dedicated political reactionary before finding his way on a path toward becoming a highly decorated philosopher in the Thomistic tradition, Maritain indeed cut a vocational and intellectual trajectory quite at odds from that of Schaff. Their myriad differences notwithstanding, what finally fascinates, though, are the structural similarities in their encounter with the United States. Here, differences take a back seat to affinities—in their estimation of American church–state arrangements, in their views on the commendable character of

American democracy and religious freedom, and, not least, in their critical assessment of high-brow European disapprobation of the United States.

Their similar assessments were arrived at, paradoxically, both despite and because of their respective Old World milieus. Both overcame certain prevalent biases about the New World and "Americanism," even as they fruitfully brought insights from their scholarly training and European experience to bear on their interpretations of the United States. Put differently: although Schaff and Maritain were separated linguistically and culturally by the Rhine, confessionally by the sixteenth-century Church split, historically by life spans occupying separate centuries, their sojourns across the Atlantic and reflections on the *novus ordo seclorum* that they discovered there, finally, brings them into a striking intellectual kinship, the contours of which invite fruitful inquiry from the student of modern religious thought and transatlantic history.

Who, then, was Jacques Maritain? What was the nature of his early cultural setting, especially vis-à-vis French attitudes toward the United States? And what brought him across the Atlantic?

America, the French Prism, and the Young Maritain

The French, to be sure, have been especially fervent and prodigious explainers of the United States. From Crèvecoeur and Chateaubriand long ago to Jean Baudrillard and Bernard-Henri Lévy in more recent times, French thinkers have left lasting guideposts of interpretation, if not always on the actual United States, then on the symbolic "America," that golem of soulless modernity, outpost of religious misfits, and hatchery of cultural mediocrity that, as we have already seen, had become part and parcel of a more general European critical discourse. Of all European nations, as Sophie Meunier has noted, France represents the country that "has always been at the forefront of anti-American animosity."[1]

In chapter three, we glanced at some negative commonplaces about America from the republican–anticlerical standpoint of the late nineteenth century. Here, another cursory glance is warranted, focusing more on the period around the time of the Great War and its aftermath—the time of Maritain's intellectual coming of age. Since the young Maritain vacillated quite extremely in political outlook—from socialism to Catholic royalism and back to the Left again—it is particularly important to consider the fabric of discourse about America at the extremities of the French ideological spectrum. In his mature years, Maritain would distance himself from these extremes, even though he continued to consider himself a Man of the Left in a general sense, eager to sympathize with the elements of socialism that highlighted the plight of the weak and downtrodden in society.[2]

At the beginning of the twentieth century, negative discourse about America in France mirrored broader patterns on the Continent: long-standing traditions of derision and dismissal, typified earlier in the nineteenth century by writers such as Stendhal and Baudelaire, were amplified by fears of America's growing industrial strength and geopolitical influence.[3] One might think that France's alliance with the United States in 1917 would have kindled some warmth and mutual feeling of good will. It did, but only briefly. More significantly, it marked the beginning in France of a sinking, embittered feeling of political, and later economic, dependency on what was widely perceived to be a culturally inferior nation. Far from engendering lasting Franco-American warmth, "the solidarity of 1917–18 would have no future. Vanished as quickly as it had appeared, this euphoric moment would soon seem like an illusory aside . . . [B]rotherhood in the trenches was replaced by a new uncomprehending transatlantic dialogue; it would last until the next war—and beyond it."[4]

The 1920s signify the high-water mark of French anti-Americanism, for both the Right and Left. As was the case in Germany, Woodrow Wilson emerged during this period as a symbol or synecdoche of the nation's soul—a soul tirelessly explained, analyzed, and denounced in myriad political, academic and journalistic outlets. At the Paris Peace Conference (1919), France's Georges Clemenceau quickly honed in on the religious dimension. "Wilson talks like Jesus Christ and acts like Lloyd George," he said and this quip made the rounds at Paris. Indeed, the "preaching president" intent to revise la vieille Europe in his moralistic image elicited from divergent ideological positions a virtually united front of critical and oppositional sentiment.[5]

From the (predominantly Catholic) Right, for whom the papal condemnation of "Americanism" remained a fresh memory, worries were voiced about the young nation's naïve democratic idealism and incomprehension of the Old World and its traditions. In this mood, the leader of *Action Française*, Charles Maurras, penned *Les trois aspects du président Wilson* (1920), characterizing Wilson as a messianic neurotic whose grasp of reality owed more to fanatical Protestant spirituality than to any genuine abilities of statesmanship. (Incidentally, this book's publication coincided with the writing of Sigmund Freud's *Thomas Woodrow Wilson: A Psychological Study*, in which the Austrian psychologist wrote that Wilson's idealism derived from "having been born in a nation which was protected from reality during the nineteenth century by inherited devotion to the ideals of Wycliffe, Calvin, and Wesley.")[6] Other figures on the Right continued to remind France of the "machine" character and spiritual nullity of America's liberal, market-driven civilization. "The monstrous alliance of speculation and machines" wafting across the Atlantic, wrote the Catholic novelist and polemicist Georges Bernanos, was undoing the "European spirit" and deserved comparison to the "invasions of Genghis Khan or Tamburlaine."[7] Such over-the-top traditionalist criticisms were not infrequent at this time.

The Left indulged in its own vituperation during the interwar years. Much of the nineteenth-century socialist literature on America, as we have seen, presented the youthful land as one of significant promise, but somehow deficient or incapacitated—too immense and immature for "appropriate" class conflict, too gullible and obscurantist for secular-critical thought. The motif of deficiency continued apace during the interwar years, but a heightened sense of fear and loathing regularly accompanied it at this time—a reaction, no doubt, to the postwar influence of the United States in Europe. Portraying America as a plutocratic dystopia of big business, trusts, and outlandish luxury, socialist critics were keen to interpret the United States as an example of a dubious or abnormal historical development, a colossal impropriety. Robert Aron's and Arnaud Dandieu's widely read *Le cancer américain* (1931), for instance, portrayed the United States as an "artificial and morbid organism" and a massive "spiritual aberration" (*aberration du spirituel*) in Western civilization, but one which, because of postwar conditions, was poised to spread its malignancy throughout Europe.[8] Numerous other works took a similar tack, either calling for heroic resistance to the "American model" or, in a wistful key, bewailing the fact that the technocratic, capitalist barbarians had already overrun the gate.

Religious issues were always present in the postwar discourse, and this topic, more than any other perhaps, illustrates the open back door between hard-Right and hard-Left positions. For French conservatives, the United States presented the spectacle of a "religious madhouse (*foire aux religions*)," as Émile Barbier had earlier opined, "a carnivalesque mixture of churches and chapels, in which the most unutterable elite of frauds and hotheads throng.... [Religious] crooks trading in illicit divinities; puppet reverends spouting pitches talk to attract loiterers in their holy shacks."[9] Such assessments never stood too far from Catholicism's longstanding critique of Protestantism, especially in its American forms. After attending a service at Washington's National Cathedral to mark the inauguration of Franklin Delano Roosevelt in 1933, the French poet and diplomat Paul Claudel (1868–1955) registered in his diary his "profound disgust" of the American Protestant character. It was all so much "nauseating humbug and hypocrisy," he wrote; "to explain the emptiness, dryness, pride, and intellectual destitution (*misère intellectuelle*) of the Protestant character and spirit, one must take part in one of these services, which open a window onto the spiritual life of all these poor souls."[10]

For the Left, America remained simply far too religious, especially if one's benchmark was the ethos behind the 1905 French laws of church–state separation or, as was sometimes even the ideal among anticlerical socialists, the aggressive anti-religious policies of the Soviet Union.[11] Despite the enlightened efforts of the American founding fathers to create a secular republic, Urbain Gohier (whom we have already encountered) complained, religion remained "everywhere in the American republic." "Everyone is able to have their own religion or found a new religion." What is more, the forms of religion that existed were infected with the spirit of capitalism: "In this land of *business*, a church is created and organized just like any other [business] enterprise."[12] Since variations on this latter line of attack often came from conservative pens as well, Roger describes "a division of the accusatory labor: clericals were indignant over unsavory American religion, while anticlericals denounced the myth of a republic that purported to be secular but where everything was done with one hand on the Bible or with the Bible in hand." One may even observe a shared "cultural hostility," which drew its strength from "the confluence of two great traditions [in France], spiritualist and secular, usually disinclined to joining ranks, but exceptionally allied against a philistine and pharisaical America."[13]

To be sure, cultural hostility might mean different things for the Left and Right, but for both it entailed the charge that Americans lacked profundity and American society displayed a derisible anti-intellectualism. Émile Boutmy's *Éléments d'une psychologie politique du peuple américain* (first printed in 1902, but several times thereafter) provides a revealing example of how this charge might involve an interpretation of American religious life. Following in the footsteps of Tocqueville and Max Weber, Boutmy placed great emphasis on the religious, particularly the Puritan, foundations of American society: "religion and the church [has] made the Yankee what he is." The religious element had undergone many permutations over time, he felt, and what remained bore little resemblance to the fire and brimstone of the days of Cotton Mather and Jonathan Edwards. Even so, superficial, watered-down forms of Christianity—a religion "without elevation or force"—maintained a worrisomely tenacious hold on the American imagination.[14] What accounted for this, Boutmy asked?

The answer, he felt, lay in Americans' deep-seated hostility to the life of the mind. Absent their own classical and Renaissance patrimony, absent a plethora of universities and scientific academies in the European tradition, "only Christianity was available to them" as a cultural building block. And even this usually came in shallow and ungainly forms—a Christianity "without generosity or bouquet." But, alas, these forms passed muster with the Americans, even if their acceptance spelled a steady stifling of the life of the mind. In America, he wrote, "no credit is given, as in Europe, to the superior mind that creates original ideas and tries to make them prevail." Boutmy even came up with his own Latinate neologisms to lend legitimacy to his investigations: "the *misonovism* or *phobonovism* of these half-enlightened men," i.e., Americans' religiously-induced fear of critical thought and original ideas. The people of the United States, in other words, had chosen superannuated attachment to the sacred as a substitute for innovative inquiry. Piety had rebuffed thought.[15]

Americans' spiritual and cultural shortcomings became the subject of many other essays and books during this era. But perhaps none were as influential as Georges Duhamel's literary sensation, *Scènes de la vie future* (1928), an alarmist tract that left no stone unturned in derogating American society and warning against its metastasizing influence in Europe. America for Duhamel was the site of a "devouring civilization," made up of "soulless machines for a crowd whose own soul seems to be disappearing." The American cityscape appeared as "a hell that lacks a Dante." Little in the New World seemed "to incline one to thoughts of harmony." Lest his readers miss the point: "The adult inhabitant of Western Europe, who is normal and educated, finds himself more at home among the troglodytes of Matmata than he does... in Chicago." Europeans attracted to the world across the Atlantic would do well, then, to examine their conscience for the "taint of America."[16]

And the ink explaining and excoriating America in France continued to flow during the formative decades of Jacques Maritain's intellect. Publications such as Lucien Romier's *Qui sera le maître, Europe ou Amérique?* (1927); Lucien Lehman's *Le grand mirage, U.S.A.* (1929); Aron and Dandieu's previously-discussed *Le cancer américain* (1931); André Maurois's *En Amérique* (1931); and Bertrand de Jouvenal's *La crise du capitalisme américain* (1933), among many others, created a formidable stockpile of anti-American images, phrases, and habits of thought that, despite the countervailing sentiments of a few notable dissenters, became fixtures within the general social imaginary of the French intelligentsia. Although it has much deeper historical roots, in a relatively short period, Roger has summed up, "French anti-Americanism produced a decisive reference point: the intellectual Americanophobia of the 1920s and 1930s remains, even now, the unsurpassed crest of French anti-Americanism."[17]

Maritain, Modernity, and a New Humanism

"I left France in January 1940 to give the courses which for several years I had been offering at the Pontifical Institute of Medieval Studies in Toronto and for a series of lectures in the United States. I planned to return to Paris at the end of June, but the tragic events of the month of June and the German stranglehold on my country, prevented me from doing so."[18]

Thus began the long sojourn of Jacques Maritain and his wife Raïssa (née Oumansov), in the United States. He had visited North America for the first time in 1933, the year Hitler came to power. He returned to lecture in 1934 and again in 1938. But 1940 marked a decisive turning point in his life, and one that would significantly affect his political and social thought. Resolved to make the best of a trying situation, he helped establish, with other French and Belgian exiles, the *École libre des hautes études* in New York, later serving as its director.[19]

He also entered upon a lecture circuit that brought him frequently to Princeton, Toronto, Chicago, and the University of Notre Dame. In 1948 he accepted an appointment on the faculty at Princeton.

Maritain lived in the United States until 1960, punctuated by a three-year period as French Ambassador to the Vatican directly after the war. His time in America, it should be underscored, corresponded to the Fascist undoing of Europe and the anxious early years of the Cold War. The decision not to attempt to return to France proved prescient. Because of the content of some his writings, the Gestapo sought Maritain, in vain, at the Institut Catholique in Paris, where he had previously taught. What is more, Raïssa came from a Russian-Jewish background, and a return to France might have proven fatal for her. Abroad in a foreign country, the Maritains sorely missed France and deplored the "abomination" that had left her "wounded, crushed, and unspeakably humiliated."[20]

The early twentieth century in Europe was a difficult time for anyone trying to find their political—indeed their existential—bearings. World War I precipitated a crisis of profound civilizational morale, already anticipated in much fin-de-siècle intellectual disquiet and uncertainty. Before the war, despair in the face of the narrow positivism and naturalism being taught at the Sorbonne had led Jacques and Raïssa to contemplate committing suicide together—a path thankfully obviated by their conversion to Catholicism and discovery of the philosophy of Thomas Aquinas. "I would have accepted a sad life, but not one that was absurd," wrote Raïssa, summing up the mood of the young couple prior to conversion. A decisive way station en route to Catholicism was the idealist philosophy of Henri Bergson, whose lectures the couple attended at the Collège de France at the invitation of their friend, Charles Péguy. It was the influence of another figure though, Léon Bloy, who finally escorted the young couple to the doors of the Catholic Church. "The only tragedy in life is not to become a saint," Bloy had impressed upon them. They dedicated their lives to the implications of this sentence.[21]

But the desire for saintliness did not immediately translate into political perspicacity. Having declared himself a socialist as a teenager, after his conversion Maritain swung sharply to the right, becoming involved with the nationalist, authoritarian movement, *Action Française*.[22] For a period, he was even considered by some to be the movement's leading philosopher. With the arch-conservative Charles Maurras (1868–1952),

Maritain helped fund, write for, and edit *La revue universelle*, which sought to convey the ideas of the movement to a broader audience. In one of Maritain's first books, *Antimoderne* (1922), he vehemently denounced the evils of "liberalism, *Americanism* [and] modernism."[23] In his subsequent *Three Reformers: Luther, Descartes, Rousseau* (1925), making appeal to a fairly common Catholic polemical narrative, he traced practically all of the ills of modern society to the Protestant Reformation, "that immense disaster for humanity."[24] Had Maritain turned his attention to the United States at this point, negative commonplaces about religious "indifferentism" and an assessment of the new land as ridden with Protestant subjectivism and individualism would have likely followed.

Maritain's docility before the Catholic Magisterium proved a grace, however, when Pope Pius XI condemned *Action Française* in 1926 as a dangerous, Right-wing movement. Many conservative Catholics in France felt that the Pope had overreacted and sloughed off the condemnation. But not Maritain. He quickly cut his ties to the movement, losing many close friends and erstwhile allies in the process. His decision also provides the essential background for his book, *La primauté du spirituel* (1927), "the primacy of the spiritual" or, in its equally provocative English title, *The Things that are Not Caesar's*. This was Maritain's first foray into what we might consider political philosophy and its theme—that the spiritual life must always takes precedence over one's attachments to any temporal order—remained a fixture of his general outlook. Christianity, in other words, ought never to be instrumentalized to achieve purely political ends, as he felt had become the case with *Action Française*. Rather, faith must occupy a suprapolitical zone and concern itself primarily with matters of spirit. When it touched the temporal order, it ought to do so as an "indirect power" (*potestas indirecta*); for only in this way can it rightly serve as a reforming leaven, conveying the Christian Gospel's message of hope, love, and human dignity.[25]

At the time of the book's publication, Europe's descent into a political nightmare was well underway. The Bolshevik Revolution had taken place in 1917 and the growing Communist Left in Western European countries now had an external pole of inspiration in the Soviet Union.[26] The Soviet state's official commitment to atheism (a political *novum* in human history) and rhetoric of world revolution helps explain why many Catholics in Europe felt that Far-Right movements represented the lesser evil and therefore tacked (far too closely in hind-sight) toward this Scylla to avoid the clutches of the Communist Charybdis. The stock market collapse of 1929 and subsequent Depression cast a further pall over the democracies of Western Europe, creating a highly confusing and polarized political atmosphere, in which the ranks of the Far Left swelled while royalists and clericals embarked on uneasy alliances with new fascist and racist forces. As we have seen, the period also witnessed a surging anti-Americanism: the political demons of Europe found not only one another, but the United States a desirable scapegoat to shore up political legitimation.

In this political climate, Maritain penned an enduring masterpiece of political and social philosophy, *Integral Humanism* (1936), the spirit of which suffuses many of his subsequent writings and is indispensable for understanding his later reflections on the United States.

Published a decade after he had left *Action Française* and three years after Hitler's assent to power, the book in some respects represents a shift back to the Left. He expressed admiration for the "great *élan*" of socialism and praised its "noble work to institute the trial of capitalist civilization." Selectively quoted, the book could—and did—provide strong support for anti-American voices who saw the United States as the site of bourgeois contamination par excellence. "And what is this man of sin?," Maritain wrote; "It is petit-bourgeois man,... [a] decadent product born of the Puritan...and the rationalist spirit." For genuine human flourishing to take place, for "integral humanism" to be achieved, bourgeois man would have to be "liquidated"—an infelicitous choice of words in the 1930s!—to make way for a higher, more virtuous form of human personality and society.[27]

But if *Integral Humanism* contains numerous leftist commonplaces from the era, it also represents decisive new ground in Maritain's thought, in his wrestling with and attempting to overcome Europe's political extremities that had led to rival totalitarian forces. It also marks his first major effort to apply the teachings of Thomas Aquinas to a theory of democracy and religious pluralism.[28] Finally, continuing themes from *La primauté du spirituel* (1927), Maritain explored, as the book's subtitle has it, "temporal and spiritual problems of a new Christendom (*nouvelle chrétienté*)," making the case that the Christian account of human nature and human flourishing possessed enduring relevance for modern secular democratic civilization. Combined with the unexpected turn of events that exiled him to America in 1940, the lines of argument advanced in *Integral Humanism* established in Maritain a mode of thinking about religion and politics that predisposed him to esteem the United States and its religious freedoms—even to the point of suggesting that America approximated his ideal of an "integral humanism" more closely than any other temporal order. That his reflections took place in the shadow of the Vatican's longstanding misgivings about religious freedom and its condemnation of "Americanism," and that his views in fact helped pave the way for the Second Vatican Council's epochal endorsement of religious liberty, renders Maritain's achievement all the more noteworthy.

But what did Maritain in fact mean by terms such as "integral humanism" and "new Christendom"? In his reading of history since the time of the Renaissance, greater focus on the *human* as a moral, intelligent agent bearing innate dignity and rights represented a development of capital significance and one profoundly tied to the Judeo–Christian conception of human beings as bearers of the image of God, *imago Dei*. Maritain esteemed this historical development as both providential and progressive. The "tragedy of humanism" in the modern era, however, lay in the fact that humanism's emancipatory aspirations had become separated from their original theological moorings. Consequently, many people, often with the best intentions, had come to champion a purely "anthropocentric humanism," which reduced human horizons to a closed immanent domain. Both anticlerical thinkers from the Enlightenment onward and ignoble elements of Christianity in the *Ancien Régime* bore the blame for this tragedy. As Maritain expressed it, "Historical processes which were in themselves normal and providential and which demanded development in a Christian sense, were in the course of the modern age, and through the fault of both Christians and their adversaries, thus forestalled, masked, and warped by anti-Christian forces."[29] The tragedy lay in the amnesia that this situation induced about the full historical significance and moral scope of modern humanism: "Western humanism has religious and transcendent sources without which it is incomprehensible to itself."[30]

The task of Christian social thought in the present, Maritain held, was to reintegrate humanism with its discarded theological moorings. The resulting "integral" or "theocentric" humanism would not constrict itself to an immanent plane, but would restore the transcendent to human life, and "reground" the worth of every person in the *imago*

Dei. Accomplishing this meant both a positive embrace of the best intentions of modern (immanent) humanism while removing the accretions of anti-religious bias: "Christian thought will have to integrate truths discerned or surmised in the effort for social emancipation carried out during the whole of modern times, and yet purify them from the anti-Christian errors derived from the milieu in which they were born."[31] What is more, it must entail regarding politics as a fundamentally moral enterprise, whereby human beings do not serve the end of politics, but the purpose of politics serves the higher purposes of the human being. Put differently, integral humanism implied "the end of Machiavellianism," the title of his celebrated 1942 essay; that is, the end of seeing politics as an amoral phenomenon, even when, perhaps especially when, done in the name of a higher good.[32]

Integral Humanism excoriates both Fascism and Communism for carrying a Machiavellian logic to its extreme, dehumanizing ends. While very different historical phenomena, Maritain felt both similarly denigrated human beings by inordinately magnifying the scope and purpose of politics.[33] He labeled them "pseudo-realisms," since both made, or assumed, certain "realistic" epistemological claims about human nature and history, while denying what Maritain felt constituted the most fundamental human truth, creational dignity of the person in the image of God. What is more, the two pseudo-realisms were engaged in a perverse dialectical struggle, arousing fears and emotional intensity in the other.[34]

For an integral or theocentric humanism to flourish against the Machiavellianism(s) of an immanent humanism, the entire political order required reenvisioning. A purely private-interest "bourgeois" liberalism, as has already been suggested, was simply not up to the task; it led to a disaggregating individualism and soulless libertarianism all too easily. Maritain called, therefore, for a "new Christendom" to guide Europe into the future and supplant the political malignancies of the day. The continuities and discontinuities of Maritain's proposal with the older medieval notion of Christendom are equally striking.

The errors and problems of premodern Christendom were numerous and Maritain welcomed its expiration. Among its principal errors was a "theocratic imperialism," the conflation of the kingdom of God with the kingdom of this world. Maritain felt that this squarely contravened Christ's words that "My Kingdom is not of this world." But since the time of Charlemagne, up through the reigns of Charles V and

Philip II, and coming to full flower in the notion of the "divine right of kings" in the seventeenth and eighteenth centuries, this theocratic impulse—the inordinate sacralizing of the *imperium*—had been the "tempting angel" of the premodern world, often having "monstrous" consequences. It had been checked at various points by the counter-assertion of ecclesiastical privilege (one thinks of the symbolic importance of Pope Gregory VII and Emperor Henry IV at Canossa, for example), but never entirely vanquished. The intellectual underpinnings of this reality might have expired with the coming of political modernity, but it tragically lived on in some respects in the quasi-divine role assigned to the state in Jacobinism, Bonapartism, and Hegelian philosophy. Insofar as Karl Marx inherited Hegel's statism, Maritain felt justified in giving Communism the paradoxical label of an "atheist theocratic imperialism."[35]

But Christendom was not uniformly bad: "it has borne its fruit."[36] Some elements Maritain desired to retrieve for a *nouvelle chrétienté*. In the realm of politics, it had achieved in its better moments a form of checks and balances between the powers of the *imperium* and the *sacerdotum*, in which neither was able to dominate society completely. This gave rise to myriad forms of local autonomy, identity, and community, where human flourishing could take place. What is more, in the realm of thought the achievement of scholasticism in general and Thomas Aquinas in particular were inseparable from the intellectual assumptions of Christendom, especially in scholasticism's universalizing aspirations to affirm natural law and human dignity. In scholastic thought, "a person is a universe of spiritual nature endowed with freedom of choice and constituting to this extent a whole which is independent in the face of the world—neither nature nor the State can prey upon this universe without its permission." Even God himself must respect this freedom, Maritain insisted, following Aquinas.[37] Such a lofty view of the human person had been extinguished under twentieth-century extremist ideologies. In Fascism, the human had devolved into an intelligent biological organism alone, which the state could mold to its "higher" uses. In Communism, the individual must submit to the collective and to the "inexorable laws of history." In both forms of totalitarianism, the freedom and spiritual dignity of the person qua person had suffocated under an ideology of statist monism. But this freedom and dignity—what Maritain calls "a common theoretic minimum" for a new Christendom—were capable of extensive expansion in a milieu of democracy, human rights, and religious freedom.[38] Indeed, the modern liberal age constituted the natural field of implementation of ideas about the person, put forth (often in rarified form) in scholastic thought, but left largely unrealized in the indigent and highly stratified society of the Middle Ages.

When Maritain speaks of a new Christendom, therefore, he emphatically does *not* have in mind the customary theocratic and coercive tendencies often associated with the term today. Instead, he means a common, supranational insistence on the freedom and dignity of the person qua person. But this was not something that could be arrived at and sustained in the abstract. It had specific (Judeo–)Christian-theological beginning points and apart from some ongoing sustenance from these roots, it could quite easily devolve into mere "bourgeois individualism," a shortsighted exchange of one's spiritual freedom and dignity for the petty porridge of pleasures, profits, and property. Even so, this "bourgeois temptation," as we might call it, must remain a "live" possibility if a loftier personalist humanism was to be achieved, for seeking to extirpate it completely—the route of totalitarianism—offered a cure worse than the disease, achieving a coerced unity about the ends of human life, but at the expense of genuine freedom.[39]

In short, then, Maritain's ideal of a *nouvelle chrétienté* significantly overlapped with modern liberalism generally, but a liberalism mindful of the theological bases of human dignity, wary of descent into libertine individualism, and rejecting both the theocratic impulses of the past and state monisms of the present. Several additional elements should also be mentioned. First, politics must unambiguously renounce coercion of conscience and accept religious pluralism: a *nouvelle chrétienté* "allows among its characteristic traits a pluralism that renders possible the convivium of Christians and non-Christians in the temporal realm."[40] Second, it should accept democracy as a vital expression of human freedom, not a negative "impersonal freedom," which he often associated with Rousseau, but one which gave rise to—and here he closely followed the Catholic social encyclicals since *Rerum Novarum* (1891)—a rich matrix of "social institutions and social bodies."[41] Third, in opposition to Marx and Lenin, Maritain does not gainsay private property and private interest: "The problem is not to suppress private interest, but to purify it and to ennoble it," to encourage through the agency of the Church and other social institutions, a sense of stewardship and fraternal obligation and discourage a purely acquisitive individualism—even if, again, the latter might remain a possible, if regrettable, outcome in a situation of "real existing" freedom.

Finally, Maritain's *nouvelle chrétienté* entailed a progressive view of history, not one of declension. Nostalgia for the "world we have lost" and a cultural pessimism about one's moment in history were not responsible options. "Authentic Christianity abhors the pessimism of inertia," he wrote. "It is pessimistic... in the sense that it knows that the creature comes from nothingness....But its optimism is incomparably more profound than its pessimism, because it knows that the creature comes from God, and that everything that comes from God tends toward God. A truly Christian humanism [holds that]...man is still a nocturnal sketch of himself, and that before attaining to his true lineaments...will have to pass through many moltings and renewals."[42]

In theological parlance, Maritain's "Thomistic" optimism about the original, irrepressible goodness of the created order takes precedent over an "Augustinian" insistence on the ubiquity of human concupiscence and the presence of evil in the world. But Augustine's point is not sloughed off. As Maritain memorably put it in his lectures on the philosophy of history, "The devil hangs like a vampire on the side of history. History goes on nonetheless, and goes on *with the vampire*."[43] Noble human achievement is possible, in other words, but the upending capacity of evil remains ever-present. Even so, in the modern world, "a new historical sky" had manifested itself, beckoning the realization of dynamically Christian potentialities in the democratic, secular political sphere.

Maritain recognized that his views were vulnerable to criticism. From the standpoint of the Catholic hierarchy, he pushed the limits of acceptable social thought in his robust embrace of democracy and religious freedom. He handled this delicately by insisting that his starting-off point was none other than the Angelic Doctor himself, Thomas Aquinas, whose thought had regained ascendancy in official Catholic teaching from the time of Leo XIII's encyclical *Aeterni Patris* (1879).[44] With respect to religious freedom and Catholic teaching, Maritain obliquely noted that "many misunderstandings arose in the time of Gregory XVI and Pius IX," in which timeless Christian truths were thought to be bound up with "a decaying temporal order."[45] But this did not placate all critics; Maritain found himself under attack in the pages of the *Civiltà Cattolica* and by the influential Argentinean priest Julio Meinvielle, whose *De Lamennais à Maritain* (1945) argued that the nineteenth-century condemnations of Lamennais' views ought to apply to Maritain's as well.[46]

Maritain was sensitive, too, to the charge that his ideas, in a time of political turmoil, amounted to the utopian musings of someone who too infrequently left his study. This charge has some teeth, insofar as many questions about the practical outworkings of his ideas were not sufficiently addressed. What is more, more than a few commentators have noted that, despite his emphasis on the limitations of the political and the "primacy of the spiritual," the actualization of the ideas presented in *Integral Humanism*, would, in fact, demand quite a lot from politics and would have to assume—against the grain of much twentieth-century experience—that human beings' better angels would rise to the occasion. Maritain sought to parry these charges by insisting that his proposal was not a "utopia," but a "concrete historical ideal," something that did not exist, but which, under favorable conditions, "is realizable—with more or less difficulty, more or less imperfection." Put differently, he offered a "rough sketch," a political blueprint "corresponding to a *relative* maximum of social and political perfection," which might vary considerably according to the actual conditions of possibility presented by any given "historical climate."[47]

Novus Ordo Seclorum and the Angelic Doctor

As Maritain became more familiar with American society after 1940, he arrived at the opinion, often to his surprise, that the United States suggestively embodied many of the ideals that he had sketched in *Integral Humanism*. Shortcomings aplenty existed in the *novus ordo seclorum*, to be sure, but the promise of what his kindred spirit, the Jesuit John Courtney Murray (1904–67), called the "American Proposition" ought to allay excessive misgivings. Accordingly, Europe's intellectual classes and reactionary elements within the Catholic Church should reconsider their assumptions about the land of "creative vigor."[48] His *Reflections on America* (1958), based on a seminar held at the University of Chicago in 1956, casts the United States in a particularly favorable light. But this work does not stand alone; his reflections in it are complemented by others in *Scholasticism and Politics* (1940), *The Rights of*

Man and Natural Law (1942), *Christianity and Democracy* (1943), *Man and the State* (1951) and *On the Philosophy of History* (1957), not to mention a few shorter essays. The composite picture of America that emerges in these works, not least with respect to the relationship of religion and the political order, offered a forceful riposte to anti-American sentiment in Europe, even as it subtly invited the Catholic Church to develop a more nuanced understanding of democracy and religious freedom.

In considering these work, however, one is confronted with an interpretative problem, especially when read in light of Maritain's criticism of "bourgeois liberalism" as expressed in *Integral Humanism*. Was not the United States, after all, the land of bourgeois liberalism par excellence among Western nations, at least in numerous Marxist interpretations? Can Maritain have it both ways—condemning bourgeois liberalism, on the one hand, but singing America's praises on the other?

The latter question has divided commentators. Some have been inclined to see Maritain, finally, as a political naïf, attested to by his youthful ideological swings and by the seeming contradiction between his anti-bourgeois sentiment and high esteem for the United States. Others have suggested that *Reflections on America* represents an anomalous work, a partial lapse in judgment, and that the "real" Maritain remained deeply anti-capitalist and anti-bourgeois, and, ipso facto, *should* have been far more critical of the United States. An element of plausibility lies in both interpretations, even as both miss the mark. I would suggest instead that his valuation of the United States represents the triumph of experience over theory, in that once residing in America Maritain gradually came to hold that many European (especially socialist and reactionary) categories of analysis simply did not apply to the United States; the two continents' historical configurations and experience of religion and modernity diverged too profoundly. What is more, Maritain's reflections bear witness to a deepening Thomistic sensibility on his part, assisted by the historical exigencies of the moment. As Ralph McInerny has written, a chief Thomistic "technique" of Maritain's was his effort to seek out the "lurking positive" in things. With Europe in the throes of destruction, finding himself abroad in land of relative stability and consensus about politics and society, Maritain attuned his mental faculties to understanding the conditions of his new home with a desire to bear witness to the "lurking positive" within them.[49] He received an assist in this endeavor by other leading Catholic intellectual exiles, such as Yves Simon (1903–61), and by the aforementioned American Jesuit, John Courtney Murray.[50] In the final analysis then, Maritain's Thomistic inclinations and his own war-time experience in America gained ascendancy in his thought over lingering socialist categories, even as the latter admittedly persisted, sometimes yielding insight, but sometimes dangling as exhausted holdovers.

In 1940, Maritain published *Scholasticism and Politics*. It is a testimony to the Catholic milieu prior to the Second Vatican Council that he insisted the word "democracy" not appear in the title, as his editors had wanted. The essays comprising the volume were originally prepared for American audiences during a lecture tour in 1938, as the political storm clouds gathered in Europe. A foreboding sense of crisis strikes the reader immediately, even as Maritain recognized that the afflictions of Europe were not necessarily those of the United States: "The dangers imperiling civilization and threatening an overwhelming crisis, due to the errors which weigh upon modern history, appear to concern Europe more immediately than the New Continent. It may be that, in America, there is still time for mankind to eliminate these errors by a creative effort of intelligence and liberty."[51]

In the book's centerpiece essay "Democracy and Authority," Maritain distinguished between an "anarchic democracy" or a "democracy of the individual," on the one hand, and a true or "organic democracy," on the other. The logic of the former, preeminently theorized and advocated by Rousseau, constituted for Maritain one of the most problematic developments of modern times—and one that had regrettably sullied the idea of democracy in the eyes of the Church. It offered a recipe for unprincipled majoritarianism, a democracy of "Number and not of reason and justice," and one that produced in citizens "a mental disposition to dislike any hierarchy." By encouraging each individual to live maximally free of all others, moreover, it attenuated the need for intermediary social institutions and shared, suprapolitical moral norms, and thus prepared conditions for a "centralized state"—based on power alone (*potestas*), not legitimate authority (*auctoritas*)—to expand its scope indefinitely as a well-intentioned prophylactic against injustice and anarchy. Democracies of the type, he concluded, "tend to engender their contrary, the totalitarian state," and the "old continent," he felt, was being swept along by such a fateful development.[52]

But fortunately this did not constitute the final word on democracy. Against this understanding, Maritain proposed another, in which law was mediated through the people, but its ultimately authority rested on natural law and a yet deeper sense of "transcendence" that, he felt, necessarily served as the guarantor of natural law. Belief in the capacity of all persons (as reflections of the *imago Dei*), and not just certain moral virtuosi, to seek out and live by this "higher" law constituted, according to Maritain, the ultimate basis of the democratic idea. "At the origin of the democratic sense," as he put it, "there is not the desire to 'obey only oneself,'" but rather the belief that all people have the potential in freedom "[to] desire to obey only whatever it is just to obey." Accordingly, justice cannot simply mean the will of the majority, inscribed into positive law at a particular point, and then enforced by the coercive powers of the state. This amounted to a form of tyranny. "Organic democracy," by contrast, "holds that an unjust law [however popular] lacks foundation in authority and hence does not oblige man in conscience." True justice requires genuine authority, not power alone, and such authority rested, finally, on supratemporal and ultimately theological forms of legitimation: "[A]ll authority derives from God as from a primordial source. An organic democracy will not commit the folly of rejecting this idea. It needs it more than any other regime. Even if, invoked in the name of the most elementary natural philosophy, and one least tinged with theology, it would in any case agree regarding this subject with an essential theme of Christian philosophy and theology."[53]

Maritain does not aver that the United States—with its founding-era appeals to "the laws of Nature and Nature's God"—purely embodied this second form of democracy, but he does indicate that the fallacy of Rousseau constituted more a European than an American burden. In his beloved France, he rued the historical legacy of eighteenth-century absolutism, revolutionary Jacobinism, and the "morbid" political theory of Rousseau. "In the Democracy of the United States," he opined, "I believe that the ideology of the eighteenth century and of Rousseau also plays a certain role, but much less than in France," surmising further that "when America criticizes herself" it has less to do with "the political structure of her democracy than with the practice of politicians."[54]

As fears spread and war gripped the Continent in the 1940s, the United States took on a yet brighter visage in the eyes of Maritain. He became particularly intrigued by the enduringly religious sense that pervaded American society, even if it often appeared to him in "diffuse and diluted" forms. Without a reservoir of spiritual vitality and moral idealism from the American people, he felt, the political demons of Europe would remain perched in their high places. A sense of gratitude for safe refuge also began to ease the Maritains' initial feelings of dislocation and homesickness. As Raïssa expressed in her memoir: "All of us who in exile have had the privilege of the large hospitality of this free country, who have known and loved its spirit... are overwhelmed with enthusiasm and gratitude."[55] In a letter to the radical social reformer Saul Alinsky (1909–72), Maritain esteemed the "soul" and "hopes" of America, "that great human dream which is permeated by the Gospel infinitely more than the Americans themselves believe."[56] Supported by the American government, Maritain took an active role in the Resistance, writing a number of essays that were clandestinely distributed in France and giving several radio messages on the "Voice of America."[57]

During the war, Maritain published two short works of political philosophy, *The Rights of Man and Natural Law* (1942) and *Christianity and Democracy* (1943). Both reflect his growing appreciation of the United States, and both made the case that without "higher" moral and religious foundations genuine democracy and freedom cannot flourish. Reminiscent of the language of Winston Churchill at times, Maritain also presented the choice facing Western democracies in stark, uncompromising terms. The future, he wrote, "will be shaped either by the totalitarian spirit or by the Christian spirit."[58] While some have dismissed such language as simplistic moralizing, beneath a philosopher of his stature, one must remember that at the time of his writing—1941 and 1942—victory over Hitler was by no means a forgone conclusion, and the looming presence of the Soviet Red Army in the East added a dark shadow to an already ominous landscape.[59] Maritain felt compelled, in other words, to identify what spiritual and intellectual forces he felt possessed the vigor to check the Machiavellian imperative animating both totalitarianisms. And as *Integral Humanism* had stipulated, liberalism alone, resting on purely Rousseauean foundations, was not up to the task and posed a political problem of its own—albeit one less immediately pressing in light of gulags and extermination camps.

Instead, the West required the reassertion of a "vitally Christian society" anchored in a historically deep conception of natural law with inviolable human rights derived therefrom. Again, Maritain did not mean a return to a premodern "Christian state": the attempted "sacral" society of the "absolutist era" had seen its day. An "integral humanism," a "new Christendom," offered instead a "personalist, communal, and pluralist" democracy, but one that did not categorically abjure "an organic link between civil society and religion." "A vitally and truly Christian political society would be Christian," not as a result of a theocratic imperium from on high, Maritain tirelessly qualified, but "by virtue of the very spirit that animates it and that gives shape to its structures."[60] Before it can become a form of government, Maritain elaborated, democracy must first be a "state of mind" or a "philosophy" of human life that accorded infinite "spiritual dignity" to the human person. This assumption, embedded in the Christian intellectual tradition if, sadly, often not practiced by its adherents, constituted the "soul of democracy"; without it, ideals such as equality and freedom would lose their "hidden stimulation."[61]

Knowledge of Thomas Aquinas and Aristotle's political thought, however, made Maritain sensitive to the risks and possible failure of democracy if citizens gave themselves up to a purely appetitive existence or did not develop wisdom commensurate with the task of self-rule. Accordingly, he held that modern democracy needed the "evangelical ferment" not only "to be realized" but "to endure." "The lasting advent of the democratic state of mind and of the democratic philosophy of life," he elaborated, "requires the energies of the Gospel to penetrate secular existence, taming the irrational to reason and...stabiliz[ing] in the depths of the subconscious those reflexes, habits, and virtues without which the intellect, which leads action, fluctuates with the wind and [a] wasting egoism prevails in man."[62] When Maritain speaks of reviving the Christian heritage, it is important to keep in mind that he never means doing this apart from reviving the natural law tradition, which of course long preceded Christian revelation. He sometimes invoked Sophocles' *Antigone* as the archetypal witness of those "unwritten laws"—grounded in "transcendence," "mystery," "Creative Wisdom" itself—higher than the political community and which the political community denies only at its peril. Christianity (at least in a Thomistic framework) never challenged this tradition, and instead made it the centerpiece of its moral philosophy. Grace does not destroy nature, but perfects it: "Only when the Gospel has penetrated to the very depth of human substance will natural law appear in its flower and its perfection."[63]

It was on this subject that Maritain (along with Yves Simon, John Courtney Murray, and a handful of others) began to draw a distinction, in the 1940s and 1950s, between the development of democracy in Continental Europe and that in the United States. Despite its largely Protestant origins and many denominational divisions, the United States in its founding documents accorded better with much older (Catholic, Thomistic) Christian and natural law elements than had been the case in the French Revolution, the more radical phases of which had in fact sought to erase the Christian legacy from cultural memory. Not the deification of human reason nor a history-bound "social contract," but the primacy of natural law and the "sovereignty of God" over the nation-state lay at the core of the "American Proposition," Murray had opined; this "radically distinguishe[d] the conservative Christian tradition of American from the Jacobin laicist tradition of Continental Europe."[64] Highlighting this distinction, figures such as Murray and Maritain held, might allow the Catholic Church to reconsider its past intransigent stances toward democracy and religious freedom; the Continental, anticlerical "religion of laicism," they held, was not an essential ingredient for either, as was often assumed.[65] As late as 1950, Murray groused about the widespread belief prevailing in Rome that "americanism and catholicism are fundamentally in conflict."[66]

What Murray proclaimed loudly in his 1960 landmark book *We Hold These Truths*, Maritain had uttered quietly in his writings in the 1940s.[67] A principal error of the eighteenth-century Enlightenment as a whole, Maritain proposed, resided in the fact that many thinkers severed the transcendental, theological underpinnings of natural law and sought to enumerate various "human rights" strictly on the basis of an immanent conception of human reason. The French *philosophes* and revolutionaries, however, erred in this direction far more egregiously than their American counterparts, he believed. "The French Declaration of the Rights of Man framed these rights in the altogether rationalist point of view of the Enlightenment and Encyclopedists and to that extent enveloped them in ambiguity." The American Declaration of Independence, in his reading, "adhered more closely to the original Christian character of human rights."[68]

The charter of American democracy, therefore, did not entail a sharp conflict between the claims of reason and those of religion, but even implied that one of the first duties of (political) reason was to establish conditions where the unmolested search for and free practice of religious truth could take place. "The very name democracy has a different ring in America and in Europe," he therefore opined. "In America...democracy has penetrated more profoundly into existence, and where it has never lost sight of its Christian origin, this name conjures up a living instinct stronger than the errors of the spirit which prey upon it."[69] Among the principal problems in Europe, he held, echoing Philip Schaff, was an overheated anticlerical and often anti-religious animus among liberals, originating in the first place as an embittered reaction against the unsavory elements of the Church of the *Ancien Régime*, and sustained in the nineteenth century as an opposing pole to the intransigent spirit of the Restoration.

Religious freedom shorn of anticlerical animus, however, approximated for Maritain something close to a universal human ideal. He expressed enthusiastic accord with a line in a speech by Franklin Delano Roosevelt that the "freedom of every person to worship God in his own way everywhere in the world" should be a shared international goal.[70] At the same time, Maritain knew his nineteenth-century papal encyclicals all too well and therefore felt the need, drawing from his American experience, to define religious freedom more precisely. Religious freedom should not mean that everyone follow every capricious whim of thought or belief, mistaking genuine liberty for its antinomian perversion. Rather, freedom constituted an *environment* or *medium* for the scrutiny of conscience and the pursuit of truth; "freedom of investigation and discussion" was among his preferred phrases. If conscience impressed upon one a religious truth, one ought to adhere to that truth. Properly understood, therefore, religious freedom only meant that the political community—the realm of Caesar—cannot coerce conscience, whether by law or force. Among the first democratic rights, as Maritain expressed it, was the right of

the human person to make his way toward his eternal destiny along the path which his conscience has recognized as the path indicated by God. *With respect to God and truth*, one has not the right to choose according to his own whim any path whatsoever, he must choose the true path, in so far as it is in his power to know it. *But with respect to the State, to the temporal community and to the temporal power*, he is free to choose his religious path at his own risk; his freedom of conscience is a natural, inviolable right.[71]

Framed in this way, Maritain sought to loosen Catholicism's longstanding connection of "religious freedom" to the error of "indifferentism," recognizing the theological concerns associated with the latter, while vigorously promoting the former, indeed grounding it in Christian theology itself. His line of reasoning bore fruit. Maritain is widely credited with helping build momentum toward the Second Vatican Council's epochal Decree on Religious Liberty (*Dignitatis humanae*). "Truth can impose itself on the mind of man only in virtue of its own truth," the Decree proclaims; the high dignity of the human person, known through Scripture and reason, is itself sufficient to ensure "the free exercise of religion in society" and "freedom from coercion" in doing so.[72]

★★★

After a three-year period as French ambassador to the Vatican after World War II, Maritain returned to the United States to teach philosophy at Princeton University. Outside of a handful of seminaries, he felt, there was no place in Europe where a professed Catholic could openly teach the philosophy of Aquinas, and he was thus moved by the generous offer extended to him by Princeton, an historically Presbyterian institution.[73] But it was the University of Chicago that provided him with the opportunity to offer two seasoned reflections, one on political philosophy and the other on the United States. In December of 1949 he gave the prestigious Walgreen Lectures, published in 1951 as *Man and the State*. In November of 1956 he offered a three-day seminar on "America" sponsored by Chicago's Committee on Social Thought; these were published in 1958 as *Reflections on America*.[74]

In the latter work, European elite criticism of the United States is never far from Maritain's mind. When unwarranted, he contravened it; when justified, he sought to present it shorn of more general antipathy toward America; throughout, he spoke in what we might call a transatlantic voice, neither American nor European, but paradoxically both· and neither, and one keen to recognize the "genuinely original" character and "infinite complexity" of his subject. Still, his stance was not dispassionate: his writings exhibit the affection of a former grateful refugee and he argues that the American constitutional order and society presented promising elements of what he sought to articulate theoretically in his own earlier works. He speaks, in fact, of a basic "congeniality" between his social and political ideas and American society, and even goes so far as to suggest that if a *nouvelle chrétienté* "is ever to come about in human history, it is on American soil that it will find its starting point."[75]

For this reason, the hostility against America in his home country and elsewhere in Europe vexed Maritain greatly. What explained the "Grand Slander," as he called it, the "utterly misleading" image of "the Yankee" prevalent across the Atlantic? In part, he felt that it stemmed from wounded pride and feelings of dependency, compounded on the political Left by powerful Marxist currents in Western Europe.[76] In part, it grew simply from the want of perspicacity that comes with the lack of first-hand knowledge; this was the case especially among spiritually or aesthetically sensitive intellectuals, he felt, who had either never crossed the Atlantic or who persisted in seeing the United States through time-worn preconceptions: "many persons endowed with a genuine spirituality may happen to detest and slander America because they don't know her." He offered one humorous example of some Carthusian friends who felt it would be "completely ridiculous" to establish a charterhouse in the spiritually arid climate of the United States—a viewpoint, Maritain felt, that the example of Thomas Merton and the Trappist monks in Kentucky had successfully rebuffed.[77]

In the final analysis, though, anti-Americanism suggested to Maritain a reflexive repugnance on the part of some, the exact origins of which lay shrouded in the murkier regions of the heart. In "the detestation and slander of America, there is a sort of mystical ardor and mysterious meaning," an inexplicable "mystical frustration" that gives birth to a "furious image." Those inclined to this attitude, he designated as "pseudo-spirituals, the false witnesses of the spirit." "Theirs is the absolute and irreducible, the mystic hatred of America." They had helped create a "monstrous America," a "world-wide scapegoat, a symbolic continent great and powerful enough to arouse mankind's hopes, and perverse enough to betray them—the nightmare of *their* America." He sought to counter this image, insisting that the United States, imperfections notwithstanding, occupied a unique position "for the hopes of mankind and the future of civilization." Its religious or spiritual "vocation" and church–state arrangements, in particular, contrasted sharply with those of Europe, and were rightly ascribed with commendable historical and philosophical significance.[78]

That Americans lacked any sense of tradition or history was a refrain among European critics, as we have seen. Maritain did not categorically dispute this charge, but he gave it a more nuanced and positive valuation. For him, an "openness to the future" was a salutary consequence of America's very historical conditions. In Europe, the "rotten stuff of past events, past hatreds, past habits" amounted to an "over-whelming historical heredity," a "sclerosis"; and it was well and good that Americans might be delivered from much of this. The Old World's past was not theirs in a direct sense; it was their "pre-history." By im-plication, Americans might possess an important vantage point to help distinguish the valuable and enduring in Europe's own history, being less constricted by national(ist) attachments, long-standing hostilities, and the state-centralized legacy of Absolutism that, as Tocqueville too had argued, continued on in the French Revolutionary and Bonapar-tist traditions of Europe.[79]

But openness to the future did not mean that Americans had no historical consciousness. Maritain was struck by how the spirit of America's founding era and a "pioneer" ethos continued to penetrate the present. This ongoing sense of a living past, not an exhausted one, and a palpable sense of a future amenable to human initiative, appeared to him to have inoculated Americans from revolutionary ideologies, claiming "historical necessity," that swept the Continent in the first part of the twentieth century. Accordingly, he posited a "root incom-patibility...between the American people and Marxist philosophy." "For Marx," he elaborated,

history is...an immense and terrible set of concatenated necessities, in the bosom of which man slaves toward his final emancipation. When he becomes at last, through communism, master of his own history, then he will drive the chariot of the Juggernaut which had previously crushed him. But for the American people it is quite another story. They are not interested in driving the chariot of the Juggernaut. They have gotten rid of the Juggernaut. It is not in any future messianic freedom of mankind, nor in mastering the neces-sities of history, it is in man's present freedom that they are interested.[80]

One might read this as Maritain's final response European socialists, who had wrung their hands for decades over the ideologically telling question, enshrined in the title of Werner Sombart's famous book of 1906, *Why is there no Socialism in the United States?*

In a chapter on "The Old Tag of American Materialism," Maritain sought to rebut the persistent charge that Americans were a people *peculiarly* given to materialistic pursuits. He did not deny that consum-erist excesses constituted a problem throughout the industrialized world, but he wondered if Americans, at least in some respects, were in fact the least materialistic among the wealthy nations. "[F]ew things," he wrote, "are as sickening as the stock remarks with which so many persons in Europe, who are themselves far from despising the earthly goods of the world, reproach this country with its so-called materialism." This reproach did not derive from empirical evidence, he felt, but drew its strength from an Old World elitist tradition of "confusing spirituality with an aristocratic contempt for any improvement in material life." This elitist or "pseudo-spiritual" critique, however, had exerted such a powerful moralistic appeal, that "you yourselves [Americans] are taken in by it."[81]

To make a countervailing case, Maritain, in the spirit of Tocqueville, pointed to the "infinite swarming" of American charitable organizations, philanthropic foundations, private schools and colleges, and religious societies, which, in size and scope, had no counterpart in modern Europe. The enormous creative energy of the American private sector, both in generating wealth and giving it away, constituted for Maritain an historically unprecedented contribution to human welfare. While he admired the efforts of America's largest foundations—"born of freedom and immune from state control"— he equally praised the voluntarist and giving spirit of average Americans as upholders of "the ancient Greek and Roman idea of the *civis preaclarus*, the dedicated citizen who spends his money [and time] in the service of the common good."[82] This spirit, he believed, was intimately connected to the fact that "this country was born of politico-religious communities whose own autonomous behavior, traditions, and self-government have left an indelible impression on the general mood of the American people."[83]

Maritain also felt the frequent charge that America lacked culture and intellect was unjustified. With others, he voiced concerns about strands of popular anti-intellectualism in American society, which might discourage the population as a whole from esteeming the life of the mind. But a flourishing *vita contemplativa*, he held, was an undeniable reality. He esteemed, in particular, the efforts of those such as Mark van Doren, Robert Hutchins, and Mortimer Adler, who sought to "overcome the dangers of overspecialization" by emphasizing general liberal learning and the "great books" of the past. The work of American philosophers such as Josiah Royce and William James demonstrated "how absurd is the notion...that the American mind has a congenital aversion for abstract ideas, and for sustained and disinterested reflection." In literature, he admired figures such as Emily Dickinson and Herman Melville for their preoccupation with the "beyond and the nameless which haunt our blood." But above all, he regarded the American penchant for open discussion and self-reproof as a marvel for others to behold: "a perpetual process of self-examination and self-criticism" appeared always underway in "every sphere of American life." He even felt that this sometimes went too far, and wondered why many "cultivated" Americans appeared "anxious to have America criticized." "Any writer who bitterly denounces the vices of this country is listened to with special care and sorrowful appreciation. . . . Americans denigrate America with ethical melancholy."[84]

But it was, finally, in the spiritual and religious realm, and especially in the juridical structure of religious life, that Maritain felt America had made a signal contribution to human flourishing—a contribution, again, that accorded well with his own notion of a *nouvelle chrétienté*. It was also in this realm that the New World departed most saliently from the Old, he believed, offering much past (and present) occasion for misapprehension and disaccord.

Maritain attributed great "spiritual importance" to the fact that the United States was not a "typical" nation, defined by ethnicity, religion or language, but a mosaic of immigrants, many forced out of Europe for religious reasons. These so-called "bruised souls" were found in the genealogy of practically all Americans—"people hunted because of their religious convictions, rejected by their national community, or offended and humiliated by distress and poverty." The cultural memory of past suffering coupled with a chance to make good in a New World had deposited "a reminiscence of the Gospel in the inner attitude of people" and a resolve that misery and want need not be the accepted lot of humankind. "Here lies," he elaborated, "a distinctive privilege of this country, and a deep human mystery concealed behind its power and prosperity. The tears and suffering of the persecuted and unfortunate are transmuted into a perpetual effort to improve human destiny and to make life bearable; they are transfigured into optimism and creativity." This "concealed" spiritual identity did not always avail itself to urbane critics of America; it was under the surface, "hidden in the secret life of souls, and covered by all the ordinary selfish desires and concerns of human nature. It exists, however, and is active in the great mass of the nation. And what is more valuable in this poor world than to find a trace of Gospel fraternal love active among men?"[85]

Serving as a repository of Europe's downtrodden and despised had contributed to "the obvious fact" of America's unusual identity. In turn, upholding basic human dignity—a dignity of "the least among us"—constituted, in Maritain's view, America's historic vocation, even if this meant, as in the incipient Civil Rights Movement, an astringent criticism of wanting social *practices* in light of founding-era *principles*.[86] This might not constitute a high calling, understood in gastronomic or aesthetic terms, but rather one at once quotidian and indispensable. Americans might lack many refinements from the standpoint of Paris or Florence, Maritain could admit, but

there is one thing that America knows well and that she teaches as a great and precious lesson to those who come into contact with her amazing adventure: that is the value and dignity of the man of common humanity....In forms so simply human that the pretentious and pedantic are at pains to perceive it, we find [in this country] a spiritual conquest of immeasurable value. The mainspring of American civilization is this dignity of each one in daily existence.[87]

In the context of discussing immigrants in America and human dignity, Maritain makes one of his more perplexing observations, one already alluded to above—namely, that the United States was "principally a middle-class nation," but "not a 'bourgeois' nation."[88] Since it is generally assumed that the two terms denote roughly the same thing, what could Maritain have meant? Unfortunately, he does not elaborate greatly on the distinction, but one might hazard a reasonable conjecture. Usually when he speaks derogatorily of "bourgeois" society, he refers to European society in the nineteenth century. Mandated by history to accumulate capital and exploit labor, at least in *bien-pensant* Marxist interpretations, European middle classes also came into their own in the shadow of centuries-old aristocratic sensibilities, which held up idle leisure as a positive good and social stratification as a historical necessity. Historians of the nineteenth century sometimes speak in shorthand of the "feudalization of the bourgeoisie" to convey how Europe's incipient middle classes often unwittingly aped and transmitted certain aristocratic conventions and attitudes. Lack of a traditional aristocracy, Maritain felt, as Philip Schaff did before him, had produced a different type of middle class in America, one much less imbued with residually aristocratic values and freer to generate its own.

The American middle-class values of particular theological significance, in Maritain's eyes, were the "dignity of work" and a "yearning to make life tolerable" for all people. The latter—a yearning ultimately "evangelical in origin"—helped account for Americans' interest in

finding pragmatic solutions to tedious problems and capacity to manu-
facture inexpensive goods to improve the material circumstances of
life. He had little patience with Europeans who pooh-poohed America's practical ingenuity in the name of putatively "higher" values. "It is
all to easy," he wrote "for certain high-brow Europeans with large
bank accounts and delicious wine in their cellars to make fun of
[American] gadgets . . . . These gadgets serve, in actual fact, to make the
material life less overwhelming for common humanity." All inventions
are not equal, of course, and some contributed little to human flourishing and deserved derision, but those that actually served "the great
mass of the people are of a nature to restore within human beings a
sense of inner freedom at the most elementary level."[89]

But inexpensive goods and practical ingenuity (however commendable) took a back seat to what Maritain regarded as America's signature
contribution to human flourishing: its ideal of religious freedom or
the voluntary nature of faith and practice. He held this to be a salutary
historical novum and, with John Courtney Murray, perhaps the sharpest point of contrast between the United States and Continental
Europe.

Reflecting on the First Amendment in the American Bill of Rights,
Maritain was struck by the pairing of its two clauses: one, the so-called
"Disestablishment Clause," forbidding an established national church;
the other, the "Free-Exercise Clause," not only allowing, but virtually
serving to "sponsor, protect, and favor religious life in general."[90] He
gave voice to the same paradox that had fascinated Tocqueville and
others: the United States evinced secularism only in a very limited
political sense, while also being "the only country in the West in which
society is conceived as being basically a *religious society*." Secularism at
the political level, i.e., the prohibition of an established church, appeared in fact to have inoculated Americans from becoming secular at
the cognitive level. "It is unlikely that, however powerful it may be, the
antagonistic trend toward secularism will ever be able to tear from
American civilization [its] religious inspiration." The founding-era
documents of the United States, while not religious in an overt sense,
were still not denuded of an "age-old heritage of Christian thought
and civilization" and therefore the nation as a whole remained imbued,
willy-nilly, with "an unshakeable religious feeling."[91] Removed from
the European legacy of *cuius regio, eius religio*, this situation accorded
well with his own view that the natural law tradition, properly

developed, upheld freedom from coercion in the pursuit of ultimate verities as a consequence of the creational dignity of the human person.

But how did Maritain, a Catholic, regard America's founding-era Protestantism and the predominantly evangelical spirituality that suffused American society? As we have seen, this reality for other Frenchmen, whether Catholic or secular, caused considerable consternation. The sixteenth-century Church split remained a vexing issue for Maritain, even if he did not quite share the ecumenical enthusiasms of other leading Catholic thinkers of his generation, such as the great Dominican ecumenist Yves Congar (1904–95).[92] Still, Maritain believed that the inscrutable ways of Providence allowed for the derivation of good even from unlikely sources. What is more, his conception of natural law was not static, but dynamic; that is, certain historical developments were capable of deepening and enriching "knowledge of the particular precepts of natural law." Religious freedom was one of these precepts that the pluralistic-sectarian Protestant setting of North America had helped illuminate, for it was "in the historical situation resulting from the very state of religious division engendered by Protestantism that in actual fact the great political achievement brought about by America took place."[93] No doubt, the divisions caused by Protestantism remained a *theological* problem for him, but even as such they had played an indispensable *historical* role in bringing into focus an hitherto under-developed facet of natural law.

To put this somewhat differently: out of the contingent and theologically compromised circumstances of America's founding era, a vital contribution to human flourishing had emerged, and one that the Catholic Church ought to recognize and build upon. Maritain, in fact, believed that American Catholics had an especially important role to play in the future: the opportunity to flesh out from the resources of their own tradition a distinctively Catholic understanding and acceptance of American democracy and religious freedom. As he put it in his lectures on the philosophy of history,

The Catholic Church plays a growing part in American life, and I think that American Catholics are called to a particularly important historic role, if they fully understand their mission, especially their intellectual mission in cooperating in the forward movement of the national community as a whole. Yet the fact remains that in its historical roots, and in the cast of mind of its Founding Fathers, as well as the moral structure of its secular consciousness, America is more of a Protestant than a Catholic country.[94]

In sizing things up in this way, we might say that Maritain's Thomistic impulse to validate the "lurking positive" in things triumphed over more conventionally Catholic anti-Protestant instincts. The "momentous temporal achievement" of American democracy and religious freedom was Protestant largely by historical accident, but much more widely applicable in its moral and political implications. For Thomas Aquinas, the true and the good, however complexly developed and under whatever contingent circumstances that they might appear, remained indefectibly the true and the good, and should be embraced as such irrespective of historical accidents.[95] Maritain's robust embrace of the American experiment, therefore, amounted to an intellectually deft elision of the nineteenth-century encyclicals, and indeed much of the legacy of the Council of Trent, and an artful return to the authority of the Angelic Doctor himself. The road forward for the Catholic Church on religious freedom, in other words, passed through the thirteenth century, not the sixteenth nor the nineteenth. And, indeed, the journey from the *Summa Theologiae* to the First Amendment, from Aquinas to James Madison, was more straightforward than one might have thought.

But in expressing esteem for American religious freedom and the consequent religious vitality of American society, Maritain could not help but notice the contrast with the direction Europe had taken since the French Revolution. The American First Amendment, for example, contrasted strongly in his mind with the 1905 French laws of church–state separation. The former emerged to guarantee peace and freedom of expression among various vital religious communities, while the latter emerged, in part, as an effort to bury, once and for all, religio-political nostalgia for the *Ancien Régime*. In the vociferous atheism and anticlericalism among the French Left in the 1950s, moreover, Maritain saw currents of thought simply not present in the American political bloodstream. Murray had recognized this too, opining in 1960 that the United States "has never known organized militant atheism on the Jacobin, doctrinaire Socialist, or Communist model; it has rejected parties and theories which erect atheism into a political principle."[96] The "unique relationship" in America between "religion, the state, and society," Maritain had noted earlier in *Reflections on America*, "constitutes the sharpest difference between American and European institutions, concepts, and traditions."[97]

During the Cold War, politicians and publicists placed great emphasis on the "Atlantic alliance" and the presumed, underlying political

patrimony of the NATO nations. Some of this reflected genuine realities, even as some testified to the exigencies of the moment—a constructed political unity more than an organic, historical one. For both
political and intellectual reasons, Maritain too desired to see this unity
realized and he knew that it required effort. During the world war, for
example, he called for greater postwar cooperation and understanding
between European countries and the United States, "for the spirit of
Europe and the spirit of America to work together [in the future] in the
common good will."[98] In *Reflections on America*, he expressed hope that
"the Atlantic Ocean [will]...become the great inner lake of Western
civilization, as the Mediterranean Sea was for classical antiquity," and
that through its contact with "the [new] Christian vocation of America," the "old Christian vocation of France" would be reinvigorated for
the challenges of a new historical moment of democracy and
freedom.[99]

But as laudable as these *political* goals might be, Maritain also recognized that formidable *historical* challenges stood in the way. In the
realm of church–state relations and in the religious dynamics of society, he saw various points of significant divergence, as we have
seen. Many of these were perhaps dimmed during the Cold War
milieu by those understandably eager to foster a shared Atlantic
identity. Scholars, equally, played a role, whether in descrying a
common "Western" civilization stretching from Athens to Los
Angeles, or, among social scientists, in presuming that the "secularization" paradigm of modernity might somehow apply equally in
Paris, France and Paris, Texas. But today as the transatlantic cultural
and religious divergences have become more salient, it is of moment
that Maritain, in the early years of the Cold War, offered a prescient
insight. In his Walgreen lectures at the University of Chicago in
1949, he put it as follows:

[A] European who comes to America is struck by the fact that the expression
"separation between Church and State"...does not have the same meaning
here and in Europe. In Europe it means...that complete isolation which
derives from century-old misunderstandings and struggles, and which has
produced most unfortunate results. Here it meant, as a matter of fact, together
with a refusal to grant any privilege to one religious denomination in preference to others and to have a State established religion, a distinction between
the State and the Churches which is compatible with good feeling and mutual
cooperation....[T]here's a historical treasure, the value of which a European

is perhaps more prepared to appreciate, because of his own bitter experiences. Please to God that you keep it carefully, and do not let your concept of separation veer round to the European one.[100]

Too grateful a former refugee? Perhaps. Still, given Maritain's transatlantic breadth, one must reckon with why he saw things the way he did.

6

Conclusion: The Double Helix and the Dialectic

Since [seminaries in America] are not under state control, they have almost no youths who are empty of heart-felt religion or who see the Gospel as a mythological fable and the Church as a cow that supplies them with butter.

—Friedrich Nietzsche, 1865

The [French] Revolution did not accept a Church. Why? Because it was a Church itself.

—Jules Michelet, 1848

On 24 October 1648 in the Westphalian city of Münster, plenipotentiary delegates of the European powers concluded "in the name of the most holy and individual Trinity" the Peace of Westphalia. Since securing "a Christian and Universal peace" among the feuding parties of the Thirty Years War was the goal of the treaty, Münster served as apt site for this to occur, as it had seen its share of religious troubles before. In the 1530s, it had witnessed one of the most violent episodes of the Reformation era. A group of maverick Anabaptists had taken over the city, prophesying the imminence of the Last Days. Their erratic religious spirit so threatened the powers of the day that once the city was retaken, the leaders of this movement were rounded up and—in a scene reminiscent of Dante's *Inferno*—their flesh pulled from their bones by red-hot iron tongs before receiving a dagger to the heart. Their bodies were then raised in cages above St. Lambert's Church—a reminder to all of the dire consequences of disturbing the religio-political order. While their bones were removed several decades later, the cages have remained until the present.

While 1648 marked a watershed in many respects, we should recognize the Peace of Westphalia's limits in preventing discriminating measures against religious minorities. Its famous doctrine—*cuius regio, eius religio*—applied only to the three major Continental confessions: Catholic, Lutheran, and Calvinist. Historians of early modern Europe refer to this age as one of "confessionalization" and are quick to remind the Whiggishly inclined that "Christendom" not only did *not* expeditiously decline from this time, but its underlying logic received powerful, official sanction and continued on in the fragmented territorial or "state churches" of the emergent European nation-states. Presiding over considerably secularized societies, remnants of these state churches, veritable "mini-Christendoms," have endured until the present.[1]

While incremental and episodic steps toward religious toleration took place after 1648, many religious minorities more readily felt the hand of the past and chose emigration over the risk of persecution.[2] As the early experiments in religious pluralism and freedom in North American colonies such as Pennsylvania and Rhode Island were entering the historical stage, the Sun King Louis XIV revoked in 1685 the short-lived Edict of Nantes (1598), prompting Bishop Bossuet to boast that France, "the eldest daughter of the Church," had reverted to being the most "intolérant" state in Europe, setting a model of religio-political propriety for others to follow.[3]

To be sure, the Puritan and Anglican establishments in New England and Virginia replicated the European state-church model. But as confessionalism and established churches held an enduring grip in Europe, the situation on the ground was rapidly changing in North America toward what Philip Schaff later called "a motley sampler of all church history." The emigration-fueled growth of religious pluralism and internal religious splits found in practically all of the colonies—combined with the principled arguments leading toward religious liberty put forth by figures such as William Penn, Roger Williams, and, later, Thomas Jefferson and James Madison—led, in meandering and often inadvertent fashion, to the principles of disestablishment and "free exercise" of religion embodied in the American Constitution's First Amendment.[4] What is more, in contrast to Enlightenment Europe, Mark Noll has noted, strong vitriol against traditional religion of the *écraser-l'infâme* sort was virtually absent in the colonies; in fact, political and intellectual elites were more often preoccupied with the challenge of how "to encourage religion without setting up a European-style church establishment."[5]

On this score, the French Revolution differed as much from the American Revolution as the preceding period of confessional absolutism differed from the experiments in Rhode Island and Pennsylvania. In France, mounting a frontal assault on the church of the *Ancien Régime*, not figuring out a *modus vivendi* with the religious status quo, was the order of the day. To realize this formidable aim, as Tocqueville observed, the French Revolution had to present itself virtually as an alternative religion, a regeneration of humanity under secular auspices—an impulse powerfully continued, as we have seen, in the intellectual projects of figures such as Saint-Simon and Comte, Marx and Durkheim.[6] "Thus in the end, it [the French Revolution] took on the appearance of a religious revolution which so astonished contemporaries. Or, rather, it itself became a new kind of religion."[7] We might even speak of a new *secularist confessionalism* that, as if taking its cue from Bossuet, sought to rigidly demarcate the limits of dissent in the name of a higher state-orchestrated anticlerical, and at times specifically anti-Christian, unity.[8]

Efforts to achieve this higher unity by attempting to break the back of religious opposition to the Revolution in the 1790s represents one of the most momentous periods of cultural discontinuity in modern Western history. A complete catalog of change or *déchristianisation* would include much more, but one should mention here the abolition of contemplative religious orders and the state's confiscation of monastic and other ecclesiastical properties; forcing the clergy to sign an oath of loyalty to the state in the Civil Constitution of the Clergy (1790); the killing of thousands of non-oath-taking priests in the Vendée uprising of 1793; pillaging churches and monasteries throughout France and Europe to finance the revolutionary armies fighting abroad; the abrogation of the Gregorian calendar and attempt to introduce a new one based on revolutionary-era sensibilities; the re-naming of streets and locales from saints' names to figures and ideals of the Revolution; the brief transformation of the venerable Notre Dame cathedral into a "Temple of Reason," dedicated "to philosophy"; and, not least, the abduction and exile of no less than two popes—Pius VI (1798) and Pius VII (1809).[9] Not surprisingly, many of Europe's devout onlookers equated the Revolution, and later its international embodiment in Napoleon Bonaparte, as a sure manifestation of the spirit of the Anti-Christ.[10]

But even as we see the 1790s as period of remarkable cultural discontinuity, we should, again, not overlook the transmuted "confessional" sensibilities, the underlying "political theology" that persisted at this time.[11] As if cribbing from the Catechism of the Council of Trent or the Heidelberg Catechism, devotees of the Revolution wrote and circulated "catechisms" that included such lines as:

Question: What is Baptism?
Answer: It is the regeneration of the French begun on 14 July 1789 and soon supported by the whole French nation.
Question: What is Communion?
Answer: It is the association proposed to all peoples by the French Republic henceforth to form on earth only one family of brothers who no longer recognize or worship any idol or tyrant.[12]

Confessional passions were eerily echoed, too, in the partisan conflicts of this era. Speaking of the civil war in the Vendée region, Michael Burleigh has observed that "this was the first occasion in history when an 'anticlerical' and self-styled 'non-religious' state embarked on a program of mass murder . . . just as capable of unimaginable barbarity as any inspired by religion, eclipsing such limited atrocities as the Inquisition or the Massacre of St. Bartholomew's Day."[13] A major goal of the Revolution, one revolutionary wrote in reference to Robespierre's Rousseau-inspired Cult of the Supreme Being, was to create "the *single universal religion* on the debris of dethroned superstition."[14]

Compelling reasons exist to see the American and French Revolutions as together forming "an age of democratic revolution," as R. R. Palmer influentially argued, but in religious matters, as much of the above suggests, the transatlantic disparities overwhelm the similarities.[15] To highlight the contrast, the political theorist Hugh Heclo has used the arresting image of a double helix to capture what he sees as the specifically American "denouement" in matters pertaining to religion and politics. Quoting him will prepare the way for some concluding reflections:

So in the end . . . there was a denouement to the puzzle of reconciling Christian religion and civil authority. . . . Instead of contraries there was a contrapositioning, not something univocal, but an equivocal coexistence of reciprocal influences. While the Christian gospel was a key long-term force shaping democratic vision, organized Christianity and democracy had had an ambiguous relationship throughout their respective histories. In America, for the first time, Christianity and democratic self-government launched themselves together in a kind of double-stranded helix spiraling through time. Christianity and civil government were both now freed from the old [European] dialectic of yes/no, unity or chaos, and became two maybes, moving together, each affecting the other.[16]

One of the principal arguments of this book might be summarized with the formula that, since the late eighteenth century, European intellectuals' gaze upon America has frequently been tantamount to the occupants of a presumed zero-sum game situation, a yes–no dialectic between organized religion and the forces of modernity, observing the behavior of occupants of the double helix. This latter metaphor, again, seeks to capture the fastidious separation of religion *from* the political order in the new American republic, but, in consequential paradox, its enduring proximity and influence *on* the political order. America's multifarious "sectarian" religiosity has bewildered reactionaries and restorationists in favor of one side of the European dialectic, while the strong "survival" of religion has confounded and disturbed secularists and progressives in favor of the other.

Various and sundry exceptions to this general rule could be offered, and there are doubtless many other constructive, mediating figures— not only beyond Tocqueville, but beyond Philip Schaff and Jacques Maritain as well. Even so, the general formula holds and offers, if not an Archimedean point, at least a wide-lens vantage point that affords insight into the distinctive patterns of religion and political modernity viewed in transatlantic comparative historical perspective.

Again, from the traditionalist or rightist side of the European dialectic, the American double helix appeared as an ill-conceived compromise with liberal, democratic and anti-establishmentarian forces. Indeed, for those defenders of the cultural stability and social cohesion afforded by state churches after the Restoration, the American example of a purely "voluntary" approach to religious matters appeared woefully problematic and blameworthy. As we have seen, figures such as Metternich, Chateaubriand, Joseph de Maistre, Samuel Wilberforce, Charles Dickens, Frances Trollope, Joseph Edmund Jörg, Ferdinand Tönnies, Matthew Arnold, Hilaire Belloc, and numerous others gave voice to this line of critique, reproaching the United States for its wanting religious conditions, the political supports undergirding them, and a concomitant "spiritual" disarray, mediocrity, or uncouthness.

The exact nature of the criticisms varied, but their limited range reflects common concerns. Lacking a religious establishment, many felt, religion became worrisomely decentralized and local, cast to the whims of everyman in a wide-open frontier environment. From this compromised situation, it followed that strange religious enthusiasms— Quakers, Shakers, Mennonites, Jews, Baptists, Methodists, revivals, camp-meetings, itinerant ministers, Unitarians, Mormons, etc.—would multiply and flourish without an official countervailing power to superintend and check them. In this land of "humbug" and "nonsense" (*Unfug*) as one Catholic traditionalist opined, cultural discord and social disharmony were the logical results; fragmentation would beget fragmentation; arbitrariness would feed upon arbitrariness.[17] No longer upheld by the state, religion would become the creature of the unseemly, the vulgar, the market, the mob. Dependent on their congregations for support, the office of the clergy would forfeit respect and esteem. As deference to appropriate authority declined, a shameful "indifferentism" would likely transfer itself from a political realm of "unlimited liberty" to the religious sensibilities of the people at large.[18]

The particular form of anti-modern, organicist, throne-and-altar and/or ultramontane conservatism animating such criticisms is, I have mentioned, largely foreign to the bloodstream of American political thought. And in Europe today this tradition is vestigial at best (and should not be confused with more recent nationalist and anti-immigrant right-wing voices). Even so, the voluminous outpouring of this line of criticism in the nineteenth and much of the twentieth century should make one think twice before pronouncing it obsolete; passionate moods of being and thought perish reluctantly in history, especially when the truth of religion and the social order is at stake; more often they live on in transmuted, residual, and unexpected forms. One might plausibly speculate, at least, that a traditionalist condescension and contempt of New World religiosity prowls about today ghost-like in the general (more secularized) European body politic and historical consciousness, an embedded element of cultural memory, a burrowed but not dormant ingredient in transatlantic disaffections.

Historically sedimented on top of this traditionalist contempt, however, is the secularist or leftist vision of the American double helix. This line of analysis—"why is America so religious?"—will be more familiar to students of contemporary affairs, even if, as I have argued, it often resembles and draws a measure of rhetorical firepower from the more hoary traditionalist approach summarized above. At several levels, *les extrêmes se touchent.*

From the Left, to recapitulate, the problem with America was not necessarily the profusion of erratic forms of religious life, but the more fundamental fact that religion in general and Christianity in particular appeared worrisomely unsusceptible to the putatively secularizing forces of modernity and the "stagist" logic of history. What chutzpah had possessed religion in this upstart land to flout the learned prophets of its demise? From this standpoint, America suffered from a congenital lack of secularizing impulses: there existed insufficient dialectical opposition, no attempted death-blow, to traditional, organized religion, as had occurred (in practice) in the French Revolution and (in theory) in many of its successor ideologies and intellectual systems in the nineteenth century. The revival-prone young republic had generated no gripping "drama of atheist humanism," to quote Henri de Lubac's famous title.[19] Consequently, traditional expressions of religion, willy-nilly, had enjoyed a more visible and enduring role in America than in Europe. This line of thinking we have glimpsed in Condorcet, various Saint-Simonians, Comte, numerous 1848ers and anticlerical republicans, Marx, Engels, Durkheim, as well as in many latter-day shapers of and subscribers to the "secularization thesis," which, again, should be understood both as an influential model of social scientific explanation and, by extension and more loosely, as a "grand narrative" about "the modern" nested in the social imaginary of the intellectual Left (broadly understood).[20] Cultured despisers of religion occupying this political space have found in American credulity an inviting target for a supercilious scorn.

★★★

The steady, often mutually-reinforcing accumulation of traditionalist–rightist and secularist–leftist disapprobation of American religious life has contributed to what Samuel Johnson, in another context, described as an "hereditary imputation," the propensity for "certain fixed and stated reproaches [from] one part of mankind... [to be] thrown upon another, which are regularly transmitted through continued successions."[21] While not downplaying other, more recent sources of anti-American sentiment in Europe, transatlantic disaffections and misapprehensions in recent decades possess a much deeper and more complex cultural (and specifically religious) backdrop or "pre-history" than contemporary commentators, often focused myopically on policy differences alone, normally suppose. It would be too simplistic, however, to conclude that long-standing religio-political differences comprise some "root" cause of anti-Americanism. Determining historical causality about a complex phenomenon is a complex matter. At the most, I hope to have established that these differences—manifested, in particular, in the longstanding efforts of denizens of the European "dialectic" to size up the American "double helix"—have left a sizable mark on the formative presuppositions or "social imaginaries" among various European elites and intellectuals in the modern era. These in turn have provided a fertile, if not a necessary, ground from which negative predispositions toward America might arise.[22]

To clarify this point, it might help to return to Charles Taylor's understanding of a social imaginary. In an effort to define the term, Taylor wrote that, in contrast to pure theory and pure experience, "it [is] the ways people imagine their social existence, how they fit together with others, how things go between them and their fellows, the expectations that are normally met, and *the deeper normative notions and images that underlie these expectations.*" Drawing from the philosopher Wittgenstein, Taylor elaborated that a "social imaginary" constitutes not the conscious foreground of our thought, but its murkier "background": a "background understanding" that results in certain *idées fixes* about "our whole predicament," ones that legitimize "normal expectations," providing currency and legitimacy to some habits of thought and perception while rendering others beyond the pale.[23]

At the outset of political modernity, for numerous European elites, statesmen, and intellectuals, the social imaginary with respect to religion and modern democratic government was imprinted with a dialectical positioning of stark contraries: a revolutionary tradition wedded to an insistent anticlerical, and often anti-religious, ethos, on the one hand, standing against a counterrevolutionary program intent on restoring traditional forms of religious life and political authority, on the other. From the standpoint of the former, a complete "break through" to the modern was hard to imagine without a secularist confessionalism robust and unremitting enough to displace and reoccupy the social and intellectual space of a church, ancestrally embedded in the social and political order of the *Ancien Régime*. One might draw a line from revolutionary-era catechisms and cults, through the "religious" musings of Saint-Simon and Comte, to the "eschatological" longings of Marx and the secularist civil ideology of Durkheim, and see among them a family resemblance, the shared genetic material of which grew out of a kind of counter-ecclesiology, a secularist architecture of human meaning and possibility truly "Gothic" in its aspirations to define the intellectual skyline of the modern age.[24]

From this dialectical standpoint, the American double helix simply looked misshapen, a curious half-measure, lackluster and lethargic in its ability to shake off traditional religion, even if that religion had been severely fractured in the "sectarian" environment of North America. To use Taylor's terms again, those confronted by it, or who set off from the Old World to expatiate upon it, had a difficult time placing it in the intellectual "repertory" afforded by the dialectical social imaginary. It did not fit into normal expectations, customary narratives, and was consequently frequently reviled, misapprehended, or shoehorned to fit into a template of historical imagination fashioned apart from its alterity. A quizzical and largely negative intellectual discourse of *longue durée* then, if not the actual cause of "anti-Americanism" in any direct or unilinear sense, makes up at least one, often overlooked, historical factor that has worked to amplify it and succor its perdurability.

But history, finally, is in motion and full of exceptions and surprise turn-abouts. The considerable legacy of Tocqueville, and the lesser legacies of Schaff and Maritain, serve to illustrate that while certain European patterns of encountering the American double helix can be ascertained, these patterns are not monolithic or entirely predictable. Nonplussed disapprobation is not the whole story. What is more, one could marshal considerable evidence among European liberals in the nineteenth century that, while not commenting on the United States directly, resonates quite well with the church–state arrangements and ideals of religious liberty within the American tradition.[25]

We should perhaps also remind ourselves not to reify the meaning of the terms "European" or "American." As I mentioned in the introduction, the former in this study mainly refers to certain influential political and intellectual trajectories in Western Europe in the post-revolutionary age, especially insofar as they differed from those afoot in the United States. "Europe," in other words, has not referred to the dazzling mosaic of regions, languages, cultural practices, and other forms of localism that still (*pace* EU forces of homogenization) make up the actual geographical Europe. And this is to say nothing of the enduring diversity today of church–state arrangements, ranging from the highly secularized state of France, the "pillarized" situation in the Netherlands, the established Orthodox Church in Greece, among others.[26] We have been trafficking all along in the world of cultural elites and intellectual history, spotlighting the curious behavior of images, perceptions, and ideas, which concurrently float free and fix themselves upon social realities that they at once reflect and shape.

To the student of the American scene since World War II, moreover, the categories of double helix and dialectic might appear far too rigid. One of the signature developments of this period might even be described as the superimposition of a more "European" dialectical set of sensibilities on top of an older American double helix. A steady stream of Supreme Court decisions since the 1940s has had the cumulative effect of severely circumscribing the public exercise of religious expression, affirming what some have called a "godless" constitution and created what others have labeled a "naked public square."[27] Concurrently, in the postwar period and markedly since the 1960s, there has arisen, most notably in the media, the academy, and the leftward wing of the Democratic Party, an intelligentsia committed to a much more aggressive secularism than has generally been the case in American history. Only partly joking, Peter Berger has spoken of the heightened "Europeanization" of American intellectual classes in the postwar period, with its leaders looking predominantly to Western Europe for models of intellectual sophistication, social or "critical theory," and political inspiration.[28] Not surprisingly, like the situation in France's Third Republic, the commitment to a more aggressive secularism among elite classes has generated a strong backlash, in the form of a populist "Religious Right," a religion-friendly "neo-conservatism," and the creation of new ecumenism among tradition-minded Protestants, Catholics, and Jews. As in the Third Republic, American politics has often become marked by a no-compromise, dialectical conflict between secularist and religious activists that does not reflect the moderate beliefs of most American citizens. America has experienced its own *guerre culturelle* or *Kulturkampf*, in short, with the major difference being that the conservative side does not harken back nostalgically to "throne and altar," but wants to reaffirm religion in general and Christianity in particular (often in idealized forms) as a bedrock of American society and democratic order.[29]

In the postwar period, the situation in Europe also has not been static. Since the crumbling legacy of Christendom has fully come undone in what Hugh McCleod has described as "the religious crisis of the 1960s," a number of Europeans have begun to rethink the significance of secularization and its social consequences.[30] The collapse of the Soviet Union and with it the actual embodiment of state-sanctioned atheism; the fresh, if ever turbulent, winds of change brought about by Vatican II and the papacy of John Paul II; the influx of Muslims into Europe in the wake of de-colonization; the rise of numerous missionary "evangelical" style churches often led by non-white, "Global South" figures; along with the recognition that the young in Europe often know little or nothing about the religious heritages of their respective countries, have led many to wonder if the legacy of an all-embracing secular canopy remains a viable option for Europe's present-day post-colonial immigration societies internally more multicultural than ever before and externally linked to a world beyond Europe's borders that appears as vibrantly and perdurably religious as ever. A once resolutely secularist thinker, the German philosopher Jürgen Habermas, for example, has in recent years spoken of the emergence of the category "post-secular" and the limits of a philosophical secularism, a legacy of a European "special path" (*Sonderweg*), that compels religious believers to articulate their intuitions about morality and the good life in an idiom foreign and often adverse to their deepest convictions.[31]

In France, the purest embodiment of a secular canopy in a political sense, the situation is especially instructive. While old-guard defenders of *laïcité* and the 1905 law of church–state separation are not in scarce supply, challengers to the status quo have recently come on the scene, arguing for greater public visibility of religious belief and less hostility on the part of the state toward religious actors in society. The Federation of French Protestants, the Union of Islamic Organizations in France, and the prestigious League of Education (historically a bastion of French secularism), for example, all have called for a move away from the traditional model of a combative secularism (*laïcité de combat*) to one of pluralism and greater openness (*laïcité plurielle*), sometimes appealing directly to the American model.[32]

These pleas have received powerful endorsement from several leading French intellectuals, including the Sorbonne scholars Jean Baubérot and Jean-Paul Willaime. Taking the American model seriously alongside a revisionist reading of French history, Baubérot, a historian, has argued that the situation no longer needs to be conceived as a zero-sum game between anticlerical secularists and anti-secular Catholics, which has colored so much of French (and Southern Catholic European) experience in the modern era. Rather, the realities of multiculturalism and globalization in France should lead to a loosening of militant secularism and a more fluid, open-ended process of negotiation and dialogue with religious currents in society. Without more open avenues of expression, religious forces, he fears, will measure their worth by their intransigence and anti-modern withdrawal, not by their ability to engage and peaceably interact with civil society.[33] Similarly, Jean-Paul Willaime, a sociologist of French secularism, has argued that France today stands in need of a "secularization of secularism" (*laïcisation de la laïcité*). By this, he means that the traditional idea of secularism in France has too often evinced a scorched-earth mentality toward religious sentiment and public expression. France, therefore, needs a "more secular secularism" (*laïcité plus laïque*), which would be less dogmatic, less "confessional," and more open to "a certain return of religion to the public sphere." "The more the secular state abandons its dominance over civil society, the more it will tend to recognize the contributions of religious groups to the public life. By doing that it becomes more secular." "The secularization of secularism is also a critique of the mystifications of science and politics, a demythologization of all the secular forms of absolutization."[34]

Curiously, in the final analysis, we might have to conclude that a "transatlantic" divide in important respects does not run through the Atlantic but within the societies on either side. We might do better simply to speak of two secularisms—a dialectical version with some sympathizers in America and a double helix version with some sympathizers in Europe.[35] The former bears the lingering confessional imprint of the *Ancien Régime* that it reacted against and has historically presented itself as a liberating, crusading ideal, a new *ecclesia militans*, or what Raymond Aron even called a "secular clericalism."[36] The latter reflects the messy, even cacophonous pluralism of the early American republic and has historically developed, sometimes haltingly, to permit, not rival or silence, a wide range of religious actors and voices.

It has been the argument of this book that, historically viewed, neither those in Europe with a lingering, nostalgic connection to the *Ancien Régime* nor their unsuspecting kin, enthusiasts for a new secularist *ecclesia militans*, have been very comfortable with the American model, the double helix, the pluralistic hodgepodge, the messy cacophony or whatever one might want to call it. It has often languished in the crossfire of disapprobation, reproached by cultured despisers of the post-revolutionary Right and the Left. But as figures such as Schaff and Maritain, and, yes, Tocqueville attest, the double helix is perhaps not beyond the pale of at least some commendation. And today, as the forces of democracy and modernity enjoy an ever-expanding reach, in a world where Saint Augustine's "restless heart" of religious desire appears as inextinguishable and complex as ever, one would do well at least to consider the double helix's historical arc, even if one recognizes, too, the propensity of all human achievements to defect and perish. The world may behold yet future, different *novi ordines seclorum*, perhaps arising far beyond our old Atlantic world. How we, American and European, ought to engage such phenomena, and engage one another, numbers among the significant undertakings of the future. Historical knowledge possesses at once the potential to serve and complicate these hard, high purposes.

Notes

CHAPTER I

1. Jeffrey Kopstein and Sven Steinmo, eds., *Growing Apart? America and Europe in the Twenty-First Century* (Cambridge: Cambridge University Press, 2008), 8–12, 24ff.; John Micklethwait and Adrian Woolridge, *God is Back: How the Global Revival of Faith is Changing the World* (New York: Penguin Press, 2009), 31ff.; and Andrei S. Markovits, *Uncouth Nation: Why Europe Dislikes America* (Princeton: Princeton University Press, 2007), 154–55.

2. Peter Schneider, "Across a Great Divide," *New York Times* (12 March 2004).

3. Kopstein and Steinmo, eds., *Growing Apart?*, 9.

4. See Andrew Kohut and Bruce Stokes, *America against the World: How we are Different and Why we are Disliked* (New York: Henry Holt and Company, 2006), 91ff., 106.

5. "Therapy of the Masses," *The Economist* (6 November 2003). Cf. Elizabeth Bryant, "Faith's Influence on Politics Alienates Secular Europe," *Washington Post* (6 November 2004).

6. Reinhard Heinisch, "'With God on Our Side': Warum Religion in den USA eine derart wichtige Rolle spielt," *Wiener Zeitung* (10 November 2000).

7. Jean-François Colosimo, *Dieu est américain: de la théodémocratie aux États-Unis* (Paris: Fayard, 2006).

8. Gret Haller, *Die Grenzen der Solidarität: Europa und die USA im Umgang mit Staat, Nation und Religion* (Berlin: Aufbau-Verlag, 2002) and *Politik der Götter: Europa und der neue Fundamentalismus* (Berlin: Aufbau-Verlag, 2005).

9. Klaus-M. Kodalle, ed., *Gott und Politik in USA: Über den Einfluß des Religiösen* (Frankfurt am Main: Athenäum, 1988), 9.

10. Peter Berger, ed., *The Desecularization of the World* (Grand Rapids: Eerdmans, 1999), 1–18. Cf. Jon Butler, *Awash in a Sea of Faith: Christianizing the American People* (Cambridge, Mass.: Harvard University Press, 1990). On the limitations of "secularization theory" applied to Europe, see Danièle Hervieu-Leger, *La religion pour mémoire* (Paris: Cerf, 1993) and Grace Davie, *Religion in Modern Europe: A Memory Mutates* (Oxford: Oxford University Press, 2000).

11. Raymond Boudon, "À quoi sert la sociologie?" *Cités* 2 (2002), 139ff.

12. A major exception to this generalization is the work of Hartmut Lehmann. See Lehmann, ed., *Transatlantische Religionsgeschichte 18. bis 20. Jahrhundert* (Göttingen: Wallstein, 2006). The present work aims to contribute to the type of "transatlantic religious history" encouraged by Lehmann. On "Atlantic history" generally, see Bernard Bailyn, *Atlantic History: Concepts and Contours* (Cambridge, Mass: Harvard University Press, 2005).

13. Jane Louise Mesick, *The English Traveller in America, 1785–1835* (New York: Columbia, 1922), 28.

14. Seymour Martin Lipset, *The First New Nation: The United States in Historical and Comparative Perspective* (New York: Basic Books, 1963), 141.

15. Hugo Münsterberg, *The Americans*, trans. E. B. Halt (New York, 1907), 500.

16. G. K. Chesterton, *What I Saw in America* (1922) in *The Collected Works of G.K. Chesterton*, vol. 21, (San Francisco: Ignatius Press, 1990), 41.

17. Quoted in Paul Wheeler, *America through British Eyes* (Rock Hill, S.C., 1935), 6.

18. Jean Baudrillard, *Amérique* (Paris: Bernard Grasset, 1986); Bernard-Henri Lévy, *American Vertigo* (New York: Random House, 2006); and Simon Schama, *The Future of America: A History* (New York: Ecco, 2009).

19. Alexis de Tocqueville, *Democracy in America*, trans. and ed. by Harvey C. Mansfield and Delba Winthrop (Chicago: University of Chicago Press, 2000), 280, 282.

20. Peter F. Drucker, "Organized Religion and the American Creed," *Review of Politics* 18 (1956), 303.

21. John T. Noonan, *The Lustre of our Country: The American Experience of Religious Freedom* (Berkeley: University of California Press, 2000), 357.

22. Philippe Roger, *The American Enemy: The History of French Anti-Americanism*, trans. Sharon Bowman (Chicago: University of Chicago Press, 2005), 53ff.

23. Achille Murat, *Esquisse morale et politique des États-Unis de l'Amérique du Nord* (Paris, 1832), 75.

24. Karl Lamprecht, *Americana: Reiseeindrücke, Betrachtungen, geschichtliche Gesamtansicht* (Freiburg im Breisgau, 1906), 45, 62.

25. Jessica C. E. Gienow-Hecht, "Always Blame the Americans: Anti-Americanism in Europe in the Twentieth Century," *American Historical Review* 111 (2007), 1067ff.

26. Piero Craveri and Gaetano Qualiariello, eds., *L'antiamericanismo in Italia e in Europa nel secondo dopoguerra* (Soveria Mannelli: Rubbettino, 2003).

27. James W. Ceaser, *Reconstructing America: The Symbol of America in Modern Thought* (New Haven: Yale University Press, 1997), 5.

28. On the "Lockean" compatability of the American and British "Enlightenments" and their contrast with the "Voltairean" Enlightenment of France, see Gertrude Himmelfarb, *The Roads to Modernity: The British,*

French, and American Enlightenments (New York: Alfred A. Knopf, 2004), 18–19.

29. As the Frenchman Constantin Comte deVolney put it in 1803, the United States was simply "a second edition of England, but produced on a much larger format than the original." Noted in Durand Echeverria, *Mirage in the West: A History of the French Image of American Society to 1815* (Princeton: Princeton University Press, 1957), 206.

30. Otto Baumgarten, "Engländerei im kirchlichen Leben," *Religion in Geschichte und Gegenwart*, vol. 1 (1910), 337–38.

31. Timothy Garton Ash, "Is Britain European?" *International Affairs* 77 (2001), 1–13.

32. Mark Noll, *America's God: From Jonathan Edwards to Abraham Lincoln* (New York: Oxford University Press, 2002), 5, 161ff. and Nathan Hatch, *The Democratization of American Christianity* (New Haven: Yale University Press, 1989), 3–16.

33. James Bryce, *The American Commonwealth*, rev. edn., vol. 2 (New York: MacMillan, 1914), 777.

34. Louis Hartz, *The Liberal Tradition in America* (New York: Harcourt, Brace, & World, 1955), 3. For a critical account of Hartz's thesis and its legacy, see James T. Kloppenberg, "In Retrospect: Louis Hartz's 'The Liberal Tradition in America,'" *Reviews in American History* 29 (2001), 460–79.

35. Lionel Trilling, *The Liberal Imagination* (New York: New York Review Books, 2008), xv. Of course, the United States possesses a conservative tradition as well, but this tradition has always had a friendlier relationship with classical economic and political liberalism than its European counterparts. See Patrick Allitt, *The Conservatives: Ideas and Personalities throughout American History* (New Haven: Yale University Press, 2009).

36. Hartz, *The Liberal Tradition in America*, 6.

37. C. Vann Woodward, *The Old World's New World* (New York: Oxford University Press, 1991), 31.

38. Charles Taylor, *A Secular Age* (Cambridge: Belknap Press of Harvard University Press, 2007), 171ff., 212ff., 387. Or, as Edward Shils, once wrote: "[M]uch of what is believed beyond first-hand experience is the product of traditions and teachings which are the gradually accumulated and attenuated products of the activities of intellectuals." See Shils, "The Intellectuals and the Powers," in *The Constitution of Society* (Chicago: University of Chicago Press, 1982), 182.

39. On my usage of the phrase "master narrative", see Allan Megill, "Grand Narrative and the Discipline of History," in Frank Ankersmit, ed., *A New Philosophy of History* (Chicago: University of Chicago Press, 1995), 151–73.

40. For an excellent primer on these trajectories, see Hartmut Lehmann, "The Christianization of America and the Dechristianization of Europe in the Nineteenth and Twentieth Centuries," *Kirchliche Zeitgeschichte* 11 (1998), 8–20.

41. John Micklethwait and Adrian Wooldridge, *The Right Nation: Conservative Power in America* (New York: Penguin Press, 2004), 343.

42. See Christopher Olaf Blum, ed., *Critics of the Enlightenment: Readings in the French Counter-Revolutionary Tradition* (Wilmington, De.: ISI Books, 2004), xvff., 157ff., *passim*.

43. Heinz Schilling, "Der Westfälische Friede und das neuzeitliche Profil Europas," in Heinz Duchhardt, ed., *Der Westfälische Friede* (Munich: R. Oldenbourg Verlag, 1998), 3–32.

44. Considerable evidence, in fact, could be marshaled to view the nineteenth century as a "second confessional age." See Olaf Blaschke, "Das 19.Jahrhundert: Ein zweites konfessionelles Zeitalter," *Geschichte und Gesellschaft* 26 (2000), 38–75.

45. James Harvey Robinson and Charles Beard, eds., *Readings in European History*, vol. 1 (Boston, 1908), 384.

46. See Rafe Blaufarb, *Bonapartists in the Borderlands: French Exiles and Refugees on the Gulf Coast, 1815–1835* (Tuscaloosa, Ala.: University of Alabama Press, 2005).

47. Cited in Günter Moltmann, "Deutscher Antiamerikanismus heute und früher," in Otmar Franz, ed., *Vom Sinn der Geschichte* (Stuttgart: Seewald, 1976), 92.

48. Johann Georg Hülsemann, *Geschichte der Democratie in den Vereinigten Staaten von Nord-America* (Göttingen, 1823), vii–viii.

49. Dan Diner, *America in the Eyes of the Germans: An Essay on Anti-Americanism*, trans. Allison Brown (Princeton: Markus Wiener, 1996), 31.

50. Friedrich von Schlegel, *The Philosophy of History*, trans. James Burton Robertson (London: Henry Bohn, 1859), 453.

51. René de Chateaubriand, *Essai sur les révolutions* (London, 1797).

52. Frederick Marryat, *A Diary in America: with Remarks on its Institutions* (New York: Alfred A. Knopf, 1962), 292, 301.

53. Quoted in Seymour Drescher, "America and French Romanticism during the July Monarchy," *American Quarterly* 11 (1959), 8.

54. Nikolaus Lenau, *Sämtliche Werke und Briefe*, vol. 3 (Frankfurt am Main: Insel-Verrl., 1971), 193.

55. Charles Baudelaire, "The Exposition Universelle 1855," in *The Mirror of Art: Critical Studies*, trans. Jonathan Mayne (London: Phaidon Press, 1955), 196.

56. On this theme, see Markovits, *Uncouth Nation*, 151ff. In part, because of its "social and religious liberty," as Jonathan Sarna has observed, "the modernity that America represented did not seem to them [European Jews] quite so threatening." Still, highly traditionalist Jewish voices from the nineteenth century could accuse the United States of being a "*trefa* [unkosher] land where even the stones are impure." Noted in Jonathan D. Sarna, *American Judaism: A History* (New Haven: Yale University Press, 2004), 153–55.

57. For an overview of nineteenth-century, rightist anti-Americanism in Europe, see J. W. Schulte, "Anti-Americanism in European Culture: Its Early Manifestations," *European Contributions to American Studies* 11 (1986), 7–19.

58. Philip Schaff, *The Principle of Protestantism*, trans. John Nevin (Chambersburg: Publication of the German Reformed Church, 1845), 149–50.

59. Friedrich Engels, Introduction to the English edition of *Socialism: Utopian and Scientific* (London, 1892), xxvii.

60. Haller, *Die Grenzen der Solidarität*, 40.

61. See Jean Baubérot, *Histoire de la laïcité en France*, 4th edn. (Paris: Presses universitaires de France, 2007).

62. Hugh Heclo, *Christianity and American Democracy* (Cambridge: Harvard University Press, 2007), 9.

63. Antoine-Nicolas de Condorcet, *Sketch for a Historical Picture of the Progress of the Human Mind*, trans. June Barraclough (Westport, Conn.: Greenwood Press, 1975), 146–47.

64. Dipesh Chakrabarty, *Provincializing Europe: Postcolonial Thought and Historical Difference* (Princeton: Princeton University Press, 2000), 6ff.

65. Manfred Hennigsen, "Das Amerika von Hegel, Marx und Engels: Zur Genealogie des europäischen Anti-Amerikanismus," *Zeitschrift für Politik* 20 (1973), 224ff. and R. Laurence Moore, *European Socialists and the American Promised Land* (New York: Oxford University Press, 1970), 103–33.

66. Chakrabarty, *Provincializing Europe*, 16.

67. Eckhart G. Franz, *Das Amerikabild der deutschen Revolution von 1848/49* (Heidelberg: C. Winter 1958).

68. August Jullien, "De la liberté en France et aux États-Unis," *Revue Encyclopédique* 52 (1831), 215–16.

69. August Comte, *Cours de philosophie positive*, vol. 5 (Paris, 1864), 470–71.

70. Philip Schaff, *America: A Sketch of the Political, Social, and Religious Character of the United States of North America* (Cambridge: Belknap Press of Harvard University Press, 1961), 36 (emphasis added).

71. See Bertram Wolfe, *Marx and America* (New York: John Day Company, 1934), 21–22.

72. Moore, *European Socialists and the American Promised Land*, 32.

73. W. T. Colyer, *America: A World Menance* (London, 1922) and Robert Aron and Armand Dandieu, *Le cancer américain* (Paris, 1931).

74. Jeffrey K. Hadden, "Toward Desacralizing Secularization Theory," *Social Forces* 65 (March 1987), 590 and David Martin, "Europa und Amerika," in Otto Kallscheuer, ed., *Das Europa der Religionen: Ein Kontinent zwischen Säkularisierung und Fundamentalismus* (Frankfurt am Main: S. Fischer, 1996), 171–72. On the specific European-Restoration context of the birth of "sociology" and its attitude toward religion, see Robert Spaemann, *Der Ursprung der Soziologie aus dem Geist der Restauration* (Munich: Kösel-Verlag,

1959).The term secularization, admittedly, presents problems in discussing someone such as Comte, for he saw himself establishing a new "religion of humanity." Cf. Irving M. Zeitlin, *Ideology and the Development of Sociological Theory* (Englewood Cliffs, NJ: Prentice-Hall, 1968).

75. David McLellan, "Religion and Socialism in Europe," in Sean Gill et al., eds., *Religion in Europe: Contemporary Perspectives* (Kampen, the Netherlands: Pharos, 1994), 159. From this period, though, one may also speak of significant rapprochement between socialist thought (at least in its non-revolutionary forms) and Christian principles, as represented in the papal encyclical *Rerum Novarum* (1891), the font of modern Catholic social thought, and the emergence of the Evangelical Social Congress (1890) in Germany, spearheaded by Friedrich Naumann and Adolf von Harnack. The British Labour Party (1900) also achieved a high degree of conciliation with religious influences and voices.

76. Karl Marx, "Critique of the Gotha Program," in *Marx and Engels on Religion* (Moscow: Foreign Languages Publishing House, 1957), 143.

77. See Delos Banning McKown, *The Classical Marxist Critiques of Religion: Marx, Engels, Lenin, Kautsky* (The Hague: Martinus Nijoff, 1975).

78. In Western Europe, the period of more *popular* dechristianization is more recent than generally thought, taking place especially between 1955 and 1975. See Hugh McLeod, *The Religious Crisis of the 1960s* (Oxford: Oxford University Press, 2007).

79. On this point, see Grace Davie, *Europe: The Exceptional Case, Parameters of Faith in the Modern World* (London: Darton, Longman & Todd, 2002).

80. José Casanova, "Beyond European and American Exceptionalisms," in Grace Davie et al., eds., *Predicting Religion: Christian, Secular, and Alternative Futures* (Aldershot: Ashgate, 2003), 24 (emphasis added).

81. For example, see the frame of reference for the American intellectual historian, David Hollinger, "Why is there so much Christianity in the United States?" *Church History* 71 (December 2002), 858–65 and "Jesus Matters in the USA," *Modern Intellectual History* 1 (April 2004), 135–49. Cf. Gregory Paul, "The Chronic Dependence of Popular Religiosity upon Dysfunctional Psychosociological Conditions," *Evolutionary Pyschology* 7 (2009), 398–441. Paul sees religion in America largely as a "psychological mechanism for coping" in a "dysfunctional" society.

82. One could, of course, turn this around and examine American perceptions of Europe, with respect to religion and other matters. The case for contemporary American "Anti-Europeanism" has been made by Timothy Garton Ash, "Anti-Europeanism in America," *New York Review of Books* (13 February 2003). Anti-Americanism and Anti-Europeanism, however, are not numerically symmetrical phenomena, as a Google search or a Library of Congress search of the two terms will quickly reveal.

83. See Philip Schaff, *Germany; its Universities, Theology, and Religion* (Edinburgh, 1857).

84. John McGreevy, *Catholicism and American Freedom* (New York: W. W. Norton, 2003), 189ff.

CHAPTER 2

1. Robert Baird, *Religion in America* (New York: Harper & Row, 1970) [an abridgement of the 1856 edition with an introduction by Henry Warner Bowden], 202, 206, 294.
2. Durand Echeverria, *Mirage in the West: A History of the French Image of American Society to 1815* (Princeton: Princeton University Press, 1957), 175ff.
3. Antonello Gerbi, *La disputa del Nuovo Mondo; storia di una polemica, 1750–1900* (Milan: R. Ricciardi, 1955).
4. The phrases are those of Cornelius de Pauw; quoted in Philippe Roger, *The American Enemy: The History of French Anti-Americanism*, trans. Sharon Bowman (Chicago: University of Chicago Press, 2005), 7.
5. Quoted in C. Vann Woodward, *The Old World's New World* (New York: Oxford University Press, 1991), 6.
6. James W. Ceaser, *Reconstructing America: the Symbol of America in Modern Thought* (New Haven: Yale University Press, 1997), 19–42.
7. Roger, *American Enemy*, 7.
8. Jean de Crèvecoeur, *Letters from an American Farmer*, in Milton B. Powell, ed., *The Voluntary Church: American Religious Life, 1740–1860, through the Eyes of European Visitors* (New York: MacMillan, 1967), 30–33.
9. On this point, see David Paul Crook, *American Democracy in English Politics, 1815–1850* (Oxford: Clarendon Press, 1965), 94ff.
10. Joseph de Maistre, "Réflexions sur le protestantisme dans ses rapports avec la souveraineté" (1798), in *Écrits sur la Révolution*, ed. Jean-Louis Darcel (Paris: Presses universitaires de France, 1989), 239.
11. Marc Pachter and Frances Wein, eds., *Abroad in America: Visitors to the New Nation, 1776–1914* (Reading, Mass.: Addison-Wesley, 1976) xiii.
12. As John Stuart Mill put it, "All who write or speak on either side of the dispute [over the desirability of democracy] are prompt enough in pressing America into their service.... America is usually cited by the two great parties...as an argument for or against democracy." See Mill's review of the first volume of Tocqueville's *Democracy in America* in John Stuart Mill, *Essays on Politics and Culture*, ed., Gertrude Himmelfarb (Garden City, NY: Anchor Books, 1963), 174.
13. Crook, *American Democracy in English Politics*, 1ff., 94ff.
14. G. H. Guttridge, *English Whiggism and the American Revolution* (Berkeley and Los Angeles: University of California Press, 1942), 2.
15. Crook, *American Democracy in English Politics*, 39.
16. For an apologia of America's "great religious experiment," see Alex MacKay, *The Western World: Travels in the United States in 1846-47*, vol. 2 (Philadelphia, 1849), 243–60.

17. See, for example, Benjamin Evans Lippincott, *Victorian Critics of Democracy* (New York: Octagon Books, 1964), 39, 77, 150.

18. Nathan O. Hatch, *Democratization of American Christianity* (New Haven: Yale University Press, 1989), 4–7.

19. Jane Louise Mesick, *The English Traveller in America, 1785–1835* (New York: Columbia University Press, 1922), 28.

20. Frederick Marryat, *A Diary in America with Remarks on its Institutions*, ed. Sydney Jackson (New York: Alfred A. Knopf, 1962), 291.

21. Samuel Wilberforce, *A History of the Protestant Episcopal Church in America* (New York, 1849), 289, 290–91.

22. Charles Lyell, *Travels in North America in the Year 1841–42 with Geological Observations on the United States, Canada, and Nova Scotia*, vol. 1 (New York, 1845), 96.

23. Thomas Hamilton, *Men and Manners in America*, vol. 2 (London, 1833), 397.

24. Marryat, *Diary in America*, 290–92.

25. John Robert Godley, *Letters from America* (1844), quoted in M. B. Powell, ed., *The Voluntary Church*, 165.

26. Godley, *Letters from America*, vol. 2 (London, 1844), 125–26.

27. Godley, *Letters from America*, vol. 2, 128.

28. Isaac Fidler, *Observations on Professions, Literature, Manners, and Emigration, in the United States and Canada* (New York, 1837), 123. In classical mythology, one descended into the "cave of Trophonius" to consult an oracle, but most consultees were frightened out of their wits, and forgot the experience entirely upon coming up. "Descending into the cave of Trophonius" became a proverb for being scared into speechlessness or incomprehensible babble.

29. Wilberforce, *History of the Protestant Episcopal Church in America*, 291.

30. Hamilton, *Men and Manners in America*, 398.

31. Fidler, *Observations . . . in the United States and Canada*, 31.

32. Fidler, *Observations . . . in the United States and Canada*, 31, 35–36.

33. Marryat, *Diary in America*, 293–94.

34. Thomas Colley Grattan, *Civilized America*, vol. 2 (London, 1859), 342.

35. Isaac Holmes, *An Account of the United States of America* (London, 1823), 388–89.

36. See Ray Allen Billington, *Land of Savagery, Land of Promise: The European Image of the American Frontier* (New York: W. W. Norton, 1981), 184–86.

37. Grattan, *Civilized America*, vol. 2, 341.

38. Grattan, *Civilized America*, vol. 2, 342–43.

39. Max Berger, *The British Traveller in America, 1836–1860* (New York: Columbia University Press, 1943), 139.

40. Grattan, *Civilized America*, vol. 2, 353. Frances Trollope writes of the "absurd" and "mischievous" Shakers, who permit "singing and dancing of the most grotesque kind." Frances Trollope, *Domestic Manners of the Americans* (New York: Penguin, 1982), 107.

41. Noted in Berger, *British Traveller in America, 1836–1860*, 140.

42. Millerism, ancestor of present-day Seventh-Day Adventism, was an apocalyptic movement begun by the Baptist layman William Miller (1782–1849) in upstate New York. Millerites believed, errantly as things turned out, that the world would end in 1844. See David L. Rowe, *Thunder and Trumpets: Millerites and Dissenting Religion in Upstate New York* (Chico, Calif.: Scholars Press, 1985).

43. Grattan, *Civilized America*, vol. 2, 348, 350. For a nineteenth-century British traveler's account of the Mormons, see R. F. Burton, *The City of the Saints: and across the Rocky Mountains to California* (London, 1861). On the Shakers in America, see Stephen J. Stein, *The Shaker Experience in America: A History of the United Society of Believers* (New Haven: Yale University Press, 1992).

44. Sir Arthur Conan Doyle, *A Study in Scarlet*, ed., Owen Dudley Edwards (Oxford: Oxford University Press, 1993). See especially the editor's commentary on Doyle's views on Mormonism, 183ff.

45. James C. Simmons, *Star-Spangled Eden: Nineteenth-Century America through the Eyes of Dickens, Wilde, Frances Trollope, Frank Harris, and other British Travelers* (New York: Carroll & Graf, 2000), 28. On Trollope's reasons for going to America, see Pamela Neville-Sington, *Fanny Trollope: The Life and Adventures of a Clever Woman* (New York: Viking, 1998).

46. Trollope, *Domestic Manners*, 314.

47. Trollope, *Domestic Manners*, 84–85.

48. Trollope, *Domestic Manners*, 59–60.

49. Trollope, *Domestic Manners*, 64–65 and 126ff.

50. Trollope, *Domestic Manners*, 84ff.

51. Andrei S. Markovits, *Uncouth Nation: Why Europe Dislikes America* (Princeton: Princeton University Press, 2007), 71.

52. Anthony Trollope, *North America*, eds., Donald Smalley and Bradford Allen Booth (New York: Alfred A. Knopf, 1951).

53. Of relevance are Dickens' highly negative portraits of nonconformist religiosity in such novels *as Pickwick Papers* and *Bleak House*. See David A. Ward, "Distorted Religion: Dickens, Dissent, and *Bleak House*," *Dickens Studies Annual* 29 (2000), 195ff.

54. Charles Dickens, *American Notes* (New York: St. Martin's Press, 1985), 226–28.

55. Dickens, *American Notes*, xi.

56. To be sure, Arnold was not a traditional Anglican in the orthodox theological sense; still, "his support of the State Church was unequivocal," seeing it especially as a bulwark against the spread of religious dissent in England, or what he called "ignorant and fanatical little sects." See David W. Ward, "Transformed Religion: Matthew Arnold and the Refining of Dissent," *Renascence: Essays in Values in Literature* 53 (2001), 100, 102ff.

57. Matthew Arnold, *Civilization in the United States: First and Last Impressions*, 6ᵗʰ edn. (Boston, 1900), 173–74, 181, 190.

58. From a letter, to whom it is unclear; quoted in James Dow McCallum, "The Apostle of Culture Meets America," *New England Quarterly Review* 2 (July 1929), 361.

59. On this point, see Lippincott, *Victorian Critics of Democracy*, 93–133.

60. Arnold, *Civilization in the United States*, 97 (emphasis added).

61. Arnold, *Civilization in the United States*, 80, 85.

62. Arnold, *Civilization in the United States*, 82–86.

63. Arnold, *Civilization in the United States*, 87.

64. Arnold, *Culture and Anarchy* (Cambridge: Cambridge University Press, 1932), 20. Cf. Donald D. Stone, "Matthew Arnold and the Pragmatics of Hellenism and Hebraism," *Poetics Today* 19 (Summer 1998), 179–98.

65. Ward, "Transformed Religion," 109.

66. Arnold, *Civilization in the United States*, 191–92.

67. Arnold, *Civilization in the United States*, 86, 181.

68. Matthew Arnold, *Friendship's Garland* (New York, 1896), 232.

69. See Raymond Guess, "Kultur, Bildung, Geist," *History and Theory* 35 (May 1996), 151–64, and Thomas Nipperdey, *Germany from Napoleon to Bismarck, 1800–1866*, trans. Daniel Nolan (Princeton: Princeton University Press, 1996), 356ff.

70. Dan Diner, *America in the Eyes of the Germans*, trans. Allison Brown (Princeton: Markus Wiener, 1996), 31–33.

71. Jörg Fisch, "Zivilization, Kultur," in Otto Brunner et alia, eds., *Geschichtliche Grundbegriffe: Historisches Lexikon zur politisch-sozialen Sprache in Deutschland*, vol. 7 (Stuttgart: E. Klett, 1992), 679–774.

72. Fritz K. Ringer, *The Decline of the German Mandarins: The German Academic Community, 1890–1933* (Cambridge: Harvard University Press, 1969), 81–90. Cf. Walter Struve, *Elites Against Democracy: Leadership Ideals in Bourgeois Political Thought in Germany, 1890–1933* (Princeton: Princeton University Press, 1973), 23ff.

73. Friedrich Nietzsche, *Die fröhliche Wissenschaft* (Stuttgart: Reclam, 2000), 216. Nietzsche expressed the hope that the philosophy of his friend Paul Rée would not be tarnished by "Americanness" (*Amerikanerthum*) during Rée's visit to the United States. See the letter of 13 October 1880 in *Nietzsche Briefwechsel*, vol. 3, 1, eds., Giorgio Colli and Mazzino Montinari (Berlin: Walter de Gruyter, 1981), 44.

74. Dietrich von Bülow, *Der Freistaat von Nordamerika in seinem neuesten Zustand* (Berlin, 1797), 38f., 133, 204ff.

75. Friedrich Schlegel, *Sämtliche Werke*, vol. 14 (Vienna, 1846), 22.

76. Paul Weber, *America in Imaginative German Literature* (New York: Columbia University Press, 1926), 53–54. Cf. Adam Müller, *Die Elemente der Staatskunst* (Jena, 1922), especially lecture 34, "Christ died not only for people, but also for governments."

77. From Friedrich Gentz, *Memoire über die Colonialfrage* (1824); quoted in Günter Moltmann, "Deutscher Antiamerikanismus heute und früher," *Vom Sinn der Geschichte*, ed. Otmar Franz (Stuttgart: Seewald, 1976), 92.

78. On Steffens and this period in Prussian history, see Thomas Albert Howard, *Protestant Theology and the Making of the Modern German University* (Oxford: Oxford University Press, 2006), 130ff.

79. Heinrich Steffens, *Die gegenwärtige Zeit und wie sie geworden* (Berlin, 1817), 328–31. See also the comments on America in his autobiography, *Was ich erlebte*, vols. 1–2 (Breslau, 1840), 77ff., 236, and 330f.

80. Material taken from Ernst Fraenkel, ed., *Amerika im Spiegel des deutschen politischen Denkens* (Cologne, 1959), 114–15.

81. The ironic story of Lenau's time in the United States is provided in Diner, *America in the Eyes of the Germans*, 36f. It is ironic because one of the main reasons that Lenau came to America was for business speculation—the very type of activity for which he later indicted American society.

82. Nikolaus Lenau, *Sämtliche Werke*, vol. 2 (Frankfurt: Insel-Verlag, 1971), 213.

83. Lenau, *Sämtliche Werke*, vol. 2, 207, 210, 214.

84. Lenau, *Sämtliche Werke*, vol. 2, 213. "Das atlantische Meer aber ist der isolierende Gürtel für den Geist und alles höhere Leben."

85. Lenau, *Sämtliche Werke*, vol. 2, 215–16 (emphasis added).

86. Lenau, *Sämtliche Werke*, vol. 2, 213, 218.

87. Noted in Ceaser, *Reconstructing America*, 184–85.

88. Diner, *America in the Eyes of the Germans*, 42f.

89. Ferdinand Kürnberger, *Der Amerikamüde* (Berlin: Freitag Verlag, 1982), 220–21.

90. Kürnberger, *Amerikamüde*, 221.

91. "'Sollte der künftige Islam dieses Weltteils nicht überhaupt *Humbug* heißen?,' fragte der Doktor." Kürnberger, *Amerikamüde*, 303.

92. Kürnberger, *Amerikamüde*, 297–303.

93. Material taken from Fraenkel, ed., *Amerika im Spiegel des deutschen politischen Denkens*, 106–07.

94. The lines are taken from Günter Moltmann, "Deutscher Antiamerikanismus heute und früher," 94 and Diner, *America in the Eyes of the Germans*, 37.

95. On this point, see Renate Schlesier, "Homeric Laughter by the Rivers of Babylon: Heinrich Heine and Karl Marx," in Mark H. Gelber, ed., *The Jewish Reception of Heinrich Heine* (Tübingen: M. Niemeyer, 1992), 21–43.

96. Letter of 14 October 1820; quoted in *Lebensnachrichten über Barthold Georg Niebuhr*, vol. 2 (Hamburg, 1838), 449.

97. Fraenkel, *Amerika im Spiegel des deutschen politischen Denkens*, 116–17. Cf. Eberhard Kessel, "Rankes Auffassung der amerikanischen Geschichte," *Jahrbuch für Amerikastudien* 7 (1962), 19–52.

98. Jacob Burckhardt, *Weltgeschichtliche Betrachtungen*, in *Gesammelte Werke*, vol. 4 (Basel: Benno Schwabe & Co., 1956), 6.

99. Ibid., 149.

100. Heinrich von Treitschke, "Bundesstaat und Einheitsstaat" (1864), in Treitschke, *Historische und politische Aufsätze*, vol. 2 (Leipzig, 1913), 96ff.

101. Heinrich von Treitschke, *Politics*, trans. Arthur James Balfour (New York, 1916), 327–28.

102. Alexander Schmidt, *Reisen in die Moderne: Der Amerika-Diskurs des deutschen Bürgertums vor dem Ersten Weltkrieg im europäischen Vergleich* (Berlin: Akademie Verlag, 1997), 1ff.

103. Stead himself, however, saw this as a mostly positive development. What is more, he endorsed American-style freedom of religion, contrasting it to Europe, where churches are "privileged to strut…bedizened in all the gorgeous livery of State." William Thomas Stead, *The Americanisation of the World or the Trend of the Twentieth Century* (New York: Garland, 1972), 100.

104. Ludwig Max Goldberger, "Die amerikanische Gefahr," *Preußischer Jahrbücher* 120 (1905), 1–33. Cf. his *Das Land der unbegrenzten Möglichkeiten: Beobachtungen über das Wirtschaftsleben der Vereinigten Staaten* (Berlin, 1903).

105. On the almost wholly derogatory meaning of "Americanism" in the German context during this period, see Otto Basler, "Amerikanismus. Geschichte des Schlagwortes," *Deutsche Rundschau*, 224 (1930), 142–46.

106. Fritz Stern, *The Politics of Cultural Despair* (Berkeley: University of California Press, 1961), xviii–xix.

107. On the enormous influence of this distinction in Wilhelmine and Weimar intellectual life, see Ringer, *Decline of the German Mandarins*, 164ff.

108. Ferdinand Tönnies, *Community and Society*, trans. Charles P. Loomis (East Lansing: Michigan State University Press, 1957), 221.

109. Ulrich Ott, *Amerika ist anders. Studien zum Amerika-Bild in deutschen Reiseberichten des 20. Jahrhundert* (Frankfurt am Main: Peter Lang, 1991), 164.

110. See Herman Georg Scheffauer, *Das geistige Amerika von heute* (Berlin, 1925).

111. J. G. Pfleiderer had noted, for example, that from the standpoint of the European press in the late nineteenth century, the United States appeared to be nothing more than "a colorful, swarming throng of noisy sects." Pfliederer, *Amerikanische Reisebilder, mit besonderer Berücksichtigung der dermaligen religiösen und kirchlichen Zustände der Vereinigten Staaten* (Bonn, 1882), 86.

112. Stephen Berger, "The Sects and the Breakthrough to the Modern World: On the Centrality of the Sects in Weber's Protestant Ethic Thesis," *Sociological Quarterly* 12 (1971), 456–99.

113. Max Weber, "Die protestantischen Sekten und der Geist des Kapitalismus," *Gesammelte Aufsätze zur Religionssoziologie*, vol. 1 (Tübingen, 1920), 208.

114. Marianne Weber, *Max Weber: A Biography*, trans. Harry Zohn (New York: John Wiley & Sons, 1975), 288, 298.

115. On this point, see Georg Kamphausen, *Die Erfindung Amerikas in der Kulturkritik der Generation von 1890* (Göttingen: Velbrück Wissenschaft, 2002), 199ff.

116. Weber, "Die protestantischen Sekten und der Geist des Kapitalismus," *Gesammelte Aufsätze zur Religionssoziologie*, vol. 1 (Tübingen, 1920), 236.

117. On this point, see Berger, "The Sects and the Breakthrough to the Modern World," 488.

118. Weber, *The Protestant Ethic and the Spirit of Capitalism*, trans, Talcott Parsons (New York: Charles Scribner's Sons, 1958), 182.

119. Kamphausen, *Die Erfindung Amerikas*.

120. The full title of the Prussian Ministry of Culture, for example, was the Ministry of Ecclesiastical (*geistlichen*), Educational and Medical Affairs." See Karl-Heinz Manegold, "Das 'Ministerium des Geistes': Zur Organisation des ehemaligen preußischen Kultusministeriums, *Die deutsche Berufs- und Fachschule* 63 (1967), 512–24.

121. Kamphausen, *Die Erfindung Amerikas*, 276–83.

122. Hans Haupt, *Die Eigenart der amerikanischen Predigt* (Gießen, 1907), 10.

123. Kamphausen, *Die Erfindung Amerikas*, 185ff.

124. Wilhelm von Polenz, *Das Land der Zukunft* (Berlin, 1903), 402.

125. From Rilke's letters; quoted and sources provided in Richard Rutland, *America in Modern European Literature: From Image to Metaphor* (New York: New York University Press, 1976), 78, 178.

126. Quoted in Ernst Fraenkel, "Das deutsche Wilsonbild," *Jahrbuch für Amerikastudien* 5 (1960), 101.

127. Tönnies, "Im Gedenken an das Reformationsfest," *Deutscher Wille* 32 (1918), 91–92.

128. Adolf Halfeld, *Amerika und Amerikanismus: Kritische Betrachtungen eines Deutschen und Europäers* (Jena, 1927), ix–xvi.

129. Halfeld, *Amerika und Amerikanismus*, 11.

130. Halfeld, *Amerika und Amerikanismus*, 11, 80–81.

131. Halfeld, *Amerika und Amerikanismus*, 92ff.

132. Halfeld, *Amerika und Amerikanismus*, 92–93.

133. Halfeld, *Amerika und Amerikanismus*, 92–93.

134. See Klaus Schwab, "Anti-Americanism within the German Right, 1917–1933," *Amerikastudien* 21 (1976), 89–107. As has been well documented, many of these anti-American motifs and images were shared and/or later used for political purpose by the Nationalist Socialists. See Gerhard L. Weinberg, "Hitler's Image of the United States," *American Historical Review* 69 (1964), 1006–21.

135. Walter Struve, *Elites Against Democracy*, 10.

136. Oswald Spengler, *Jahre der Entscheidung* (Munich, 1933), 51.

137. Ceaser, *Reconstructing America*, 187. My discussion of Heidegger owes a debt to Ceaser's analysis.

138. Ceaser, *Reconstructing America*, 190. See especially Jean Baudrillard's *Amèrique* (Paris: B. Grasset, 1986).

139. Michael Ermarth, "Heidegger on Americanism: *Ruinanz* and the End of Modernity," *Modernism/Modernity* 7 (2000), 385.

140. Martin Heidegger, *Einführung in die Metaphysik*, in *Gesamtausgabe* vol. 40 (Frankfurt am Main: Klostermann, 1975), 40–41.

141. Heidegger, "Hölderlins Hymne," in *Gesamtausgabe* vol. 53, 86 (emphasis added).

142. Heidegger, *Holzwege* (Frankfurt:Vittoria Klostermann, 1957), 103.

143. Heidegger, "Hölderlins Hymne," in *Gesamtausgabe* vol. 53, 86.

144. Heidegger, "Hölderlins Hymne," in *Gesamtausgabe* vol. 53, 86.

145. Michael Allen Gillespie, *Hegel, Heidegger, and the Ground of History* (Chicago: University of Chicago Press, 1984), 132.

146. On this topic, see Richard Wolin, *The Seduction of Unreason:The Intellectual Romance with Fascism from Nietzsche to Postmodernism* (Princeton: Princeton University Press, 2004).

147. See especially his interview with *Der Spiegel*, translated as "Only a God Can Save Us," in Thomas Sheehan, ed., *Heidegger: the Man and the Thinker* (Chicago: Precedent, 1981), 46–67.

148. Heidegger, "Andenken: Erläuterung zu Hölderlins Dichtung," in *Gesamtausgabe*, vol. 52, 37.

149. Hugo Ott, *Martin Heidegger: Unterwegs zu seiner Biographie* (Frankfurt: Campus Verlag, 1988), 45ff.

150. On the firm association of modern liberalism and representative government with Protestantism and its problems, see the Jesuit Luigi Tapparelli d'Azeglio's influential *Esame critico degli ordini rappresentativi nella società moderna*, 2 vols. (Rome, 1854).

151. Jaime Balmes, *European Civilization, Protestantism and Catholicism*; quoted in Béla Menczer, ed., *Tensions of Order and Freedom: Catholic Political Thought, 1789–1848* (New Brunswick:Transaction Publishers, 1994), 187.

152. "In tantis [...] quibis quotidie augimur [sic] angustiis, ac in tantis catholicae fidei in Europa illatis vulneribus, a provinciis americanis expectamus solacium." Quoted in Luca Codignola, "Rome and North America, 1622–1799:The Interpretive Framework," *Storia Nordamericana* 1 (1984), 23.

153. See, for example, *Articles de l'Avenir*, vol. 2 (Louvain, 1831), 163–64.

154. "Atque ex hoc putidissimo indifferentismi fonte absurda illa fluit ac erronea sententia, seu potius deliramentum asserendam esse ac vindicandam cuilibet libertatem conscientiae." *Acta Gregorii Papae XVI*, vol. 1 (Rome, 1900), 172; English translation in Claudia Carlen, ed., *The Papal*

Encyclicals, 1740–1878, vol. 1 (Pierian Press, 1990), 238 (translation modified).

155. Claudia Carlen, ed., *The Papal Encyclicals, 1740–1878,* vol. 1 (Pierian Press, 1990), 238 (translation modified); *Papal Encyclicals,* vol. 1, 238–39. Cf. "indifferentismo" in *Enciclopedia Cattolica,* vol. 6 (1951), 1830–32.

156. Anthony J. Mioni, ed., *The Popes against Modern Errors* (Rockford, Illinois: Tan Books, 1999), 14ff.

157. See the encyclical "Respcientes," in C. Carlen, ed., *Papal Encyclicals,* vol. 1, 394. On anticlericalism, see Guido Verucci, *L'Italia laica prima e dopo l'unita, 1848–1876: anticlericalismo, libero pensiero e ateismo* (Rome: Laterza, 1981).

158. Joseph de Maistre, *Œuvres complètes,* vols. 1–2 (Geneva: Slatkine Reprints, 1979), 86–87.

159. Giovanni Antonio Grassi, *Notizie varie sullo stato presente della repubblica degli Stati Uniti dell'America* (Rome, 1818), 49–50.

160. Count Metternich, *Mémoires;* excerpted in Menzer, ed., *Tensions of Order and Freedom,* 142–44, 153.

161. Archbishop Maréchal's Report to Propaganda (16 October 1818); in John Tracy Ellis, ed., *Documents of American Catholic History* (Milwaukee: Bruce Publishing Company, 1956), 213–19.

162. Camille Ferri-Pisani, *Lettres sur les États-Unis d'Amérique* (Paris, 1862), 67.

163. Karl August von Reisach, "Il Mormonismo nelle sue attinenze col moderno Protestanismo," *Civiltà Cattolica* (19 May 1860), 391–413.

164. Joseph Edmund Jörg, *Geschichte des Protestantismus in seiner neuesten Entwicklung,* vol. 2 (Freiburg im Breisgau, 1858), 457, 469, 499ff.

165. Jörg, *Geschichte des Protestantismus,* vol. 2, 412-13, passim; 457f.

166. Jörg, *Geschichte des Protestantismus,* vol. 2, 414.

167. Jörg, *Geschichte des Protestantismus,* vol. 2, 431, 437, 457.

168. See especially the section entitled "Das Yankeethum als Produkt des Sektengeistes." Jörg, *Geschichte des Protestantismus,* vol. 2, 425ff.

169. Jörg, *Geschichte des Protestantismus,* vol. 2, 437–38.

170. Max LeClerc, *Choses d'Amérique* (Paris, 1895); excerpted in Ellis, *Documents of American Catholic History,* 513.

171. For other dimensions of Americanism as understood from a European Catholic perspective, see the entry on "américanisme" in *Dictionnaire de théologie catholique,* vol. 1 (Paris, 1930), 1043–49, and the entry on "americanismo" in *Enciclopedia cattolica,* vol. 1 (Florence, 1948), 1054–56.

172. See, for example, David F. Sweeny, "Herman Schell, 1850–1906: A German Dimension to the Americanist Controversy," *Catholic Historical Review* 76 (January 1990), 44–71.

173. John T. McGreevy, *Catholicism and American Freedom* (New York: W. W. Norton, 2003), 47, 87. Mention should also be made of the *Historisch-politische Blätter für das katholische Deutschland* (founded in 1838), which served as the mouthpiece of German Catholic traditionalism against political liberalism. Joseph Edmund Jörg, in fact, served as its editor from

1852 to 1901. See his article, "Die beginnenden Sonderbunds-Kämpfe der nordamerikanischen Union" 47 (1861), 270ff. In it, he makes a firm connection between the activities of Cavour and Garbaldi against the Church on the Italian peninsula and the example of the United States. For foreign Catholic views of the American Civil War in general, see Mark A. Noll, *The Civil War as a Theological Crisis* (Chapel Hill: University of North Carolina Press, 2006), 125–55.

174. For an example of the liberal (pro-American) position see, Edoardo Laboulaye, *La separazione della chiesa e dello stato studiata nella storia e nella legislazione degli Stati Uniti d'America* (Rome, 1874).

175. Matteo Liberatore, "Il liberalismo e gli Stati Uniti d'America," *Civiltà Cattolica* (22 February 1876), 272ff., 534ff.

176. John Ciani, "Cardinal Camillo Mazzella, S. J.," in Jeffrey von Arx, ed., *Varieties of Ultramontanism* (Washington DC: Catholic University of America Press, 1998), 105. In the 1970s Woodstock was absorbed into Georgetown University and exists today as the Woodstock Theological Center.

177. McGreevy, *Catholicism and American Freedom*, 107–08.

178. Quoted in Gerald McKevitt, *Brokers of Culture: Italian Jesuits in the American West, 1848–1919* (Stanford: Stanford University Press, 2007), 82.

179. "The Golden Jubilee, 1869–1919," *Woodstock Letters* 49 (1920), 43–44.

180. Quoted in McKevitt, *Brokers of Culture*, 84.

181. Quoted in Ciani, "Cardinal Camillo Mazella, S. J.," in Arx, ed., *Varieties of Ultramontanism* , 107.

182. Quoted in McKevitt, *Brokers of Culture*, 69.

183. McKevitt, *Brokers of Culture*, 72ff.

184. John Ciani, "Across a Wide Ocean: Salvatore Maria Brandi, S. J., and the '*Civiltà Cattolica*,' from Americanism to Modernism," Ph.D. diss. (University of Virginia, 1992), 222.

185. "…gratia legum fruatur patrocinioque publicae potestatis." *Acta Leonis XIII*, vol. 15 (Rome, 1896), 7; *Papal Encyclicals*, vol. 2, 364–65 (translation modified). Cf. Leo XIII's "Immortale Dei" (1885) and "Libertas humana" (1888), in *Papal Encyclicals*, vol. 2, 107–19, 169–81. It should also be recognized that Leo's *Aeterni Patris* (1878), reviving Thomism, and *Rerum novarum* (1891), chartering modern Catholic social thought, greatly shaped the intellectual milieu, which provided figures such as Jacques Maritain (and John Courtney Murray et al.) the intellectual tools to esteem American religious liberty and limited government. On this point, see Russell Hittinger, "Introduction to Modern Catholicism," in John Witte Jr. et al., eds., *The Teachings of Modern Christianity on Law, Politics, and Human Nature*, vol. 1 (New York: Columbia University Press, 2006), 3–38.

186. Charles Maignen, *Père Hecker, est-il un saint?* (Paris, 1898), 390 and Gerald P. Fogarty, *The Vatican and the American Hierarchy, 1870–1965* (Collegeville, MN: The Liturgical Press, 1982), 160ff.

187. Ornella Confessore, *L'americanismo cattolico in Italia* (Rome: Edizioni Studium, 1984), 67ff.
188. *Acta Leonis XIII*, vol. 19, 5–20; Fogarty, *The Vatican and the American Hierarchy*, 178–9.
189. This was the influential line taken by Felix Klein in his *Americanism: A Phantom Heresy* (Atchison, Ka., 1951).
190. Delassus, *L'Américanisme et la conjuration anti-chrétienne* (Paris, 1899); see especially, 85ff., 101ff.
191. Salvatore Maria Brandi, "Leone XIII e l'americanismo," *Civiltà Cattolica* (6 March 1899), 641, 643–4, 648–53.
192. Carlen, ed., *The Papal Encyclicals*, vol. 2, 89.
193. Fogarty, *The Vatican and the American Hierarchy*, 194.
194. Henry Bargy, *La religion dans la société aux États-Unis* (Paris, 1902), i ff.
195. Charles Maignen, "A French View of Religion in America," *The Review* 10 (1903), 292.
196. Hilaire Belloc, *The Contrast* (New York, 1924), 9–15.
197. Belloc, *The Contrast*, 150, 166.

CHAPTER 3

1. Karl Marx and Friedrich Engels, *Werke*, vol. 36 (Berlin: Dietz Verlag, 1967), 532–33, 560ff.
2. Dipesh Chakrabarty, *Provincializing Europe: Postcolonial Thought and Historical Difference* (Princeton: Princeton University Press, 2000), 6ff.
3. Robert Stuart, "Marxism and Anticlericalism: The Parti Ouvrier Français and the War against Religion, 1882–1905," *Journal of Religious History* 22 (October 1998), 287.
4. Karl Marx, "The Eighteenth Brumaire of Louis Bonaparte" (1852), in Robert C. Tucker, ed., *The Marx-Engels Reader*, 2nd edn. (New York: W. W. Norton, 1972), 597.
5. Manfred Henningsen, "Das Amerika von Hegel, Marx und Engels: Zur Genealogie des europäischen Anti-Amerikanismus," *Zeitschrift für Politik* 20 (1973), 251.
6. Peter Berger, Grace Davie, and Effie Fokas, *Religious America, Secular Europe? A Theme and Variations* (Hampshire: Ashgate, 2008), 6ff., 31–32.
7. Charles Taylor, *A Secular Age* (Cambridge: Mass.: Belknap Press of Harvard University Press, 2007), 125, 425.
8. Jean Réville, "Anticlericalism in France," *American Journal of Theology* 9 (1905), 615–16, 619.
9. Condorcet, *Selected Writings*, ed., Keith Michael Baker (Indianapolis: Bobbs-Merrill, 1976), 237.
10. *Oeuvres complètes de Condorcet*, vol. 4; quoted in David Williams, *Condorcet and Modernity* (Cambridge: Cambridge University Press, 2004), 123.
11. Quoted in Williams, *Condorcet and Modernity*, 250–53.

12. Condorcet, *Selected Writings*, 76.

13. Condorcet, *Equisse d'un tableau historique des progrès de l'esprit humain* (Paris, 1966), 202ff.

14. Henri Saint-Simon, *Selected Writings on Science, Industry, and Social Organization*, trans. Keith Taylor (New York: Holmes and Meier, 1975), 162.

15. Ibid., 162.

16. Anthony Pagden, ed., *The Idea of Europe: from Antiquity to the European Union* (Cambridge: Cambridge University Press, 2002), 13.

17. Saint-Simon, *Selected Writings*, 223, 292, 295ff.

18. Quoted in Richard G. Olson, *Science and Scientism in Nineteenth-Century Europe* (Urbana, Il.: University of Illinois Press, 2008), 52.

19. Georg Iggers, ed., *The Doctrine of Saint-Simon: An Exposition* (Boston: Beacon Press, 1958), ix–xii and G. D. H. Cole, *A History of Socialist Thought: Vol. 1: The Forerunners, 1789–1850* (London: MacMillan, 1955), 44.

20. A. S. Tillett, "Some Saint-Simonian Criticism of the United States before 1835," *Romantic Review* 52 (1961), 3–16.

21. It is doubtful if this was from the pen of Saint-Simon, but its exact authorship is disputed.

22. Saint-Simon, *Catéchisme politique des industriels*, 2nd edn. (Paris, 1832), 167–73.

23. See Iggers, ed., *Doctrine of Saint-Simon*, 34 and Tillett, "Some Saint-Simonian Criticism of the United States before 1835," *Romantic Review*, 13. Cf. Anne Wharton Smith, "Criticism of American Life and Letters in the *Revue encyclopédique*," Ph.D. Diss., Northwestern University (Evanston, Illinois, 1943), 182ff.

24. Auguste Jullien, "De la liberté en France et aux États-Unis," *Revue encyclopédique* 52 (1831), 215–16.

25. Michel Chevalier, *Lettres sur l'Amérique du Nord*, vol. 1 (Paris, 1836), 234.

26. Chevalier, *Lettres sur l'Amérique du Nord*, vol. 2, 213.

27. Chevalier, *Lettres sur l'Amérique du Nord*, vol. 2, 281–82.

28. Chevalier, *Lettres sur l'Amérique du Nord*, vol. 1, 342; vol. 2, 119, 125.

29. Chevalier, *Lettres sur l'Amérique du Nord*, vol. 2, 306–08.

30. Chevalier, *Lettres sur l'Amérique du Nord*, vol. 2, 285.

31. Chevalier, *Lettres sur l'Amérique du Nord*, vol. 1, 344.

32. Chevalier, *Lettres sur l'Amérique du Nord*, vol. 2, 186.

33. Pierre-Joseph Proudhon, *Selected Writings*, ed. Stewart Edwards and trans. Elizabeth Fraser (London: MacMillan, 1970), 184–85.

34. Proudhon, *The Principle of Federation*, trans. Richard Vernon (Toronto: University of Toronto Press, 1979), 54–56.

35. Raymond Aron, *Main Currents in Sociological Thought*, trans. Richard Howard and Helen Weaver, vol. 1 (London: Weidenfeld Nicolson, 1965), 61.

36. Comte, *Cours de philosophie positive*, 5th edn., vol. 6 (Paris, 1894), 277.
37. Comte served as the personal secretary to Saint-Simon from 1817 to 1824.
38. On this theme generally in post-revolutionary thought, see Mona Ozouf, "La révolution français et l'idée de l'homme nouveau," in Colin Lucas, ed., *The French Revolution and the Creation of Modern Political Culture*, vol. 2 (Oxford: Pergamon Press, 1988), 213ff. On Comte's relationship to Saint-Simon and his followers, see Mary Pickering, "Auguste Comte and the Saint-Simonians," *French Historical Studies* 18 (1993), 211–36.
39. Comte, *Cours de philosophie positive*, vol. 6, 279.
40. See Jacques Bénigne Bossuet, *Discours sur l'histoire universelle*, 2 vols. (Paris, 1679) and *Historie des variations des églises protestantes*, 4 vols. (Paris, 1688).
41. Quoted material, without precise sources provided, in Aron, *Main Currents in Sociological Thought*, vol. 1, 78–80 (emphasis added).
42. Michael Burleigh, *Earthly Powers: The Clash of Religion and Politics in Europe from the French Revolution to the Great War* (New York: HarperCollins, 2005), 230.
43. Henri de Lubac, *Le drame de l'humanisme athée* (Paris, Spes, 1944). This book remains one of the most trenchant analyses of Comte's project and its relationship to Catholicism.
44. Quoted material taken from R. L. Hawkins, *Auguste Comte and the United States* (Cambridge: Harvard University Press, 1936), 11.
45. Comte, *Le Producteur*, vol. 1, 610–11; quoted in C. Bouglé and E. Halvéy, *Doctrine de Saint-Simon* (Paris, 1924), 169–70.
46. Comte, *Cours de philosophie positive*, vol. 4, 121; vol. 5, 269.
47. Comte, *Cours de philosophie positive*, vol. 6, 283.
48. Comte, *Cours de philosophie positive*, vol. 5, 538–39. Despite his harsh words about America, it should be pointed out that Comte obtained a small, but committed following in the United States in the second half of the nineteenth century. See Gillis J. Harp, *Positivist Republic: Auguste Comte and the Reconstruction of American Liberalism, 1865–1920* (University Park, Pa.: Pennsylvania State University Press, 1995).
49. Comte, *Cours de philosophie positive*, vol. 6, 283–84 (emphasis added).
50. Comte, *Cours de philosophie positive*, vol. 6, 284.
51. Quoted material taken from Hawkins, *Auguste Comte and the United States*, 10–14.
52. From Hegel's lectures on the philosophy of history; quoted in Andrew Prior, *Revolution and Philosophy: The Significance of the French Revolution for Hegel and Marx* (Cape Town: David Philip, 1972), 73–74.
53. On the background to this point, see Hans Meier, *Die ältere deutsche Staats- und Verwaltungslehre*, 2nd edn. (Munich: C. H. Beck, 1980).

54. G. W. F. Hegel, *Die Vernunft in der Geschichte*, 5th ed. (Hamburg: Felix Meiner, 1955), 112. My translations owe a significant debt to those of Leo Rauch; see Hegel, *Introduction to the Philosophy of History*, trans. Leo Rauch (Indiannapolis: Hackett, 1988).

55. Hegel, *Philosophy of Right*, trans. T. M. Knox (Oxford: Clarendon Press, 1952), 279.

56. See Matthew Levinger, *Enlightened Nationalism: The Transformation of Prussian Political Culture, 1806–1848* (New York: Oxford University Press, 2000).

57. Quoted in Karl Barth, *Protestant Theology in the Nineteenth Century*, trans. John Bowden (London: SCM Press, 1972), 604.

58. Hajo Holborn, "Der deutsche Idealismus in sozialgeschichtlicher Beleuchtung," *Historische Zeitschrift* 174 (1952), 359ff.

59. Of course, Hegel, a product of a Protestant background, did not share Saint-Simon and Comte's lingering esteem for Catholicism. Indeed, he saw the Protestant Reformation as a major stepping stone toward the modern world, a precursor to the French Revolution and his own philosophy. See Joachim Ritter, *Hegel und die französische Revolution* (Cologne: Westdeutscher Verlag, 1957), 32. Cf. Lawrence S. Stepelevich, "Hegel and Roman Catholicism," *Journal of the American Academy of Religion* 60 (1992), 673–91.

60. Hegel, *Philosophy of Right*, 171.

61. Henningsen, "Das Amerika von Hegel, Marx und Engels," *Zeitschrfit für Politik*, 232.

62. Hegel, *Philosophy of Right*, 171.

63. Hegel, *Die Vernunft in der Geschichte*, 206.

64. Hegel, *Die Vernunft in der Geschichte*, 206–07.

65. Hegel, *Die Vernunft in der Geschichte*, 202.

66. See Antonello Gerbi, *The Dispute of the New World: The History of a Polemic, 1750–1900*, trans. Jeremy Moyle (Pittsburgh: University of Pittsburgh Press, 1973), 423.

67. Hegel, *Die Vernunft in der Geschichte*, 209–10.

68. Henningsen, "Das Amerika von Hegel, Marx und Engels," *Zeitschrift für Politik*, 236–37.

69. Gerbi, *The Dispute of the New World*, 417ff. and Hegel, *Die Vernunft in der Geschichte*, 206–07. Hegel's thought, to be sure, has also served highly optimistic readings of America's world-historical purpose, not least among the so-called "St. Louis Hegelians." On this movement in American philosophy, see William H. Goetzmann, ed., *The American Hegelians: An Intellectual Episode in the History of Western America* (New York: Alfred A. Knopf, 1973).

70. On developments after Hegel, see John Edward Toews, *Hegelianism: The Path toward Dialectial Humanism, 1805–1841* (Cambridge: Cambridge University Press, 1980), 203ff.

71. See, for example, Herbert Marcuse, *Reason and Revolution: Hegel and the Rise of Social Theory* (New York: Humanities Press, 1954) and George Lichtheim, *The Origins of Socialism* (New York: Praeger, 1969).

72. Marx, *Writings of the Young Marx on Philosophy and Society*, ed. and trans. L. D. Easton and K. H. Guddat (New York, 1967), 205.

73. Marx and Engels, *Marx and Engels on Religion* (New York: Schocken Books, 1964), 41, 50 (translation modified).

74. In this paragraph, I borrow material from N. Lobkowicz, "Karl Marx's Attitude toward Religion," *Review of Politics* 26 (1964), 326ff.

75. Manfred Henningsen, *Der Fall Amerika: Zur Sozial- und Bewußtseinsgeschichte einer Verdrängung* (Munich: List Verlag, 1974), 76ff.

76. Karl Marx and Friedrich Engels, "Zur Judenfrage," *Werke*, vol. 1 (Berlin: Dietz Verlag, 1976), 352.

77. Marx, "Zur Judenfrage," *Werke*, vol. 1, 352–53.

78. See Karl Marx, *On America and the Civil War*, ed. and trans. Saul K. Padover (New York: McGraw-Hill, 1972).

79. Henningsen, "Das Amerika von Hegel, Marx und Engels," *Zeitschrift für Politik*, 240.

80. *Marx and Engels on Religion*, 135.

81. "Judaism" here is Marx's crude (anti-Semitic) shorthand for a capitalist mentality and practice. See Julius Carlebach, *Karl Marx and the Radical Critique of Judaism* (London: Routledge Kegan Paul, 1978).

82. *Werke*, vol. 1, 373–74.

83. Karl Marx, "The Eighteenth Brumaire of Louis Bonaparte," in Robert C. Tucker, ed., *The Marx-Engels Reader* (New York: W. W. Norton, 1978), 597, 602 (translation modified).

84. On the persistence of this question, see Robin Archer, *Why is there no Labor Party in the United States?* (Princeton: Princton University Press, 2007). See especially chapter seven on religion and labor in America. Werner Sombart also left the dubious legacy of associating American Puritanism and Judaism. Because of their strident moralizing and economic productivity, he wrote of a "close spiritual connection" between the two. See Sombart, *Die Juden und das Wirtschaftsleben* (Leipzig, 1911), 292.

85. Engels to Sorge (8 August 1887) in Marx and Engels, *Letters to Americans, 1848–1895*, trans. Leonard E. Mins (New York, 1953), 190.

86. Karl Kautsky, "Der amerikanische Arbeiter," *Die Neue Zeit*, vol. 1 22/34 (1905–06), 740–44.

87. Delos B. McKown, *The Classical Marxist Critiques of Religion: Marx, Engels, Lenin, Kautsky* (The Hague: Martinus Nijhoff, 1975), 148.

88. Karl Liebknecht, *Gesammelte Reden und Schriften*, vol. 3 (Berlin: Dietz Verlag, 1960), 512.

89. Edward Aveling and Eleanor Marx Aveling, *The Working-Class Movement in America* (London, 1891), 13 and R. Laurence Moore, *European Socialist and the American Promised Land* (New York: Oxford University Press, 1970), 32.

90. Noted in Alexander Schmidt, *Reisen in die Moderne: Der Amerika-Diskurs des deutschen Bürgertums vor dem Ersten Weltkrieg im europäischen Vergleich* (Berlin: Akademie Verlag, 1997), 170.

91. Philippe Roger, *The American Enemy: The History of French Anti-Americanism*, trans. Sharon Bowman (Chicago: University of Chicago Press, 2005), 257ff.

92. W. T. Coyler, *Americanism: A World Menace* (London, 1922), 2–5. See how this discourse became embedded in the legitimation strategies of the early Soviet Union in Frederick C. Barhoorn, *The Soviet Image of the United States* (New York: Harcourt, Brace, and Company, 1950), xiff.

93. Coyler, *Americanism*, 11, 121–33.

94. Thompson first advanced this influential thesis, focusing largely on English Methodism, in *The Making of the English Working Class* (London: Victor Gollancz, 1963), 375–400. Cf. Harvey J. Kaye, *The British Marxist Historians* (New York: St. Martin's Press, 1995).

95. Antonio Gramsci, *Americanismo e fordismo* (Milano: Riuniti, 1991), 42f.

96. Jean Baudrillard, *America*, trans. Chris Turner (London: Verso, 1988), 2, 7, 90–91.

97. René Rémond, *L'anticléricalisme en France de 1815 à nos jours* (Paris: Fayard, 1976), 3ff. and Hugh McLeod, *Secularisation in Western Europe, 1848–1914* (London: MacMillan, 2000), 31ff.

98. On this point, see Ahmet T. Kuru, "Passive and Assertive Secularism: Historical Conditions, Ideological Struggles, and State Policies toward Religion," *World Politics* 59 (July 2007), 568ff. Cf. Jean Baubérot, *Histoire de la laïcité en France* 2nd edn., (Paris: Presses Universitaires de France, 2005), 75–92.

99. James J. Sheehan, *German History, 1770–1866* (Oxford: Oxford University Press, 1989), 697–710.

100. M. Hedwigis Overmoehle, "The Anticlerical Activities of the Forty-Eighters in Wisconsin, 1848-1860," Ph.D. diss. (St. Louis University, 1941), 124.

101. La Vern J. Rippley, *The German-Americans* (Boston: Twayne Publishers, 1976), 53.

102. Chester Verne Easum, *The Americanization of Carl Schurz* (Chicago: University of Illinois Press, 1929), 125.

103. Friedrich Nietzsche, "Die kirchliche Zustände der Deutschen in Nordamerika," in Nietzsche, *Kritische Gesamtausgabe*, vol. 4 (1). eds., Girogio Colli and Mazzino Montinari et al. (Berlin: Walter de Gruyter, 1999), 24–25.

104. On the legacy of the German émigré press, see Elliott Shore et al., eds., *The German-American Press: The Shaping of a Left Political Culture, 1850–1940* (Urbana, Il.: University of Illinois Press, 1992).

105. Quoted material taken from Overmoehle, "The Anticlerical Activities of the Forty-Eighters," 135, 194.

106. *Wisconsin Banner* (8 February 1854); quoted in Overmoehle, "The Anticlerical Activities of the Forty-Eighters," 190.

107. Maria Wagner, "The Forty-Eighters in their Struggle against American Puritanism: The Case Study of Newark, New Jersey," in Charlotte L. Brancaforte, ed., *The German Forty-Eighters in the United States* (New York: Peter Lang, 1989), 219–29.

108. Quoted in Overmoehle, "The Anticlerical Activities of the Forty-Eighters," 200–01.

109. Hildegard Binder Johnson, "Adjustment to the United States," in A. E. Zucker, *The Forty-Eighters: Political Refugees of the German Revolution of 1848* (New York: Columbia University Press, 1950), 58. On Mencken and religion, see S. T. Joshi, ed., *Mencken on Religion* (Amherst, NY: Prometheus Press, 2002).

110. Ray Allen Billington, *The Protestant Crusade, 1800–1860* (Chicago: Quadrangle Books, 1964), 242.

111. Alessandro Gavazzi, *Father Gavazzi's Lectures in New York*, trans. Madame Julie de Marguerittes (New York, 1853), 276 and John T. McGreevy, *Catholicism and American Freedom* (New York: W. W. Norton, 2003), 24–25.

112. Donald S. Spencer, *Louis Kossuth and Young America* (Columbia: University of Missouri Press, 1977), 129. Cf. Daniel R. Miller, "American Christians and the Visit of Louis Kossuth," *Fides et Historia* 20 (1988), 6–17.

113. Heinrich Börnstein, *Die Geheimnisse von St. Louis* (Cassel: H. Hotop, 1851). It was soon translated into English and several other languages. See Steven Rowan, "Anticlericalism, Atheism, and Socialism in German St. Louis, 1850–1853: Heinrich Börstein and Franz Schmidt," in Henry Geitz, ed., *The German-American Press* (Madison, Wisconsin: Max Kade Institute, 1992), 43–56.

114. Quoted in Overmoehle, "The Anticlerical Activities of the Forty-Eighters," 245.

115. The "Louisville Platform," from Heinrich Tolzmann, ed., *The German-American Forty-Eighters, 1848–1998* (Indianapolis: Publication of the Max Kade German-American Center, 1998), 99–102.

116. Carl Wittke, *Refugees of Revolution: The German Forty-Eighters in America* (Philadelphia: University of Pennsylvania Press, 1952), 134.

117. Quoted in Rippley, *The German-Americans*, 53.

118. Geitz, ed., *The German-American Press*, 64.

119. *Atlantis*, vol. 2 (May 1855), 392–93; quoted in Overmoehle, "The Anticlerical Activities of the Forty-Eighters," 253.

120. Quoted without precise source in Wittke, *Refugees of Revolution*, 126.

121. Carlton J. H. Hayes, *A Generation of Materialism, 1871–1900* (New York: Harper & Row, 1941), 124 and A. N. Wilson, *God's Funeral* (New York: W. W. Norton, 1999). For a view contravening Wilson's, see Timothy Larsen,

Crisis of Doubt: Honest Faith in Nineteenth-Century England (Oxford: Oxford University Press 2006).

122. Emile Poulat, *Liberté, laïcité: La guerre des deux France et le principe de la modernité* (Paris: Cerf, 1987).

123. Stuart, "Marxism and Anticlericalism," *Journal of Religious History*, 289.

124. Jean-Paul Willaime, "Laïcité, religions et construction européenne," in Jean Baubérot et al., eds., *Laïcité et séparation des Églises et de l'État* (Limoges: Pulim, 2006), 213–24.

125. Noted in Roger, *American Enemy*, 99.

126. Victorien Sardou, *L'Oncle Sam*, 3rd edn. (Paris, 1882), 10–12.

127. Roger, *American Enemy*, 100–01.

128. Frédéric Gaillardet, *Aristocratie en Amérique* (Paris, 1883), 146.

129. Gaillardet, *Aristocratie en Amérique*, 152.

130. Frédéric Gaillardet, *Sketches of Early Texas and Louisiana*, trans. James L. Shepherd (Austin: University of Texas Press, 1966), 61.

131. Gaillardet, *Aristocratie en Amérique*, 153–55.

132. Gaillardet, *Aristocratie en Amérique*, 162ff.

133. Urbain Gohier, *Le peuple du xxe siècle aux États-Unis* (Paris: Fasquelle, 1903), 115. Cf. Jacques Portes, *Fascination and Misgivings: The United States in French Opinion, 1870–1914*, trans. Elborg Forster (Cambridge: Cambridge University Press, 2000), 288ff.

134. Jules Huret, *En Amérique; de New-York à Nouvelle-Orléans* (Paris, 1904), 94.

135. Huret, *En Amérique*, 328.

136. On Durkheim's life, see the magisterial recent biography by Marcel Fournier, *Émile Durkheim, 1858–1917* (Paris: Fayard, 2007). Cf. Henry Alpert, *Emile Durkheim and his Sociology* (New York, 1939).

137. Durkheim, *The Division of Labor in Society* (New York: MacMillan, 1933); quoted in Christian Smith, ed., *The Secular Revolution: Power, Interests, and Conflict in the Secularization of American Public Life* (Berkeley: University of California Press, 2003), 15–16.

138. Riccardo Calimani, "The Jewish Intellectual in France: Durkheim and Mauss," *European Judaism* 36 (Spring 2003), 63. Cf. his essay, "The Principles of 1789 and Sociology," in Robert Bellah, ed., *Emile Durkheim on Morality and Society: Selected Writings* (Chicago: University of Chicago Press, 1973). One should note that Durkheim had great appreciation for the social function of religion as a cement for society; and though a prophet of secularization he also recognized the socially disaggregating consequences of religious decline.

139. See Robert Wuthnow, *Boundless Faith: The Global Outreach of American Christianity* (Berkeley: University of California Press, 2009); Philip Jenkins, *The Next Christendom: The Coming of Global Christianity*, rev. and exp. ed. (New York: Oxford University Press, 2007); and Mark Noll, *The New Shape of World Christianity: How American Experience Shapes Global Faith* (Downers Grove, IL: IVP Academic, 2009). For statistics of world

Christianity between 1910 and the present, see Todd Johnson and Kenneth R. Ross, eds., *Atlas of Global Christianity* (Edinburgh: Edinburgh University Press, 2009).

140. See Peter Berger, ed., *The Desecularization of the World* (Grand Rapids: Eerdmans, 1999), 1ff. and "After Secularization," an issue of the journal *Hedgehog Review* (Spring/Sumer 2006) devoted to the global resurgence of religion—or at least the growing awareness of religion's persistence among scholars.

141. Berger, ed., *Desecularization of the World*, 11.

142. John Micklethwait and Adrian Woolridge, *God is Back: How the Global Revival of Faith is Changing the World* (New York: Penguin Press, 2009).

143. Grace Davie, *Europe the Exceptional Case: Parameters of Faith in the Modern World* (London: Darton, Longman and Todd, 2002) and R. Stephen Warner, "Toward a New Paradigm for the Sociological Study of Religion in the United States," *American Journal of Sociology* 98 (March 1993), 1044–93.

144. Talcott Parsons, *The Social System* (New York: Free Press, 1959), 32 (emphasis added).

145. Jeffrey K. Hadden, "Toward Desacralizing Secularization Theory," *Social Forces* 65 (March 1987), 590.

146. David Martin, *The Religious and the Secular: Studies in Secularization* (London: Routledge & Kegan Paul, 1969), 65.

147. Peter Berger et al., *Religious America, Secular Europe? A Theme and Variations* (Burlington, Vt: Ashgate, 2008), 9ff.

148. e.g., Steve Bruce, *God is Dead: Secularization in the West* (Oxford: Blackwell, 2002).

149. See Hans Blumenberg, *Die Legitimität der Neuzeit* (Frankfurt am Main: Suhrkamp, 1996) and Marcel Gauchet, *Le désenchantement du monde: une histoire politique de la religion* (Paris: Gallimard, 1985).

150. Jean-Paul Willaime, "Laïcité, religions et construction européenne," in Baubérot et al., eds., *Laïcité et séparation des Églises et de l'État*, 222. One does well, however, to recognize that there are other forms of "secularism" in Europe.

151. Jeffrey Cox, "Secularization and Other Master Narratives of Religion in Modern Europe," *Kirchliche Zeitgeschichte* 14 (2001), 30–32.

152. José Casanova, "Religion, European Secular Identities, and European Integration," in Timothy A. Byrnes and Peter J. Katzenstein, eds., *Religion in an Expanding Europe* (Cambridge: Cambridge University Press, 2006), 83–85. Still, one must recognize limits and qualifications of applying secularization even to Western Europe. See Hervieu-Leger, *La religion pour mémoire* (Paris: Cerf, 1993).

153. Martin, *The Religious and the Secular*, 10.

154. Rainer Prätorius, *In God We Trust: Religion und Politik in den U.S.A.* (Munich: C. H. Beck, 2003), 8.

155. Micklethwait and Woolridge, *God is Back*, 11.

156. Andrei S. Markovits, *Uncouth Nation: Why Europe Dislikes America* (Princeton: Princeton Unversity Press, 2007), 26.
157. José Casanova, "Religion, European Secular Identities, and European Integration," in Byrnes and Katzenstein, eds., *Religion in an Expanding Europe*, 32.
158. See Edward Shils, *The Constitution of Society*, (Chicago: University of Chicago Press, 1972), 224ff.
159. Max Weber, "'Churches' and 'Sects' in North America: An Ecclesiastical Socio-Political Sketch" (trans. Colin Loader), *Sociological Theory* 3 (Spring 1985), 7.
160. Christian Smith, ed., *The Secular Revolution*, 35, 57–59.
161. Drawing from some of the latest social science, a *New York Times* reporter wrote in 1968: "By the 21st century religious believers are likely to be small sects, huddled together to resist a worldwide secular culture." "A Bleak Outlook is Seen for Religion," *New York Times* (25 February 1968).
162. From his poem, "A Postcard from the Volcano."

CHAPTER 4

1. One finds an especially sanguine image of America, for example, in the writings of the Dutch statesman and intellectual, Abraham Kuyper (1837–1920). See John Bolt, "Abraham Kuyper and the Holland-America Line of Liberty," *Journal of Markets and Morality* 1 (Spring 1998), 35–59.
2. See Günther Markus, *Auf dem Weg in die Neue Welt: die Atlantiküberquerung im Zeitalter der Massenauswanderung 1818–1914* (Augsburg: Wissner, 2005), 49–54 and Jonathan D. Sarna, *American Judaism: A History* (New Haven: Yale University Press, 2004), 154–56.
3. Of relevance here, too, is John Stuart Mill's lengthy review of *Democracy in America*, which originally appeared in the *Edinburgh Review* (October 1840). See J. S. Mill, *Dissertations and Discussions: Political, Philosophical, and Historical*, vol. 2 (London, 1859), 1–83.
4. See the bibliography in Milton Powell, ed., *The Voluntary Church: American Religious, 1740–1860, Life Seen Through the Eyes of European Visitors* (New York: MacMillan, 1967), 196–97. Cf. Adolf Keller, *Dynamis: Formen und Kräfte des amerikanischen Protestantismus* (Tübingen, 1922), a little-known work by an accomplished Swiss theologian.
5. Sadly, Schaff is largely neglected in Germany today. A leading scholar of Schaff, Klaus Penzel, relates the story of how the editors of one of the dominant German-language theological reference works, *Theologische Realenzyklopädie*, almost excluded an entry on Schaff (personal letter from Penzel, 13 October 2005).
6. On Schaff's scholarly legacy, see Henry W. Bowden, ed., *A Century of Church History: The Legacy of Philip Schaff* (Carbondale Il.: Southern

Illinois University Press, 1988) and Thomas Albert Howard, "German Academic Theology in America: The Case of Edward Robinson and Philip Schaff," *History of Universities* 18 (2003), 102–23.

7. David S. Schaff, *The Life of Philip Schaff in Part Autobiographical* (New York, 1897), 409.

8. See the "Congratulatory Address from the Theological Faculty of the University of Berlin," in Klaus Penzel, ed., *Philip Schaff: Historian and Ambassador of the Universal Church: Selected Writings* (Macon, Ga.: Mercer University Press, 1991), 344.

9. Penzel, ed., *Schaff*, 15.

10. On Schaff's early years in Switzerland, see Ulrich Gäbler, "Philip Schaff in Chur, 1819–1834," *Zwingliana* 18 (1989), 143–65.

11. D. Schaff, *Life of Philip Schaff*, 2, 6.

12. On Schaff's theological training in German universities, see Klaus Penzel, *The German Education of Christian Scholar Philip Schaff: The Formative Years, 1819–1844* (Lewiston: Edwin Mellen Press, 2004), 11–126 and David Schaff, *The Life of Philip Schaff*, 17–37.

13. Philip Schaff, *Germany; its Universities, Theology, and Religion* (Philadelphia, 1857), 8.

14. The German Reformed community accounted for less than 1% of the churches in America in the 1840s. See Stephen R. Graham, *Cosmos in the Chaos: Philip Schaff's Interpretation of Nineteenth-Century Amerian Religion* (Grand Rapids: Eerdmans, 1995), 2.

15. Graham, *Cosmos in the Chaos*, 54.

16. Schaff and Nevin are generally credited as the founders of the so-called "Mercersburg theology," a vigorous, if short-lived, theological movement in the nineteenth century, which in the name of tradition, ecclesial authority, and church unity sought to combat "the highly individualistic and subjectivist tradition of American evangelicalism." See Claude Welch, *Protestant Thought in the Nineteenth Century, 1799–1870*, vol. 1 (New Haven: Yale University Press, 1972), 227.

17. On Schaff at Union, see Robert T. Handy, *A History of Union Theological Seminary in New York* (New York: Columbia University Press, 1987), 35, 38, 47–51, passim.

18. Schaff, "Ordination of Professor Schaff," *Weekly Messenger* 9 (4 September 1844), 1869–70.

19. On the Prussian Union Church, see Walter Elliger, ed., *Die evangelische Kirche der Union* (Witten: Luther-Verlag, 1967).

20. D. Schaff, *Life of Philip Schaff*, 81.

21. Schaff refers to the New Testament book of Acts, which conveys the story of the Apostle Paul's vision of a man from Macedonia (a Roman province) who pled for his help, prompting Paul in fact to set sail for Macedonia. See Acts 16: 8–10.

22. Before crossing the Atlantic, Schaff spent six weeks in England, where he reported developing a deeper appreciation of the "Anglo-Saxon" mind. D. Schaff, *Life of Philip Schaff*, 82ff.

23. It was soon published, first in German and then in an English translation by his colleague John Nevin. See Schaff, *Das Princip des Protestantismus* (Chambersburg, Pa., 1845) and *The Principle of Protestantism as Related to the Present State of the Church*, trans. John Nevin (Chambersburg, Pa., 1845). The English translation was reprinted in 1964. I cite from this edition.

24. Schaff, *Principle of Protestantism*, 154.

25. Schaff, *Principle of Protestantism*, 145. Cf. Paul's Epistle to the Romans 10:2 (RSV).

26. Schaff, *Principle of Protestantism*, 149–50. As one might surmise, Schaff's inaugural lecture was not taken well by all hearers. To some, he took a critique of Protestantism too far and thus veered close to "Romanizing tendencies" or "Puseyism," a term associated with the high-church views of Edward Bouverie Pusey (1800–1882), a leader of the Oxford Movement in England. In fact, Schaff was even tried for heresy (on two occassions) by the German Reformed Church, but acquitted. On this episode in his life, see George H. Schriver, "Philip Schaff: Heresy at Mercersburg," in Schriver, ed., *American Religious Heretics: Formal and Informal Trials* (Nashville: Abingdon, 1966), 18–55.

27. Penzel, ed., *Schaff*, 93–94.

28. Jacques Maritain, *The Things that are not Caesar's*, trans. J. F. Scanlan (New York: C. Scribner's Sons, 1931).

29. On state–church arrangements in nineteenth-century Germany, see John Groh, *Nineteenth-Century German Protestantism* (Washington: University Press of America, 1982) and Kurt Novak, *Geschichte des Christentums in Deutschland: Religion, Politik und Gesellschaft vom Ende der Aufklärung bis zur Mitte des 20.Jahrhunderts* (Munich: C. H. Beck, 1995).

30. Quoted in D. Schaff, *Life of Philip Schaff*, 144.

31. Quoted in D. Schaff, *Life of Philip Schaff*, 140–41.

32. The article series, "Introduction to the Church History of the United States," appeared in the *German Reformed Messenger* from December 20, 1848 through February 21, 1849, pp. 2754, 2760, 2768, 2772, 2776, 2784, 2788, and 2792. My quotations of this source are taken from Stephen R. Graham, *Cosmos in the Chaos*, 24–28.

33. See Eberhard Reichmann et al., eds., *Emigration and Settlement Patterns of German Communities in North America* (Indianapolis: Max Kade German-American Center, 1995).

34. D. Schaff, *Life of Philip Schaff*, 156.

35. D. Schaff, *Life of Philip Schaff*, 157. Reflecting fairly typical views of the time, Schaff thought in highly ethnic terms; he was especially eager to champion what he referred to as the genius of "Anglogermanismus." See his *Anglogermanismus. Eine Rede gehalten den 10ten März, 1846, vor der*

Schillergesellschaft des Marshall-Collegiums zu Mercersburg, Pa. (Chambersburg, Pa., 1846).

36. The lectures were first published in German as *Amerika: Die politischen, socialen, und kirchlich-religiösen Zustände der Vereinigten Staaten von Nord-Amerika mit besonderer Rücksicht auf die Deutschen, aus eigener Anschauung dargestellt* (Berlin, 1854; subsequent editions in eitions in 1858 and 1865). The English translation—*America: A Sketch of the Political, Social, and Religious Character of the United States of North America*—appeared in 1855, published in New York, translated by Edward D. Yeomans. Harvard University Press reprinted the English edition in 1961 with an introduction by Perry Miller. I quote from this text unless otherwise noted.

37. *Der Bürgerkrieg und das christliche Leben in Nord-Amerika* (Berlin, 1865) was based on lectures delivered in Germany and Switzerland. It was translated by C. C. Starbuck and published in installments in the *Christian Intelligencer* in the spring of 1866.

38. Hans Rudolf Guggisberg, "Philip Schaff's Vision of America," *Yearbook of German-American Studies* 25 (1990), 32.

39. Schaff, *America*, 212.

40. On Schaff's providentialist conception of historical development and the role of America therein, see Klaus Penzel, "The Reformation goes West: The Notion of Historical Development in the Thought of Philip Schaff," *Journal of Religion* 62 (July 1982), 219–41.

41. Schaff, *America*, 213.

42. Frederick Jackson Turner, *The Frontier in American History* (New York: Holt, Rinehart and Winston, 1962), 38.

43. On European images and interpretations of the American frontier, see Ray Allen Billington, *Land of Savagery, Land of Promise: The European Image of the American Frontier* (New York: W. W. Norton, 1981).

44. Turner, *The Frontier in American History*, 36. For discussions of the significance of Turner's "frontier thesis" and its place in the historiography of the United States, see George Rogers Taylor, *The Turner Thesis Concerning the Role of the Frontier in American History*, 3rd ed. (Lexington, Ma.: Heath, 1972) and Ray Allen Billington, *The Frontier Thesis: Valid Interpretation of American History?* (New York: Holt, Rinehart and Winston, 1966). Cf. the excellent study by Matthias Waechter, *Die Erfindung des amerikanischen Westens: die Geschichte der Frontier-Debatte* (Freiburg: Rombach, 1995).

45. Schaff, "Progress of Christianity in the United States of America," *Princeton Review* 55 (September 1876), 211.

46. Schaff, *Der deutsche Kirchenfreund* 5 (1852), 175.

47. Schaff, *Theological Propaedeutic: A General Introduction to the Study of Theology*, 7th ed. (New York, 1907), 294.

48. Schaff, "Christianity in the United States," 18.

49. From editor's introduction; Schaff, *America*, xxx.

50. Schaff, *America*, 19.

51. Schaff, *America*, 5.
52. "If your right eye causes you to sin, tear it out and throw it away; it is better for you to lose one of your members than for your whole body to be thrown into hell" (NRSV).
53. Schaff refers to an article on America in volume nine of the *Kirchen-Lexikon: oder, Encyklopädie der katholischen Theologie und ihrer Hilfswissen-schaften,* edited by Heinrich Joseph Wetzer and Benedikt Welte (Freiburg im Breisgau, 1854). See Schaff, *America*, 104–05.
54. Graham, *Cosmos in the Chaos,* 34ff.
55. Schaff, *America*, 14.
56. Schaff, *America*, 100–01. Of course, Schaff recognized Mormonism as an exception to this rule.
57. Schaff, *America*, 14.
58. Schaff, *America*, 13–14.
59. Schaff, *America*, 191ff. Schaff's developmental view of history was fairly common for his time. His views bear witness, in direct and indirect ways, to the thought of Hegel, F. C. Baur, and August Neander. On his conception of history, see especially Schaff, *What is Church History? A Vindication of the Idea of Historical Development* (Philadelphia, 1846). On the various ideas concerning "historical development" afoot in nineteenth-century European thought, see Maurice Mandelbaum, *History, Man, and Reason: A Study in Nineteenth-Century Thought* (Baltimore: John Hopkins University Press, 1971), 41ff.
60. Schaff, *Germany; its Universities, Theology, and Religion,* 70.
61. Schaff, *America*, 12.
62. Schaff, *Germany; its Universities, Theology, and Religion,* 13 and Schaff, *Church and State in the United States,* 6.
63. Schaff, "The State Church System in Europe," *The Mercersburg Review* 9 (1857), 151–52. Even so, he recognized that Europe could not simply replicate American conditions, for fundamentally different historical dynamics were at work.
64. Schaff often qualified this observation by recognizing the vestiges of a European aristocracy in the planters of the American south and the vestiges of established churches in the New England states.
65. Schaff, *America*, 27–31.
66. Schaff, *America*, 29.
67. Elisabeth Fehrenbach and Elisabeth Müller-Luckner, eds., *Adel und Bürgertum in Deutschland, 1770–1848* (Munich: Oldenbourg, 1994), 187ff. and Deirdre N. McClosky, *Bourgeois Virtues: Ethics for an Age of Commerce* (Chicago: University of Chicago Press, 2007).
68. Schaff, *America*, 33.
69. Schaff, *America*, 31ff.
70. Schaff, *America*, xxix, 47.
71. Schaff, *America*, 36.
72. Schaff, "Progress of Christianity," *Princeton Review*, 221.

73. Schaff, "The State-Church System in Europe," 159.
74. Schaff, *Der Bürgerkrieg und das christliche Leben in Nord-Amerika*, 34.
75. This actually refers to the fictitious donation of Constantine, which was exposed as fraudulent by Lorenzo Valla during the Renaissance. Schaff, *Church and State in the United States* (New York, 1888), 11.
76. Schaff, *Church and State in the United States* (New York, 1888), 12.
77. Schaff, *Der Bürgerkrieg und das christliche Leben in Nord-Amerika*, 43–44; Schaff, *Church and State in the United States*, 9–12.
78. Schaff, *Church and State in the United States*, 23.
79. Schaff, *Church and State in the United States*, 16.
80. Schaff, "Christianity in America," a reprinted article from the *Princeton Review* (1857) in Charles Yrigoyen and George M. Bricker, eds., *Reformed and Catholic: Selected Historical and Theological Writings of Philip Schaff* (Pittsburgh: Pickwick Press, 1979), 359–60.
81. On this point in particular, see Sidney E. Mead, *The Lively Experiment: The Shaping of Christianity in America* (New York: Harper & Row, 1963).
82. Cf. Abraham Kuyper, "Calvinism: Source and Stronghold of Our Constitutional Liberties (1874)," in James D. Bratt, ed., *Abraham Kuyper: A Centennial Reader* (Grand Rapids, Mich.: Eerdmans, 1998), 279–322.
83. Schaff, *America*, 88.
84. Schaff, "Christianity in America," 352.
85. Indeed, Schaff did not want the divisions of the sixteenth century to be reified in perpetuity. Until his last days he hoped that America would be the site of an evangelical-catholic unity, where "from the Phoenix ashes of all Christian denomiantions" there would arise "the truly universal, evangelical Catholic bride of the Lord." If this did not happen—at some indeterminant future point—and if Protestantism's "centrifugal and unchurchly tendencies" predominated, then "a greater triumph of Catholicism" would have been prepared on American soil. Schaff, *America*, 215. On Schaff's ecumenical longings, see the address, "The Reunion of Christendom," prepared for the World's Parliament of Religions held in conjunction with the World's Columbian Exhibition at Chicago in 1893. This is reprinted in Klaus Penzel, ed., *Philip Schaff: Historian and Ambassador of the Universal Church: Selected Writings* (Macon, Ga.: Mercer University Press, 1991), 293–340.
86. Schaff, "Christianity in the United States," Report at the Seventh General Council of the Evangelical Alliance (New York, 1879), 42.
87. Schaff, *America*, 181.
88. Schaff, *America*, 191.
89. Schaff, *America*, 178ff., 197.

CHAPTER 5

1. Sophie Meunier, "Anti-Americanisms in France," *French Politics, Culture, and Society* 23 (2005), 126.

2. Jacques Maritain, *The Peasant of the Garonne* (New York: Macmillan, 1968), 36–37.

3. Jacques Portes, *Fascination and Misgivings: The United States in French Opinion, 1870–1914,* trans. Elborg Forster (Cambridge: Cambridge University Press, 2000), 399ff.

4. Philippe Roger, *The American Enemy: The History of French Anti-Americanism,* trans. Sharon Bowman (Chicago: University of Chicago Press, 2005), 259. For the remainder of this section, I owe a particular debt to Roger.

5. Roger, *American Enemy,* 264.

6. Sigmund Freud and William C. Bullitt, *Thomas Woodrow Wilson: A Psychological Study* (Cambridge, MA: Riverside Press, 1967), 71.

7. Georges Bernanos, *The Last Essays of George Bernanos,* trans. Joan and Barry Ulanov (Chicago: Henry Regnery, 1955), 129–30, 151ff.

8. Robert Aron and Arnaud Dandieu, *Le cancer américain* (Paris, 1931), 16, 19.

9. Émile Barbier, *Voyage au pays des dollars* (Paris, 1893), 167–68.

10. Paul Claudel, *Journal II,* 1933–1955, ed., F. Varillon and J. Petit (Paris: Gallimard, 1969), 10–11.

11. David Drake, *French Intellectuals and Politics from the Dreyfus Affair to the Occupation* (New York: Palgrave MacMillan, 2005).

12. Urbain Gohier, *Le peuple du xxe siècle aux États-Unis* (Paris: Fasquelle, 1903), 109, 117.

13. Roger, *American Enemy,* 411, 413.

14. Émile Boutmy, *Éléments d'une psychologie politique du peuple américain: la nation, la patrie, l'état, la religion,* 3rd edn. (Paris: Armand Colin, 1911), 89ff.

15. Boutmy, *Éléments d'une psychologie politique du peuple américain,* 94, 288ff.

16. Georges Duhamel, *Scènes de la vie future,* 5th edn. (Paris, 1930) 18f., 49, 109, 114.

17. Roger, *American Enemy,* 273. On the persistence in the twentieth century of images of America forged in the 1920s and 1930s, see Jean-Philippe Mathy, *Extrême Occident: French Intellectuals and America* (Chicago: Chicago University Press, 1993). For particular examples, see Simone de Beauvoir, *America Day by Day,* trans. Carol Cosman (Berkeley: University of California Press, 1999) and Jean Cau, *Discours de la décadence* (Paris: Copernic, 1978). For a pointedly dissenting view, see the many remarks about the United States in Raymond Aron, *The Opium of the Intellectuals,* trans. Terence Kilmartin (London: Secker & Warburg, 1957).

18. Jacques Maritain, *France, My Country through the Disaster* (New York, 1941), v.

19. This institution functioned sort of as a university-in-exile for French academics during World War II. See Aristide R. Zolberg, "The Ecole Libre at the New School 1941–1946," *Social Research* 65 (Winter 1998), 921–51.

20. Maritain, *France, My Country through the Disaster,* 1.

21. Ralph McInerny, *The Very Rich Hours of Jacques Maritain* (Notre Dame: University of Notre Dame Press, 2003), 12ff.

22. Eugen Weber, *Action Française: Royalism and Reaction in Twentieth-Century France* (Stanford: Stanford University Press, 1962).

23. Jacques Maritain, *Antimoderne* (Paris, 1922), 184 (emphasis added).

24. Jacques Maritain, *Three Reformers* (Westport, Conn.: Greenwood Press, 1950), 13.

25. Jacques Maritain, *La primauté du spirituel* (Paris, 1927), 3ff.

26. Ludmila Stern, *Western Intellectuals and the Soviet Union: From Red Square to the Left Bank* (London: Routledge, 2007). Cf. Paul Hollander, *Political Pilgrims: Travels of Western Intellectuals to the Soviet Union, China, and Cuba* (Oxford: Oxford University Press, 1981).

27. Jacques Maritain, *Humanisme intégral*, in Jacques and Raïssa Maritain *Œvres complètes* (Paris: Éditions Saint-Paul, 1984), 382ff. In what follows, translations of this work closely follow those of Joseph W. Evans: see Maritain, *Integral Humanism: Temporal and Spiritual Problems of a New Christendom*, trans. Joseph W. Evans (New York: Charles Scribner's Sons, 1968).

28. Indeed, this book bears out Raïssa's description of her husband's life calling: "Jacques' vocation...[was] to bring to light the vital forces of Thomism, to carry the light of this great doctrine to all the problems of our times, to widen its frontiers, while holding in the strictest fashion to its principles." As Maritain often quipped, *vae mihi si non thomistizavero*, or "woe to me if I do not Thomistize." See Raïssa Maritain, *We Have Been Friends Together / Adventures in Grace*, trans. Julie Kernan (Garden City, NY: Image Books, 1945), 352. Maritain owed a particular debt to the work of John of St. Thomas (1589–1644), one of Thomas Aquinas's leading seventeenth-century commentators. Cf. Maritain, *St. Thomas Aquinas*, trans. Joseph Evans and Peter O'Reilly (New York: Meridian Books, 1958) and Gerald A. McCool, "Jacques Maritain: A Neo-Thomist Classic," *Journal of Religion* 58 (October 1978), 380–404.

29. *Humanisme intégral*, 547.

30. *Humanisme intégral*, 301.

31. *Humanisme intégral*, 558.

32. Maritain, "The End of Machiavellianism," in Joseph W. Evans and Leo R. Ward, eds., *The Social and Political Philosophy of Jacques Maritain* (Notre Dame: University of Notre Dame Press, 1976), 292–325.

33. Compare Maritain on this point to that of Hannah Arendt, *The Origins of Totalitarianism* (New York: Harcourt Brace, 1951).

34. *Humanisme intégral*, 542ff., 599.

35. *Humanisme intégral*, 415.

36. *Humanisme intégral*, 451.

37. *Humanisme intégral*, 306. On this point, see Coleen P. Zoller, "Determined but Free: Aquinas's Compatibilist Theory of Freedom," *Philosophy & Theology* 16 (2004), 25–44.

38. *Humanisme intégral*, 522.

39. Unfortunately, Maritain does not express this latter idea sufficiently, but I think that this is a fair extrapolation of his thought, given that the brunt of his criticism falls on the *freedom-ending* capacities of Fascism and Communism.

40. *Humanisme intégral*, 523.

41. *Humanisme intégral*, 517.

42. *Humanisme intégral,* 358.

43. Maritain, *On the Philosophy of History* (New York: Charles Scribner's Sons, 1957), 54 (my italics). In this book, Maritain writes of the "law" of the "double antagonistic movement" in history; that is, all progress and any goodness in the here-and-now will always be intermingled with regressive and disordered elements. Progress does not lie in fully eliminating the latter, but in incrementally attenuating their influence. Cf. his *Saint Thomas and the Problem of Evil* (Milwaukee: Marquette University Press, 1942).

44. On the Neo-Thomist or Neo-Scholastic revival in modern Catholic learning, see Philip Gleason, *Contending with Modernity: Catholic Higher Education in the Twentieth Century* (New York: Oxford University Press, 1995), 105–23.

45. *Humanisme intégral*, 472–73.

46. A. Messineo, "Democrazia e libertà religiosa," *Civiltà Cattolica* 102 (14 April 1951), 126–37 and Julio Meinvielle, *De Lamennais à Maritain* (Buenos Aires: Ediciones Nuestro Tiempo, 1945).

47. *Humanisme intégral*, 437ff.

48. Jean-Luc Barré, *Jacques and Raïssa Maritain: Beggars for Heaven*, trans. Bernard Doering (Notre Dame: University of Notre Dame Press, 2005), 397.

49. McInerny, *The Very Rich Hours of Jacques Maritain*, 159. I emphasize the word "relative" in this sentence because Maritain was well aware of America's race problem and later a strong supporter of the Civil Rights Movement.

50. See Yves Simon, ed., *La civilisation américaine* (Bruges: Desclée de Brouwer et Cie, 1950) and John Courtney Murray, S. J., "Freedom of Religion," *Theological Studies* 6 (1945), 229–86. Maritain's views on the United States also owe a significant debt to his friend John U. Nef, an historian of economics at the University of Chicago and the founder of Chicago's Committee on Social Thought. See especially Nef's *The United States and Civilization* (Chicago: University of Chicago Press, 1942).

51. Jacques Maritain, *Scholasticism and Politics*, trans. Mortimer Adler (Garden City, NY: Images Books, 1940), 7–8. Even before he left France, he had written Yves Simon: "And who knows? A living Thomism will perhaps

take root more easily over there [in the United States] than on our with-
ered soil?" Quoted in McGreevy, *Catholicism and American Freedom*, 204.

52. *Scholasticism and Politics*, 92, 94ff.

53. *Scholasticism and Politics*, 104. Cf. *Summa Theologiae* II-I, 95.2.

54. *Scholasticism and Politics*, 92.

55. Raïssa Maritain, *Adventures in Grace*, 169–70.

56. Letter to Saul Alinsky (20 August 1945), in Bernard Doering, ed., *The Philosopher and the Provocateur: The Correspondence of Jacques Maritain and Saul Alinsky* (Notre Dame: University of Notre Dame Press, 1994), 10–11.

57. Renée Bédarida, *Les Catholiques dans la guerre 1939–1945: Entre Vichy et la Résistance* (Paris: Hachette littératures, 1998), 142ff.

58. Jacques Maritain, *Rights of Man and Natural Law*, trans. Doris C. Anson (San Francisco: Ignatius Press, 1986), 107.

59. Jacques Maritain, *Christianity and Democracy*, trans. Doris C. Anson (San Francisco: Ignatius Press, 1986), 11.

60. *Rights of Man and Natural Law*, 107–08.

61. *Christianity and Democracy*, 25–27, 30.

62. *Christianity and Democracy*, 51–52.

63. Maritain, *Rights of Man and Natural Law*, 144. For a primer on classical and scholastic conceptions of natural law, see Yves Simon, *The Tradition of Natural Law*, ed.,Vukan Kuic, intro. Russell Hittinger (New York: Fordham University Press, 1992), 129.

64. John Courtney Murray S. J., *We Hold These Truths: Catholic Reflections on the American Proposition* (New York: Sheed and Ward, 1960), 28.

65. See John Courtney Murray, S. J., "Leo XIII: Separation of Church and State," *Theological Studies* 14 (1953), 145–214.

66. From a memorandum of Murray's, "The Crisis in Church-State Relations" (1950); quoted in Joseph A. Komonchak, "The Silencing of John Courtney Murray," in Alberto Melloni et al., eds., *Cristianesimo nella storia: Saggi in onore di Giuseppe Alberigo* (Bologna: Il Mulino, 1996), 661.

67. But some of Murray's earlier writings had influenced Maritain. On relations and similarities between the two men, see McGreevy, *Catholicism and American Freedom*, 189–215.

68. Maritain, *Rights of Man and Natural Law*, 159.

69. *Christianity and Democracy*, 23.

70. *Rights of Man and Natural Law*, 160.

71. *Rights of Man and Natural Law*, 160.

72. "Decree on Religious Liberty" (*Dignitatis Humanae*) in Austin Flannery, O.P., ed., *Vatican Council II, vol. 1, The Conciliar and Post-Conciliar Documents* (Northport, NY: Costello Publishing Company, 2004), 799–802. On Maritain's influence on the Second Vatican Council, see Barré, *Jacques and Raïssa Maritain*, 418ff. and Philippe Chenaux, *Paul VI et Maritain* (Rome:

Edizioni Studium, 1994). *Dignitatis Humanae* proved to be one of the most controversial outcomes of the Council. See John Noonan, Jr., *The Church that Can and Cannot Change* (Notre Dame: University of Notre Dame Press, 2005), 154–58.

73. Maritain, *Reflections on America* (New York: Charles Scribner's Sons, 1958), 149. Maneuvering around some skepticism of Maritain within Princeton's faculty, Princeton's President, Harold Dodds, made provision for a special resident professorship for Maritain.

74. The original title of the seminar was "random reflections on the American scene." It took place on the 6th, 7th, and 8th of November, 1956.

75. *Reflections on America*, 15, 29, 188.

76. On the postwar attractions of Communism for French intellectuals and the implications of this for anti-American sentiment during this period, see Tony Judt, *Past Imperfect: French Intellectuals, 1944–1956* (Berkeley: University of California Press, 1992), 187–204.

77. *Reflections on America*, 40, 124–26.

78. *Reflections on America*, 17, 125–27.

79. *Reflections on America*, 26. Cf. Alexis de Tocqueville, *The Old Regime and the French Revolution*, trans. Stuart Gilbert (Garden City, NY: Doubleday, 1955), 32–40.

80. *Reflections on America*, 27 and Barré, *Jacques and Raïssa Maritain*, 397.

81. *Reflections on America*, 90.

82. *Reflections on America*, 34–35, 162ff. On the persistent "transatlantic charity gap" with respect to private-sector philanthropy and volunteering of time between Western Europe and the United States, see Arthur C. Brooks, ed., *Gifts of Time and Money: The Role of Charity in America's Communities* (Lanham, Md.: Rowman & Littlefield, 2005), 3ff.

83. *Reflections on America*, 162–63.

84. *Relfections on America*, 38–47, 64.

85. *Reflections on America*, 83–86.

86. Maritain was quite taken by the work of Martin Luther King and regularly held him up as an example of American religious vitality and social idealism. See *On the Philosophy of History*, 74–75.

87. *Christianity and Democracy*, 79–80.

88. *Reflections on America*, 87.

89. *Reflections on America*, 90.

90. The entire First Amendment of the American Bill of Rights reads: *"Congress shall make no law respecting an establishment of religion, or prohibiting the free exercise thereof; or abridging the freedom of speech, or of the press; or the right of the people peaceably to assemble, and to petition the Government for a redress of grievances."*

91. *Reflections on America*, 180–83. Maritain draws in his work from an article by Peter Drucker, "Organized Religion and the American Creed," *Review of Politics* 18 (1956), 296–304.

92. Yves Congar, *Chrétiens Désunis* (Paris: Cerf, 1937). Still, toward the end of his life, Maritain turned his attention to ecclesiology and ecumenism. See *On the Church of Christ*, trans. Joseph W. Evans (Notre Dame: University of Notre Dame Press, 1973).

93. *On the Philosophy of History*, 105, 58.

94. *On the Philosophy of History*, 160–61.

95. In this sense, Thomas embraced much of Aristotle's corpus against considerable criticism from his opponents. On this point, see Josef Pieper, *Guide to Thomas Aquinas*, trans. Richard and Clara Winston (San Francisco: Ignatius Press, 1962), 50f.

96. Murray, *We Hold These Truths*, 29.

97. *Reflections on America*, 180.

98. *Christianity and Democracy*, 84.

99. *Reflections on America*, 189–90.

100. Maritain, *Man and the State* (Chicago: University of Chicago Press, 1951), 182–83.

CHAPTER 6

1. Heinz Schilling, *Konfessionalisierung und Staatsinteressen: internationale Beziehungen, 1559–1660* (Paderborn: Schöningh, 2007).

2. On early modern Europe and steps toward or examples of religious toleration, see Perez Zagorin, *How the Idea of Religious Toleration Came to the West* (Princeton: Princeton University Press, 2003), 46ff. and Benjamin J. Kaplan, *Divided by Faith: Religious Conflict and the Practice of Toleration in Early Modern Europe* (Cambridge: Belknap Press of Harvard University Press, 2007). The Peace of Westphalia did make some provision for the emigration of religious minorities.

3. Janine Garrison, *L'Édit de Nantes et sa révocation: histoire d'une intolérance* (Paris: Editions de Seuil, 1985).

4. Thomas J. Curry, *The First Freedoms: Church and State in America to the Passage of the First Amendment* (New York: Oxford University Press, 1986).

5. Mark Noll, *The Old Religion in a New World: The History of North American Christianity* (Grand Rapids: Eerdmans, 2002), 82–83. Cf. Gertrude Himmelfarb, *The Roads to Modernity* (New York: Alfred A. Knopf, 2004), 18–19.

6. See T. Ferneuil, *Les principes de 1789 et la science sociale* (Paris, 1889) and Durkheim's review of this book in *Revue internationale de l'enseignement* 19 (1890), 450–56.

7. Alexis de Tocqueville, *The Old Regime and the Revolution*, vol. 1, trans. Alan Kahan (Chicago: University of Chicago Press, 1998), 101.

8. On the notion of secularist confessionalism, I borrow from Brad S. Gregory, "The Other Confessional History: On Secular Bias in the Study of Religion," *History and Theory* 45 (2006), 132–49.

9. See Jean de Viguerie, *Christianisme et révolution: cinq leçons d'histoire de la révolution* (Paris: Nouvelles Éditions Latines, 1986) and Nigel Aston, *Religion and Revolution in France, 1780–1804* (Washington, DC: Catholic University Press of America, 2000).

10. See C. D. A. Leighton, "Antichrist's Revolution: Some Anglican Apocalypticists in the Age of the French Wars," *Journal of Religious History* 24 (2000), 125–42.

11. On the notion of political theology or political religion, I draw from Jean-Pierre Sionneau, *Sécularisation et religions politiques* (The Hague: Mounton, 1982) and Philippe Burrin, "Political Religion: The Relevance of a Concept," *History & Memory* 9 (1997), 321–49.

12. See Emmet Kennedy, "The French Revolutionary Catechisms: Ruptures and Continuities with Classical, Christian, and Enlightenment Moralities," *Studies on Voltaire and the Eighteenth Century* 199 (1981), 353–62.

13. Michael Burleigh, *Earthly Powers: The Clash of Religion and Politics from the French Revolution to the Great War* (New York: HarperCollins, 2005), 97.

14. M.-J. Chènier (November 1793); quoted in Aston, *Religion and Revolution in France*, 185 (emphasis added).

15. R. R. Palmer, *The Age of Democratic Revolution: A Political History of Europe and America, 1760–1800*, 2 vols. (Princeton: Princeton University Press, 1959–64).

16. Hugh Heclo, *Christianity and American Democracy* (Cambridge: Harvard University Press, 2007), 34–35.

17. Kuno Damian Freiheer von Schütz zu Hölzhausen, "Die Krisis in Washington und die Zustände überhaupt," *Historisch-politische Blätter für das katholische Deutschland* 59 (1867), 136.

18. Giovanni Antonio Grassi, *Notizie varie sullo stato presente della repubblica degli Stati Uniti dell'America* (Rome, 1818), 49ff.

19. Henri de Lubac, *Le drame de l'humanisme athée* (Paris: Spes, 1944).

20. Jeffrey Cox, "Secularization and Other Master Narratives of Religion in Modern Europe," *Kirchliche Zeitgeschichte* 14 (2001), 30–32.

21. Samuel Johnson, *Rasselas, Poems, and Selected Prose* (New York: Holt, Rinehart and Winston, 1958), 74–75.

22. Of course, one could turn the tables and examine Americans' perceptions of Europe; but that would require another book. For starters, see Foster Rhea Dulles, *Americans Abroad: Two Centuries of European Travel* (Ann Arbor: University of Michigan Press, 1964).

23. Charles Taylor, *Modern Social Imaginaries* (Durham: Duke University Press, 2004), 23–24 (emphasis added).

24. Sionneau, *Sécularisation et religions politiques*, 578–79.

25. See, for instance, Helena Rosenblatt, *Liberal Values: Benjamin Constant and the Politics of Religion* (Cambridge: Cambridge University Press, 2008).

26. Lasia Bloss, *Cuius religio-EU ius regio? Komparative Betrachtung europäischer staatskirchenrechtlicher Systeme, status quo und Perspektiven eines europäischen Religionsverfassungsrecht* (Tübingen: Mohr Siebeck, 2008).

27. Richard John Neuhaus, *The Naked Public Square: Religion and Democracy in America*, 2nd edn. (Grand Rapids: Eerdmans, 1986).

28. Transcript of "Religious America, Secular Europe: Implications for Transatlantic Relations" (21 April 2005), Pew Forum on Religion and Public Life, at http://pewforum.org/events/?EventID=76 (accessed on 24 May 2010).

29. As José Casanova has written: "What is new in the last decades is the fact that for the first time in American political history, the contemporary culture wars are beginning to resemble the secular-religious cleavage that were endemic to continental European politics in the past." See Casanova, "Rethinking Secularization: A Comparative Global Perspective," *Hedgehog Review* 8 (Spring/Summer 2006), 21. Cf. James Davison Hunter, *Culture Wars: The Struggle to Define America* (New York: Basic Books, 1991); Gertrude Himmelfarb, *One Nation, Two Cultures* (New York: Alfred E. Knopf, 1999); and Wilfred W. McClay, "Two Concepts of Secularism," *Journal of Policy History* 13 (2001), 47–72.

30. Hugh McCleod, *The Religious Crisis of the 1960s* (Oxford: Oxford University Press, 2007).

31. Jürgen Habermas, "Die Dialektik der Säkularisierung," *Blätter für deutsche und internationale Politik* 4 (2008), 33–46. "[T]he democratic state," he writes, "must not pre-emptively reduce the polyphonic complexity of the diverse public voices, because it cannot know whether it is not otherwise cutting society off from scarce resources for the generation of meanings and shaping identities. Particularly with regard to social relations, religious traditions possess the power to convincingly articulate moral sensitivities and solidaristic intuitions. What puts pressure on secularism, then, is the expectation that secular citizens in civil society and the political public sphere must be able to meet their religious fellow citizens as equals" (p. 46).

32. Noted in Ahmet T. Kuru, *Secularism and State Policies toward Religion in the United States, France, and Turkey* (Cambridge: Cambridge University Press, 2009), 103–06, passim. Before he became President of France, Nicolas Sarkozy made a similar argument. See his *La République, les religions, l'espérance* (Paris: Cerf, 2004).

33. Jean Baubérot, *Histoire de la laïcité en France*, 4th edn. (Paris: Presses universitaires de France, 2007), 4. The dilemmas of this approach have been spelled out by Christopher Caldwell, *Reflections on the Revolution in Europe: Immigration, Islam, and the West* (New York: Doubleday, 2009).

34. Williame as quoted in Kuru, *Secularism and State Policies*, 118.

35. I am indebted here to McClay, "Two Concepts of Secularism," *Journal of Policy History*.

36. Raymond Aron, *The Opium of the Intellectuals*, trans. Terence Kilmartin (New York: W. W. Norton & Co., 1957), 284.

Index